HOW TO
INSTANT POT

HOW TO INSTANT POT

MASTERING ALL *the* FUNCTIONS *of the* ONE POT *that will* CHANGE THE WAY YOU COOK

DANIEL SHUMSKI

Author of *Will It Waffle?*

Workman Publishing • New York

Library of Congress Cataloging-in-Publication Data is available.
ISBN: 978-1-5235-0206-6

Design by Becky Terhune
Cover and interior photos by Waterbury Publications, Inc., Des Moines, IA
Ken Carlson, Photographer
Food Stylists: Charles Worthington, Jennifer Peterson
Author photograph by Alex Tran

Workman books are available at special discounts when purchased in bulk for premiums and sales promotions as well as for fundraising or educational use. Special editions or book excerpts can also be created to specification. For details, contact the Special Sales Director at the address below, or send an email to specialmarkets@workman.com.

Workman Publishing Co., Inc.
225 Varick Street
New York, NY 10014-4381
workman.com

Printed in China
First printing September 2017

10 9 8 7

ACKNOWLEDGMENTS

My second-favorite thing about food is its power to bring people together. I'm just being real here; my favorite thing about food is its power to be so freaking delicious.

As with food, writing a cookbook brings people together. This book could never have happened without the work and wisdom of a lot of people. It's tough to find the words to say how grateful I am, which is awkward because my job is, you know, finding words. But here we are.

Let me start by saying thank you to Amy Matthews and Kerrie Ahern, whose attention to detail and kitchen know-how saved us all from some recipe blunders.

Without exaggeration, every book of mine owes a debt of gratitude to Megan Nicolay, who took a gamble on a waffle blogger a few years back. I hope she thinks it paid off.

Kylie Foxx McDonald, the editor of this book, who has been such a good sport about the twists and turns along the road to publication: Now that the book is out, I promise not to email or call you for at least a week. That's pretty much the best

thank-you gift ever, no? (Full disclosure: I originally wrote "for at least a month," but I'm trying not to set myself up for failure here. So I rolled it back. Talk soon!)

My thanks also to Rachael Mt. Pleasant for her behind-the-scenes heavy lifting. Probably I should be thankful to her for doing work I don't even know about, which is so often the work for which a person should be extra grateful.

I am so appreciative of Chloe Puton, Rebecca Carlisle, Selina Meere, Kate Karol, Ian Gross, and too many others to name at Workman Publishing for the amazing work they do to help put this book in people's hands and kitchens.

Thank you also to Becky Terhune, Anne Kerman, and the people at Waterbury Publications for making me look good and making it look easy.

To Sarah Curley, who did so much wrangling and shepherding for the updates to this book: I really appreciate the work you put into this.

You want to know who's really been a good sport? The guy who asks, "What's for dinner?" each night and never has a cross word to say about the answer. He's the same guy who told me that he believed in me when I was halfway through writing this book and I couldn't quite see the light at the end of the tunnel. Thank you, Bryan.

My agent for this project, Stacey Glick, has been a trouper about dotting i's and crossing t's. I'm very grateful to have worked with her.

Nicholas Day and Mark Lucera have been so patient, smart, and good-humored. I wonder if they know how much I appreciate that. They do now, assuming they read this book.

Now, some late-breaking gratitude: Since this book first came out, so many people have taken the time to post reviews online, to recommend the book to friends, and to send me notes of appreciation for the information in this book. Thank you.

This is probably a good place to mention that my mom bought me my first Instant Pot as a birthday gift. Neither of us had any idea where it would lead, but now this book is a thing. I can't help but feel that I owe her big-time for something beyond that first Instant Pot, though—maybe it's the decades of unwavering support? That's probably it. I love you, Mom.

CONTENTS

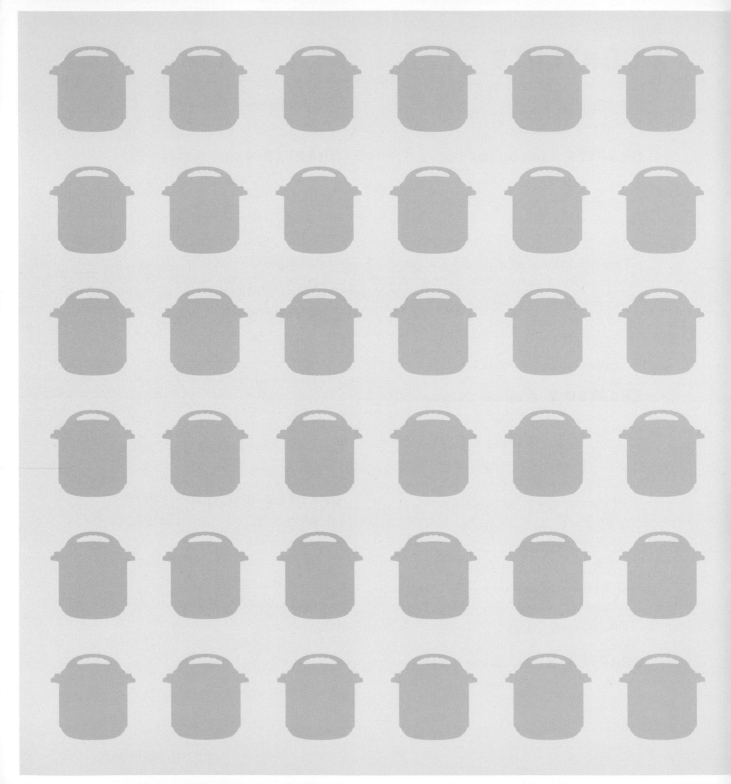

INTRODUCTION

Maybe your initial reaction to seeing the Instant Pot was like mine: "It does all those things? Really? Hmm. . . . Okay. But does it do them *well*?"

Was the Instant Pot just a trendy kitchen appliance trying to tackle too much? I already owned a slow cooker. And I could steam things and make rice on the stovetop. True, I didn't own a pressure cooker. But neither did I own an Elvis costume. Was either really necessary? Bottom line, did I need an Instant Pot?

As it turns out, the answer was yes. (For the Instant Pot, not the Elvis costume.)

Yes, to yogurt that all but makes itself while I sleep. Yes, to dinners I can prep in the morning and leave to cook all day. Yes, to dried beans that I can make for dinner without the foresight to presoak them. Yes, to steaming vegetables without having to fiddle with the stovetop temperature. Yes, to rice that comes together quickly without moving it on and off the heat. Yes, to things I couldn't have imagined I would be saying "yes" to: quick-pickled vegetables, no-fuss hard-boiled eggs, mulled cider.

In short, yes to the Instant Pot.

On the day my Instant Pot arrived, I opened the package but had only begun to unwrap the mystery. I was excited but . . . what had I gotten myself into? I thought I grasped the idea of a Rice function, but why were there so many settings and valves?

How did I use this thing? I know how to bake, boil, skillet, and waffle (I've written books on the last two). But how to Instant Pot?

Cooking in an opaque, sealed chamber requires a culinary leap of faith. After the lid is locked tight, you can't cook by sight or smell. Was I willing to take the plunge? Sure, but I had two goals:

1. Don't ruin dinner.
and
2. Don't anger the machine.

I was willing to sacrifice No. 2 if it meant that No. 1 could be accomplished.

I'm here to tell you that you can have it both ways. Not only that, you can take advantage of a unique and useful tool that may nudge its way onto center stage in your kitchen and change the way you cook. In short, you can master the Instant Pot.

The Instant Pot presents a new paradigm even for experienced cooks, but it's one that you can master regardless of your experience or comfort level in the kitchen. While there is a bit of a learning curve, this book is here to make it more of a gentle slope—and one that lets you eat as you progress.

The Instant Pot is useful but not immediately intuitive. That's where this book comes in. The main functions of the Instant Pot are covered—pressure cooker, slow cooker, rice cooker, yogurt maker, steamer—as well as the auxiliary functions that allow you to sauté food and to keep food warm.

You'll learn:

• What the buttons mean

• How to decipher the LCD screen

• How to convert your favorite recipes for the Instant Pot

• How to clean your Instant Pot

• How the Instant Pot is different from other pressure cookers

• Which optional accessories you might want for your Instant Pot

In short, you'll learn how to Instant Pot. Now, let's get cooking.

HOW TO USE THIS BOOK

This book arranges its chapters by function. You have a machine that offers many functions in one. What better way to master those functions than by breaking out and exploring each one separately? That said, there are two functions that are used mainly in conjunction with others and do not have their own chapters:

• The Sauté function plays a key role in many slow-cooker and pressure-cooker recipes.

• The Keep Warm function can serve a valuable purpose, but is perhaps less useful on its own.

For information on how to use each, see pages 10–12 of Instant Pot Basics.

Chapter 1

INSTANT POT BASICS

L ook, I get it. You were hoping this book would help you avoid reading the Instant Pot manual. If that's the case, go to your happy place (puppies! kittens!) as you read this next bit: While this section covers the basics of the Instant Pot and hits the highlights of using and maintaining the machine, it's worth looking over the manual that came with it. There won't be a test later, but you might learn a few things.

The following pages cover all the ins and outs of this marvelous (and occasionally maddening) machine, but if it all feels like a bit much, take heart—the chapter introductions explain the use of each of the pot's main functions, and the recipes tell you which buttons to push and when. No guesswork needed.

One final note up front: The recipes in this book were developed for a 6-quart Instant Pot (models IP-DUO60 and IP-DUO Plus60). They can also be used with other models. See boxes in this section. If you have a 3-quart or an 8-quart model, you can use the recipes with just a little modification.

3-QUART AND 8-QUART MODELS

While the Instant Pot at first came only with a 6-quart capacity, the machine now comes in other sizes, too. All the basics in this book still apply and the recipes can be used with just a little modification:

• For a 3-quart model, simply cut the listed ingredient amounts in half. Do not change the cooking time. The times to build and release pressure may be a little less than stated in the recipe.

• For 8-quart models, increase the ingredient amounts by 33%. (So, 1 cup becomes 1⅓ cups.) Keep the cooking time the same. The time to come up to pressure and release pressure may be a bit longer than what's stated in the recipe.

The Instant Pot family has sprouted up from the original 6-quart multicooker to a cavalcade of multicookers in all sizes (3 quart, 6 quart, and 8 quart) and model lines (Duo, Duo Plus, Viva, Lux, Ultra, Max). Probably by the time I finish this sentence, there will be a new size or model line. (Oh, look! Duo Nova and Duo Evo Plus.) Here's what matters: While the interface may get tweaked, the principles of pressure cooking and slow cooking remain the same.

Sit back and I'll tell you a story about the measurement markings on the inner pot and how they have evolved from . . . No? You're right. It's not a terribly interesting story. Here's the gist: Depending on your Instant Pot model, the measurement marks on the inner pot may be correct for liters but not for standard 8-ounce cups. Instead, the cup lines were designed as a rough guide for the amount of water to add for the number of "cups" of rice. Why "cups" in quotes? Because it refers to the included Instant Pot plastic cup, which is 6 fluid ounces, or three-quarters of a standard 8-ounce cup. Confused yet? Me too. **The bottom line:** Ignore the markings on the inner pot and use standard measuring cups and spoons. (Many newer versions of the inner pot have liters and quarts rather than cups marked; those are correct, but I still find it easier to rely on my measuring cups.)

Another quirk of the markers on the inside of the inner pot: On some models, the "maximum" line near the top is useful for slow-cooking but is not intended for pressure-cooking, when the inner pot should be filled no more than two-thirds full for most foods, or halfway full for foods that expand during cooking such as dried beans or grains. Many newer inner pots have clearly marked lines that show half full and two-thirds full.

MEETING YOUR INSTANT POT: EQUIPMENT AND SET-UP

Although the specifics vary depending on the model of Instant Pot and manufacturer modifications, the Instant Pot includes everything you need to get started:

Stainless steel inner pot: The dishwasher-safe inner pot is the bedrock of Instant Pot cooking. Everything happens inside here. Although one is included, it can be useful to have more than one if you use the Instant Pot frequently. (I have five. Wait. Did I just admit that?) A second inner pot can be useful if you want to slow-cook or pressure-cook an entrée and then quickly make some rice to go with it—in this case, you would carefully lift out the hot, just-used inner pot and insert the fresh one. Covered with plastic wrap or the optional silicone cover, the inner pot may also be used to store leftovers in the refrigerator.

Lid and anti-block shield: The lid, largely black plastic on the top, contains the pressure-release valve and anti-block shield, which is the removable metal cage-like piece on the underside. There are no

ABOUT THE INSTANT POT ULTRA

The Instant Pot Ultra features the same fundamental features as other Instant Pot models and works beautifully with the recipes in this book, with a few differences:

New Controls: The Ultra features a dial and just two buttons. The dial doubles as a button in that you can press it. Turn the dial to select the function, then press the dial and use it to select temperature and time. Lock in your selections by pressing the dial again. Press the Start button to begin cooking.

Venting vs. Sealing: The valve is automatically set to Sealing when you lock the lid in place. To select Venting, press down for a moment on the black Steam Release button. (It says "Press" on it.) That locks the button into the Venting position.

Pressure Release: Natural release occurs as described in this book—just let the appliance release pressure slowly on its own. For quick release, use the same black Steam Release button as above. Note that while it is a separate button from the valve where the steam emerges, be careful of that steam, which will be released from the large black steam release valve nearby.

The Ultra Function: This model's namesake function allows the Instant Pot to maintain a constant temperature and allows you to experiment with cooking sous-vide, though it is **not** a replacement for a proper sous-vide immersion circulator. (The Ultra allows the temperature to fluctuate 5°F and does not circulate the water.)

The Ultra adds a few nice-to-have features, too: A digital readout keeps you posted on the Instant Pot's cooking progress. You can also set your elevation (this adjusts cooking times automatically for you if you're using a sea-level recipe) and switch between Celsius and Fahrenheit. To access these settings, press and hold the dial.

---

electronic components inside the lid; it's all mechanical and safe for the dishwasher (see Cleaning the Machine, page 17).

Silicone sealing ring: The heatproof sealing ring fits snugly on the inside of the lid. It helps seal the Instant Pot and allows it to build pressure. Because the ring can absorb cooking odors, some Instant Pot owners find it useful to have more than one (say, one for cooking seafood and other pungent items and one for more neutral foods such as rice), and fortunately they're pretty inexpensive. That said, with proper cleaning the silicone ring has never posed a problem for me with intermingling food aromas.

Stainless steel steaming rack: This rests on the bottom of the inner pot and supports a steaming basket (not included) so that the basket does not sit directly in the water or other steaming liquid. Without a basket, the steaming rack can be used for larger foods, such as potatoes and eggs.

Condensation collector: This transparent plastic cup slides into a slot on the side of the cooking base and prevents condensation on the lid from dripping down around the Instant Pot and making a mess when using the slow-cooking function.

Rice paddle and soup spoon: You may prefer a deeper ladle for soups and stews, but the rice paddle does come in handy for scooping and stirring.

Measuring cup: Though this is standard-issue with the Instant Pot, note that it is not a standard 8-ounce cup. A large glass or sturdy plastic measuring cup with a handle is generally more useful.

OPTIONAL ACCESSORIES

Check online or at a retailer that sells the Instant Pot for the following items, which are not always included and may help you make better use of your machine:

Silicone steaming basket: While it's sometimes possible to steam food directly on the included metal steaming rack (see page 4), many foods are too small and will

fall through the slats, making a steaming basket a welcome addition. A metal basket will work if it's the right size, but silicone is my material of choice because it is flexible. I also like that it is dishwasher-safe.

Glass lid: Useful for slow-cooker recipes, the glass lid allows a view of what's happening inside the Instant Pot. It cannot be used for pressure-cooker or steamer settings because it does not seal tightly enough.

Mini silicone mitt: Any oven mitt can be handy for removing the inner pot or steaming basket—but the miniature one offered by the manufacturer is particularly handy for safely gripping the lip of the very hot inner pot.

Silicone cover: This tight-fitting cover from the manufacturer seals the inner pot for refrigerating leftovers.

SETTING UP YOUR POT

Before using the machine to make a meal for the first time, you'll want to clean the equipment (minus the electronic base) and then do a test run. This introduces you to the buttons of the Instant Pot, cleans out any residue from the manufacturing process, and ensures your machine is working properly.

1. Install the silicone sealing ring in the lid by pressing the groove in the silicone ring into the metal ring on the inside of the lid.

2. Place 3 cups of water in the inner pot and place the inner pot in the appliance.

3. Close and lock the lid: Fit the part of the lid with the Sealing/Venting indicator into the enlarged portion of the appliance's lip with the arrows on it. Turn the lid clockwise until it won't turn any farther.

4. Make sure the black pressure-release valve on the top of the lid is pointing to Sealing.

5. Press the Steam button on the control panel and use the – or + button to set the time to 2 minutes.

6. As the Instant Pot builds pressure, steam may be released from the valve on the lid until the small metal float valve pops into place to seal the unit. This is normal. It will take about 10 minutes for the Instant Pot to reach pressure and seal itself, at which point the timer will begin counting down.

7. When the countdown ends, the machine will beep and the pressure will begin to dissipate. You won't see any steam, but some clicking sounds are normal. Wait until the small metal float valve next to the pressure-release valve sinks back into the lid and the lid is no longer locked, about

25 minutes; this means the pressure has been released. Remove the lid by turning it counterclockwise and then lifting it up.

FUNCTION AND BUTTON OVERVIEW

Most Instant Pot models have five main functions (excluding the preset buttons which, as you'll see on page 12, are not all that useful):

• Pressure cooker

• Slow cooker

• Rice maker

• Yogurt maker

• Steamer

The Instant Pot also features two auxiliary functions used mostly in conjunction with the modes listed above:

• Sauté

• Keep Warm

Depending on the marketing flavor of your Instant Pot, it may say it's a "9-in-1" or a "7-in-1" cooker. Sometimes there is only a tenuous connection between the number of claimed functions and the actual capabilities of the machine. That's not to say your Instant Pot can't do a lot, because

MEET MAX

With touchscreen controls and a dial, the Max is a bit different from other Instant Pot models. And yet it can still do the same things—you can still use the recipes and principles in this book.

• Some notes on the controls: Once the Pressure Cook button has been pressed, touch the Pressure icon on the screen to select High Pressure. (While a higher setting, called "Max Pressure," does cook things more quickly, it also takes longer to build and release pressure, so the ultimate cooking time is not much different.) The venting setting is not adjusted by touching anything on the lid, but rather through the touch screen. When you touch Venting, you are offered three release options: natural, intermittent (the icon in the middle), and manual.

• While the Max offers a sous-vide function, I have never found that it regulates temperature precisely and satisfactorily, which is essential to sous-vide cooking. For that reason, I cannot recommend it for that purpose.

• The Max offers a canning feature. To see whether it's worthwhile, I turned to my go-to source on all things canning: cookbook author and blogger Marisa McClellan. She writes that while the company has commissioned testing to make sure the pressure and timing conform to canning standards, as of this writing there is no seal of approval from the National Center for Home Food Preservation. As such, she does not recommend buying an Instant Pot Max expressly for canning. I would recommend staying away from the canning function until more testing is done and the relevant authorities weigh in.

---

it can. But, for example, at some point Instant Pot started listing egg cooker as a discrete function. The thing is, all Instant Pot pressure cookers can cook eggs—and they could cook them before the company started listing the capability separately.

MAIN FUNCTION BUTTONS

These buttons get to the heart of the many functions of the Instant Pot. Note that one of the functions of the Instant Pot—rice maker—gets its own button ("Rice"), even though it's often best to use the Manual or Pressure Cook button to make rice.

Slow Cook: This function should be familiar to anyone who has used a slow cooker. After pressing Slow Cook, the Slow Cook or Adjust button switches among low, medium, and high temperatures and the - and + buttons adjust the cooking time. For details, see the Slow Cooker chapter (page 117).

Manual or Pressure Cook: The name of this button may vary depending on the model, but the function is the same: It's the pressure-cooking button. It begins a pressure-cooking program and allows you to set the time using the – or + buttons. All of the pressure-cooking recipes in this book use this button.

Yogurt: This button has three settings: pasteurizing milk, making yogurt, and making a fermented rice dish called Jiu Niang. For details, see the Yogurt Maker chapter (page 221).

Sauté: This button is used—always with the lid off—to sauté or brown meat or vegetables before slow-cooking or pressure-cooking. It can also be used after slow-cooking or pressure-cooking to reduce the volume of liquids. With this function, the Sauté button itself or the Adjust button changes the cooking temperature (to "Less," "Normal," and "More").

Steam: This button comes with three preset times; the Steam or Adjust button cycles among cooking times of 3, 10, and 15 minutes (or use the + or - buttons to customize the time). I place this button in this category because steaming is one of the basic functions of the Instant Pot.

For details, see the Steamer chapter (page 247).

MODIFYING BUTTONS

These buttons are generally used in conjunction with the function buttons to select settings or timings. I've given you the basic rundown below, but each recipe specifies exactly which buttons to press and in what order, so no need to memorize any of the following.

Pressure or Pressure Level: Once a pressure-cooking cycle has been selected, this button switches between low and high pressure. The recipes in this book use only high pressure. This button has no effect on the Slow Cook, Sauté, or Yogurt functions.

Adjust: Whether your Instant Pot has this button will depend on the specific model. The purpose of this button depends on the function selected. Most commonly in the recipes in this book, it is used to change the temperature of the Slow Cook and Sauté functions. It is also used to change programs in the Yogurt function. For models *without* this button, pressing the cooking function button again generally performs the same Adjust function. (For example, rather than press Sauté and then Adjust to change temperatures, just press Sauté again.)

Timer or Delay Start: This button allows you to delay the cooking start time for all

LIFE IN THE LUX LANE

On the Lux model, there is no Pressure Level button. That's OK. The Lux model operates on high pressure all the time. No need to push a button to select a pressure level. Another Lux quirk: the model has no yogurt-making function.

programs except Sauté and Yogurt. First, select the desired cooking function and time. Then, within 10 seconds, press this key and use the – or + buttons to set the delay before cooking. Two caveats:

- This can be convenient but tricky to use with foods such as beans, rice, and oatmeal, since the soaking time will shorten the ultimate cooking time. Experiment to find what works for you.

- Do not use this setting with perishable foods such as meat or fish. Even frozen meat or fish may hover at unsafe temperatures before the cooking begins.

Keep Warm/Cancel: On models where this is a single button: If the Instant Pot is being programmed or is in use, pressing this button cancels the program and turns the Instant Pot off. When the Instant Pot is off, pressing this button activates the Keep Warm function. Once Keep Warm is activated, the display counts up, allowing you to keep track of how long the function has been on.

On models where these are two separate buttons: The Keep Warm button controls whether the Instant Pot enters Keep Warm mode after it finishes cooking. The light on the top of the button will be on when it is selected. The Cancel button ends cooking at any time or turns the machine off. (Note that if you press Cancel during pressure-cooking, you still must safely release the pressure before opening the lid.)

SO YOU WANT TO SAUTÉ

The Sauté function is a big part of what makes the Instant Pot so convenient and is key to many recipes in this book. In simplest terms, the Sauté function can do much of what a pan on the stovetop can do—without creating more dishes to wash. While some slow-cooker recipes out there would have you sauté aromatics such as onion and garlic separately on the stovetop before adding them to the slow cooker, in the Instant Pot, you can do this right in the inner pot.

TIMING

On some models, you can set a time for the Sauté function, not to exceed 30 minutes. The time will not be displayed as it counts down. Instead, "On" or "Hot" will be displayed until the time elapses, at which point the machine will turn off. On other models, there is no time setting for the Sauté function. Once selected, the Sauté function will remain active for up to 30 minutes or until canceled. The readout will display "30" and will not count down. The recipes in this book call for pressing Cancel and switching to either pressure cooking or slow-cooking well before the 30 minutes have elapsed.

HEAT SETTINGS

The Sauté function has three settings. Pressing the Adjust button cycles among:

• Less: 221°F

• Normal: 320°F

• More: 338°F

There is no easy way to equate these settings to stovetop heat levels, but it helps to think of them as low, medium, and high. Keep in mind that the difference between "Less" and "Normal" is about 100°F, while the difference between "Normal" and "More" is only about 20°F. Rely on your senses and lower the temperature if you see or smell something burning.

USES FOR THE SAUTÉ SETTING

• Browning or softening aromatics such as onions or garlic before pressure-cooking or slow-cooking

- Browning meat before pressure-cooking or slow-cooking

- Thickening sauces or soups after pressure-cooking or slow-cooking

- Finishing beans that are slightly underdone after pressure-cooking

THINGS TO KNOW

- Always use the Sauté function with the lid off. If the lid is locked on, the display will show "Lid."

- The display will show "Hot" when the Sauté function reaches the selected temperature, but you can begin cooking before that. If you want an idea of how hot the inner pot is, flick a bit of water on it and see how quickly it "dances."

- Do not leave the Instant Pot unattended while using Sauté mode.

- Food browns better when it has a little breathing room. If the inner pot is crowded, consider browning in batches.

THE KEEP WARM FUNCTION

Keep Warm is the function that you can use without even knowing it. I'll explain: After the Instant Pot completes its slow-cooking, pressure-cooking, or steaming cycles, it switches automatically into Keep Warm mode. (On some models, you can control whether it does this or not by pressing the

Tip: Turn off the beeping. The Instant Pot likes to beep—when you start a cycle, when you finish a cycle, when the lid goes on, when the lid comes off. . . . On some models, the sound can be suppressed by pressing and holding the - button for 4 seconds when the Instant Pot is plugged in and turned off. The display will show "S Off" to indicate that the sound is off. (Some models will display a sound icon with an "X" next to it.) Enjoy the silence.

Keep Warm button, which will light up when this feature is activated.) The Instant Pot will then keep the food between 145°F and 172°F for up to 10 hours.

Keep Warm can also be activated manually by pressing the Keep Warm/Cancel button and then adjusting the time using the − or + buttons.

The USDA says that if you are not serving hot food right away, it should be kept above 140°F to avoid the temperature danger zone in which bacteria can thrive. While the Keep Warm setting does hold food at a safe temperature, some dishes do better than others at those temperatures. Rice, for instance, may scorch if left on the Keep Warm cycle. The recipes in this book are best left on Keep Warm for no more than 1 hour. After that, vegetables may get too soft, meat may begin to dry out, and evaporation could reduce any liquid. A better idea for keeping food warm for short periods (say, during dinner): Turn off the machine and keep the lid on. The trapped residual heat will keep the food warm without danger of scorching.

PRESET BUTTONS

These are the buttons with food-specific labels (e.g., "Bean/Chili" or "Poultry"). They correspond to pressure-cooking times preset by the manufacturer. Your model may or may not have all of these buttons, but don't worry: There's not much of a connection between the buttons and what your machine can actually *do*. (So, for instance, if your machine has no Egg button, you can still make eggs. When it comes to pressure-cooking, the recipes in this book use the Manual or Pressure-Cook button to help you learn typical cooking times for various ingredients and allow you to easily fine-tune the cooking times. Don't worry too much about the preset buttons. There is nothing magical about them; the Instant Pot cannot, for example, sense when your beans are cooked. In other words: **You can use all the functions of your Instant Pot without ever touching these preset buttons.** (Saying that means a lot of people will skip this section; I can live with that. See you in the next section!)

Soup or Soup/Broth: This is a pressure-cooking function designed for making soups and broths. Pressing the button again or pressing the Adjust button cycles among 20, 30, and 40 minutes. (On some models, the highest setting is 4 hours rather than 40 minutes.)

Meat/Stew: This is also a pressure-cooking function designed for meats (other than poultry) and stews. Pressing the button again or pressing the Adjust button toggles among 20, 35, and 45 minutes.

Bean/Chili: Like the two buttons above, this pressure-cooking preset can be modified by pressing the button again or pressing the Adjust button—to 25, 30, or 40 minutes—with a longer cooking time yielding softer beans.

Cake: This is a pressure-cooking preset on some models that can be modified by pressing the button again to cycle among 25, 40, or 50 minutes.

Egg: This pressure-cooking preset, available on some models, is intended for extra-large eggs and can be cycled among 4, 5, or 6 minutes.

Poultry: This is a pressure-cooking preset on some models with a cooking time of

15 minutes meant for poultry. The Adjust button also lets you select 5 minutes or 30 minutes.

Rice: This is a pressure-cooking preset that uses low pressure to make white rice. It adjusts the cooking time slightly according to the amount of rice. The manufacturer recommends rinsing and draining the rice before placing it in the inner pot with a 1:1 rice-to-water ratio. Because there are many kinds of rice and varying cooking times, I prefer to use the Manual or Pressure-Cook button. For details, see the Rice Maker chapter (page 207).

Multigrain: This pressure-cooking preset is meant for cooking wild rice, brown rice, and other long-cooking grains. Pressing the Multigrain button or the Adjust button modifies the program: Pressing it until the "Less" setting is selected gives 20 minutes of high-pressure cooking. The "Normal" setting gives 40 minutes of high-pressure cooking time. One quirk: The "More" setting provides a warm soak for 45 minutes followed by 60 minutes of cooking at high pressure. This may be used for very hard dry grains, such as hominy or pozole.

Porridge: This pressure-cooking preset uses the Porridge or Adjust button to cycle among 15, 20, and 30 minutes.

Sterilize: This button, available on some models, performs three functions. "Less" performs no-pressure sterilization at about 180°F. "Normal" performs low-pressure sterilization at about 230°F. "More" performs high-pressure sterilization at about 239°F. Note that while recipes for canning meats typically call for a pressure canner, that is not a safe and approved use of the Instant Pot or this function.

HOW TO SPEAK INSTANT POT: DECIPHERING THE LCD READOUT

The digital readout can cause some head-scratching. Some terms that might pop up on the screen:

Boil: After pressing the Yogurt and Adjust buttons, this appears on screen to indicate that the milk in the inner pot will be boiled.

C1, C2, C6: The Instant Pot's electronics are malfunctioning. Contact customer support.

C5: The temperature is too high, either because the inner pot is not properly in place or because there is no liquid in the inner pot.

Hot: When using the Sauté function, this appears after the selected temperature is reached.

Lid: This flashes on the screen when the lid is not in the correct position for the selected program, which is either open for Sauté or closed for pressure-cooking.

NoPr: If this is displayed, it means the Instant Pot cannot build any pressure. Be sure the silicone sealing ring is installed in the lid and the pressure-release valve is set to Sealing (take care because the machine and food may be quite hot). Check that there is sufficient liquid in the inner pot. If you are starting with frozen food, it may be that the Instant Pot did not reach pressure quickly enough and gave up; try running the program again.

OvHt or Burn: The Instant Pot has detected overheating. Cancel the cooking program, safely release any built-up pressure (see "Quick Release," page 26), and check to see if there is food burnt to the bottom of the inner pot.

Yogt: This means the Instant Pot has completed either the first step of the yogurt-making process (boiling—which generally takes 30 minutes) or the second step of that process (gentle heating—typically 8 hours).

CONVERTING YOUR FAVORITE RECIPES TO THE INSTANT POT

While the recipes in this book are tailored for the Instant Pot, not every recipe out there is. There is no magic formula for converting a recipe to the Instant Pot, but these guidelines and a little experimentation will help.

Four tips upfront:

- Save yourself some hassle and take notes on what works for a particular recipe.

- There is a learning curve, but it can be fun to experiment. And the lessons build upon one another; converting your tenth recipe will be much easier than your first.

- The Instant Pot doesn't reinvent all the rules. Consider that even in a pressure cooker, a continuum of cooking times holds true. So, as a rough sketch: Greens will cook faster than fish, which cooks faster than chicken, which cooks faster than beef and pork. (I owe this useful and succinct notion to writer and podcaster Matthew Amster-Burton.)

• While 1 cup of water is recommended for a 6-quart Instant Pot to build pressure, less is possible—especially with juicy or wet ingredients. So those tomatoes, with their high water content, are contributing to the water in your recipe. That starchy potato? Not so much. Onions are a strange case—quite dry by the looks of them but able to release quite a bit of moisture as they cook.

TIPS ON CHANGING A RECIPE FROM SLOW COOKER TO PRESSURE COOKER

You may already have a slow cooker and some favorite slow-cooker recipes. You'll be happy to discover that many of those recipes can be modified to work in the Instant Pot's pressure-cooker function, taking a fraction of the time and turning out the same tasty results. This means that, say, the stew that slow-cooked all day can be ready in about an hour. Keep these tips in mind (and refer to pages 24–29 for more of the nitty-gritty on cooking under pressure):

Templates: Use the recipes in this book as guidelines. If you find a pressure-cooker recipe with similar ingredients to those in your favorite slow-cooker recipe, try substituting your ingredients and using the pressure-cooking timing and instructions as the guiding method.

Timing: As a very general rule, dishes based on beef, pork, or lamb made in 4 hours on high or 8 hours on low in the slow cooker can be made in 30 minutes in the pressure cooker. Poultry-based dishes may need only 20 minutes in the pressure cooker.

Weight: The total weight of meat does not affect pressure-cooking time, but the size of the pieces does. So, for example, if you're cooking beef and lentils together, try cutting the beef into pieces that will be cooked through at the same time as the lentils (see the charts on pages 268–271 for some general guidelines).

Staggered cooking times: Sometimes it won't be ideal to change the size of the meat, and the cooking times of components will be different enough to require two stages. A recipe that includes, for example, cubed beef and cubed potatoes could be done in two parts: Cook the beef for 30 minutes, then release the pressure. Next, add the potatoes and pressure-cook everything for 5 minutes more. The principle here is that the 5 extra minutes of cooking time for a tough, stewing cut of beef will not do it any harm, whereas overcooking the potatoes by 25 minutes may make them unpleasantly soft. If the recipe also includes aromatics such as onion, garlic, or herbs, add those early on so that they can contribute their flavors to the meat as it cooks.

Liquids: While most recipes for the slow cooker include liquid, it is particularly important to double-check the amount when translating the recipe to the pressure cooker. The recipe should include at least 1 cup of liquid, whether water or broth. Keep in mind that too much liquid can also be an issue: Because there is practically no evaporation when pressure-cooking, all the liquid added will stay in the dish. In some cases, this may result in a dish being too watery. Consider cutting the amount of liquid slightly or reducing the liquid by cooking the dish on the Sauté function after the pressure-cooking has finished.

Frozen meat: Although cooking frozen meat in a slow cooker is discouraged because the meat may hover at unsafe temperatures while it warms, that is not a problem in the pressure cooker because the pressure and temperature are higher. Note that this works best with chunks of meat; a large frozen roast may cook unevenly, even in the pressure cooker. As a rule, add 50 percent to the normal cooking time when using frozen cubed or ground meat. Always check the temperature of the finished meat to verify that it is thoroughly cooked. In some instances, frozen meat may mean that the Instant Pot displays "NoPr" and doesn't reach cooking pressure. (This is because the appliance only allows so much time to come to pressure and frozen food can slow the process.) If this happens, don't be deterred, just start the pressure-cooking cycle over again.

Thickeners: If using flour or starch to thicken a recipe, always add this after the pressure-cooking cycle. Adding it before pressure-cooking risks burning the starch on the bottom of the inner pot.

Dairy: If a slow-cooker recipe calls for cheese, milk, or cream, add these ingredients after the pressure-cooking cycle to avoid curdling.

Alcohol: Red wine can be great in a slow-cooker stew, but keep in mind that in a pressure cooker there is no opportunity for the alcohol to evaporate. If your recipe calls for red wine, try cutting the quantity in half and reducing the wine using the

> **Tip:** Be sure to place food in the inner pot and not directly into the appliance. This sounds obvious, no? And yet . . . Do not, for example, absentmindedly pour water into the appliance and then realize too late that you are pouring water into the electronics of your beloved Instant Pot. I won't tell you how I came up with that example. One trick: Place a wooden spoon or cutting board over the Instant Pot when the inner pot is not in place.

Sauté setting before starting the pressure-cooking. Beer quantity can be maintained, but you'll want to evaporate some of the alcohol: Allow some of the liquid to reduce using the Sauté setting after the pressure-cooking cycle.

Overall volume: Remember that when using the pressure cooker, the inner pot should not be more than two-thirds full, or half full for recipes with foods that expand with cooking, such as beans and grains.

Natural release vs. quick release: Using natural release when converting a slow cooker recipe often achieves better results and avoids unpleasant surprises; this is particularly true with any ingredients that could interfere with a manual pressure release (for example, foamy foods such as beans).

CLEANING THE MACHINE

The Instant Pot is easy to clean, but it can be tricky at first to sort out which parts need to be cleaned and how to clean them. It's not a one-size-fits-all approach.

GENERAL CLEANING

- Unplug the appliance and allow it to cool down if it has been in use.

- Use a damp cloth to wipe down the Instant Pot's base. This is the "brains" of your Instant Pot and contains electronics. **Never immerse this part in water or clean it in the dishwasher.**

- Use a dry brush (a toothbrush works well) to remove any caked-on food or residue from the recessed area around the lip of the base.

CLEANING THE LID, ANTI-BLOCK SHIELD, AND SILICONE SEALING RING

- These parts can all be washed in the dishwasher, though the black plastic of the lid may become slightly discolored over time. As someone who frequently tosses the lid in the dishwasher, I can tell you that any merely cosmetic consequences are a small price to pay for the convenience. I also find that the dishwasher typically does a better job of eliminating clingy odors than I do by hand-washing.

- The black plastic pressure-release valve is loose-fitting and can be removed by pulling up on it. Clean it with warm, soapy water or place it in the silverware basket of the dishwasher, checking to make sure it is clear of any food and debris.

- Remove the anti-block shield from the underside of the lid. Grip it tightly and pull to remove. There are two versions of the anti-block shield and the round version can be particularly difficult to remove with bare hands. Here's a trick: Use a rubber jar opener or silicone mitt to grasp it firmly, pushing it slightly to one side before pulling it out. Wash the anti-block shield with warm, soapy water or place it in the silverware basket of the dishwasher.

- If necessary, the small metal float valve can be cleaned by removing the small silicone rubber ring from the underside of the lid.

- The silicone sealing ring can be hand-washed in warm, soapy water or cleaned in the dishwasher. Because it is crucial to the Instant Pot's ability to form a tight seal, it should be inspected periodically for cracks and damage and replaced when necessary. (The manufacturer says the ring will last two to three years under normal conditions. For what it's worth, I'm fairly certain that writing a cookbook and making breakfast, lunch, and dinner in the Instant Pot for months on end is not a normal condition, but even so, mine are still going strong.)

To remove stubborn odors from the sealing ring, use one of two methods:

- Soak the ring in white vinegar overnight and then wash with warm, soapy water or place on the top rack of the dishwasher.

- Steam-clean the sealing ring. Use the test run procedure described in Setting Up Your Pot, page 5.

CLEANING THE INNER POT AND STEAMING RACK

- As with other stainless steel cookware, these may be cleaned in the dishwasher.

- To clean by hand, use warm, soapy water. To remove any stubborn bits, soak for 30 minutes in warm water, drain, and then use a sponge to scour the metal, using a generous sprinkle of baking soda as a gentle abrasive if necessary.

CLEANING THE CONDENSATION COLLECTOR

• This small plastic cup can be hand-washed with soap and warm water or placed upside-down in the silverware rack of the dishwasher.

INSTANT POT FAQS

If you have questions about a particular Instant Pot function, check the chapter introductions or look in the index.

Q. The lid is difficult to open after pressure has been released. I try to lift the lid and the entire appliance wants to come with it. What's going on?

A. After pressure-cooking and using natural release, the valve will still be in the Sealing position. Sometimes the cooling process creates a bit of a vacuum between the lid and the inner pot and makes the lid difficult to remove. To break that vacuum, turn the valve to Venting, allow a moment for air to flow into the appliance, and then turn the lid counterclockwise; it should lift off the appliance more easily.

Q. My Instant Pot is making clicking and cracking noises as it cooks and cools. Is this normal?

A. Yes, this is normal. The noises could be due to the Instant Pot cycling on or off its heat for temperature control or the expansion or contraction of parts as the appliance heats or cools. It's all totally normal.

Q. I set the valve to Sealing, but there is still steam coming out. What's happening?

A. There are two possibilities here, but either way that steam is just your Instant Pot at work.

• **The first possibility:** When pressure-cooking, the Instant Pot may release steam before it comes to pressure and starts its cooking time. This steam is released through the small metal float valve. That's because the liquid in the inner pot is boiling but the appliance has not yet come to pressure and pushed the metal float valve into the sealing position. Once the metal float valve seals the lid and that steam is trapped inside the appliance, it achieves the necessary pressure.

• **The second possibility:** Steam is sometimes released through the black plastic valve during cooking. The Instant Pot does that to regulate pressure, automatically keeping the pressure within a safe range.

Q. The black plastic valve on the lid of my Instant Pot is very loose. That can't be normal, can it?

A. It's totally normal. The black plastic valve needs to be loose to allow the Instant Pot to vent steam as necessary during cooking to regulate pressure.

Q. When I use natural release and allow the appliance to cool on its own after pressure-cooking, I don't see any steam coming out. Where does it all go?

A. There's a big difference between the spectacular release of steam from a quick release and the total lack of steam in a natural release. When you allow the Instant Pot to cool on its own with a natural release, the heat dissipates via the metal on the lid. Once the pressure and heat have dissipated, there simply is no steam left when you open the lid; it has all turned back to liquid.

Q. Can the recipes in this book be halved?

A. Most often the answer is yes, as long as the liquid does not fall below the amount required to build pressure for pressure-cooker recipes (generally 1 cup). The cooking time stays the same. If you're asking this because you're not using a 6-quart Instant Pot, see 3-Quart and 8-Quart Models, page 2.

Q. Can the recipes in this book be doubled?

A. Many can. Some cannot. To identify those recipes that will double well, keep an eye out for a **X2** icon. Some chapter-by-chapter considerations:

Yogurt Maker: A recipe such as Homemade Plain Yogurt (page 226) will not double because there would be too much liquid for the machine to handle, but Do-It-Yourself Ricotta and Crème Fraîche will double. The time that you set on the Instant Pot remains the same as given in the recipe. So, for example, making a double batch of Crème Fraîche requires setting a time of 8 hours on the Instant Pot.

Slow Cooker: Recipes where ingredients are first sautéed generally require enough space on the bottom of the inner pot for the ingredients to move around. Also, only so much meat will fit in the inner pot. (That tends to be around 3 pounds of roast.) For the recipes that will double, the time that you set on the Instant Pot remains the same as given in the recipe.

Pressure Cooker: The space considerations are much the same as with slow-cooker recipes. One big caveat: Recipes with foods that expand—

THE *HOW TO INSTANT POT* ICONS AND WHAT THEY MEAN

Many of the recipes in this book are identified with icons to highlight special features, like if the recipe is vegan, doubles well, or is speedy enough for a weeknight dinner. You may see the following icons alone or in combination:

V Vegetarian

VN Vegan

DF Dairy-Free

X2 Recipe can be doubled

30 30 minutes or less

60 60 minutes or less

 INSTANT POT QUICK FIX
Look for recipes labeled Quick Fix sprinkled throughout this book. These recipes let the Instant Pot shine in ways you might not expect, whether by taking a time-consuming or tricky dish and making it faster and simpler, or by teaching you to make something you never expected. You'll find these recipes labeled in the Contents for each chapter. Here are just two examples:

- How many methods are there for hard-boiling eggs? Too many. Now you only need one and it couldn't be simpler (see Hard-Boiled Eggs, page 80).

- Crème Fraiche (page 233) has a rich taste that rivals sour cream and an elegant name to boot, but there's nothing complicated about making it yourself with the Instant Pot.

 1, 2, 3 RECIPES
A big part of learning to use the Instant Pot is seeing how easily you can create an entirely new dish by swapping out some ingredients and largely sticking with the Master method in the original recipe. That's the idea behind a recipe such as Winter Squash Soup 1, 2, 3 (page 83), which turns out three different meals using the same basic method. Meanwhile, recipes such as Chickpea Salad 1, 2, 3 (page 94) show you how easy it is to make a single ingredient in the Instant Pot and then turn it into three unique salads.

Look for 1, 2, 3 recipes throughout the book and use them as a starting place for your own recipes, too, by personalizing the methods with your own flavors as you master the Instant Pot.

such as dried beans or grains—cannot fill the inner pot more than halfway. The time that you set on the Instant Pot remains the same as given in the recipe. But, because of the volume of food, it will take longer for the Instant Pot to build and to later release pressure naturally.

Rice Maker: Many of these recipes will indeed double, though something like Thai-Style Sticky Rice (page 214) would overrun most steaming baskets. The time that you set on the Instant Pot remains the same as given in the recipe, though it will take longer for the Instant Pot to build pressure.

Steamer: Again, the consideration is volume. Most of the recipes in this book already fill a typical steaming basket, so there's not much room for doubling.

Chapter 2
PRESSURE COOKER

....

Some of us can picture a pressure cooker in our parents' or grandparents' kitchen but haven't felt comfortable using one ourselves. Probably whoever was using it at the time didn't offer up a physics lesson, so it may be shrouded in a bit of mystery. Also, a lot of families seem to have stories about, shall we say, "incidents"—a surprisingly common element of which is food that ended up on the ceiling. (That's not how it's supposed to go, as we can gather from the now-quaint cookbooks of decades ago that did not depict this; gelatin mold salads, yes—food on the ceiling, no.)

The Instant Pot's circuitry and safety features have eliminated that messy food-on-the-ceiling problem. And it's not necessary to understand how a pressure cooker works in order to use one. But it *is* fun to know. This chapter and a little practice will unwrap the mystery and help make you a pressure-cooker power user.

HOW A PRESSURE COOKER WORKS

At its most basic, a pressure cooker is just a pot with a very tight lid. When the liquid inside that pot heats up, the steam is trapped, raising the temperature and pressure inside the pot. That's because water boiled in an open pot at sea level cannot get hotter than 212°F—when the water molecules get too hot, they simply fly off into the air as steam. But in a well-sealed pot, those molecules have nowhere else to go. They bounce around the pot faster and faster, raising the temperature.

At the Instant Pot's pressure of about 11 pounds per square inch, the temperature reaches about 240°F. Yes, your oven has higher temperature settings than this, but that would only matter if every inch of

your oven were filled with liquid or steam, since the air in the oven is a much worse conductor of heat than the liquid and steam in the Instant Pot. Essentially, the heat in your oven is lazing around, occasionally hitting your food, but also escaping out the vents and the oven door. Meanwhile, by comparison, the heat in the Instant Pot is pummeling the food, bouncing off the food nonstop and transferring its energy to your meal. The result: The higher temperature cooks food more quickly, while the vapor keeps food moist.

Crucial in this system is some sort of valve to regulate the vapor buildup and prevent the uncontrolled release of pressure. ("Explosion" is such an ugly word.) The Instant Pot not only regulates the heat that builds up the pressure, but also regulates the pressure itself. That's what keeps the pressure and heat safely trapped inside the Instant Pot until it's ready to be released.

HOW A PRESSURE-COOKER RECIPE WORKS

Here's a quick overview of the steps typically involved in pressure-cooking:

1. Sauté some of the ingredients: This step is not in every recipe but is frequently used with meats to brown them and begin to develop flavor. Because the Instant Pot has a Sauté function, this all happens in the appliance with no need to dirty a separate frying pan.

2. Place the other ingredients in the inner pot: These ingredients must include liquid. The liquid is what helps develop the pressure inside the Instant Pot. Water is the most obvious contributor of liquid, but broth may also be called for. Many vegetables also contribute some liquid as they cook, but it's usually not enough to build sufficient pressure.

3. Seal the Instant Pot: Without a tight seal, pressure will not build. This means ensuring that the sealing ring is installed in the lid (see page 4) and that the valve is set to Sealing. Even when the valve is

set to Sealing, some steam will escape at first before the metal float valve rises and becomes flush with the lid, thereby sealing the pot. This is normal.

4. Set the cooking time: This time does not include the time it takes for the machine to build pressure or any time it takes to release pressure; it only includes the time that the food is cooked at pressure. Many models emit a single beep when the machine is at pressure and the cooking time starts. The Total Time given for the recipes in this book includes the time it takes for the pressure to build and release.

5. Release pressure: Once the cooking time has elapsed, it's time for the pressure to be released. This may be done naturally by allowing the heat and pressure to dissipate on their own, or quickly by releasing the valve on the lid. (See Natural Release vs. Quick Release, page 26.)

6. Reduce liquid or continue cooking: Soups or stews may need to be reduced slightly because no liquid has evaporated. Dried foods such as beans may require a bit of additional cooking. In both cases, you can achieve this by using the Sauté function and cooking with the lid off until the desired consistency is reached.

NATURAL RELEASE VS. QUICK RELEASE

At the end of the cooking cycle, the built-up pressure must go somewhere. There are two ways to release the pressure:

Natural release: You won't see any steam released. Using this method allows the heat and pressure to dissipate naturally and involves not fiddling with the valve and simply waiting for the pressure to release on its own, usually 10 to 30 minutes. (The time depends on the amount of food cooked.) Where this method is called for, an estimated release time is specified in the instructions and is taken into account as part of the Total Time. This means that manually releasing the pressure early in a "quick release" (see below) may result in undercooked food. Natural release is recommended particularly for foods that might clog the valve if quick release were used; this includes food with a lot of liquid or starch (such as oatmeal). You will know the pressure is released when the small metal float valve sinks back into the lid and the lid is no longer locked.

Quick release: This method releases the pressure immediately after cooking. While the food retains heat, quick release essentially stops the cooking. This is done by turning (or pressing on some models)

the black plastic valve on the top of the lid to release the pressure. This immediately sends steam shooting out of the top. This is no joke and you must be very careful to have every part of your body away from the valve when you release the pressure. Stand back from the pot and use something like a long-handled wooden spoon to turn the knob and release the steam. The knob may feel loose, as though it is not on tightly; this is normal.

THE DIFFERENCES BETWEEN INSTANT POT AND OTHER PRESSURE COOKERS

The Instant Pot has two main differences from many other pressure cookers:

- One difference is evident at a glance: The Instant Pot is electric and, unlike many older pressure cookers, does not need to be—should not be—used on the stovetop. Using it on the stovetop means risking damage to the Instant Pot if the heat is accidentally turned on.

- The second difference is less immediately evident: The Instant Pot operates at a lower pressure (and thus lower temperature) than many other pressure cookers. The recipes in this book are all tailored specifically to the Instant Pot. If you use pressure-cooker recipes not specifically for the Instant Pot, there is an easy rule of thumb for converting them: Add 15 percent more cooking time and then check the results at the end of the cooking time. Pressure-cook for a few more minutes if necessary and then make a note on the recipe for next time.

PRESSURE-COOKER TIPS AND POTENTIAL PITFALLS

Pressure-cooking may at first contain an element of mystery for novice and experienced cooks alike. If a dish goes awry, here are some factors to consider:

Too much liquid: Pressure cookers seal in liquid during cooking, which means there is practically no evaporation. Because of this, and because some ingredients—particularly fruits and vegetables—contain a lot of water, you do not need as much liquid as with many other cooking methods.

Too little liquid: You do, however, need a minimum amount of liquid (about 1 cup) for the Instant Pot to build sufficient pressure.

Cooking with the inner pot too full: Remember that foods that expand when cooked, such as raw grains and dried beans, should not fill more than half of the inner pot. Other foods should occupy no more than two thirds of the inner pot.

Overcooking delicate foods: Cooking under pressure means that foods cook quickly. This can sometimes mean that foods *overcook* quickly. Quick-cooking, delicate foods are best left to other cooking methods.

Setup glitches: Before pressure-cooking, be sure the valve is set to Sealing and the lid is in place with the silicone ring installed; otherwise the machine will not build and maintain pressure.

Expecting crispness: Pressure-cooking is a moist cooking method. Although browning some ingredients first is useful in developing flavor, food will not emerge golden brown and crispy. Part of enjoying your pressure cooker is knowing what it excels at; think less along the lines of a whole chicken with glistening brown skin and more along the lines of satisfying stews with tender chunks of meat.

RECIPE TIMING

You may see that a recipe calls for setting the pressure-cooking time for 10 minutes, and yet somehow the recipe takes twice that long to complete. Here's why: The pressure cooker takes time to build up the required pressure. Although the food does cook inside while the heat and pressure build, that time does not figure into the countdown the machine displays.

One quirk of pressure-cooking: Increasing the volume of food does not require increasing the cooking time. (That said, the time required to reach pressure will increase as volume increases.) Be cautious: While some recipe quantities may be increased, never fill the inner pot more than halfway with beans, grains, or other legumes, or more than two thirds with other foods. While recipes can often be halved, do not use less than 1 cup of liquid. See the FAQs (page 17) for more information on doubling recipes.

HIGH-ALTITUDE MODIFICATIONS

Anyone cooking at high altitudes may know that water boils at a lower temperature at higher elevations; less energy is needed for the water molecules to fly into the air as steam because less air pressure is keeping those molecules down. The pressure cooker works at high altitudes because it replaces some of that pressure and raises the boiling temperature of water. However, some modifications may be necessary (unless you have an Ultra, see page 4): Experiment to find out what works for you, but adding 5 percent to the cooking time for every 1,000 feet above sea level is a good starting point.

PRESSURE-COOKER SAFETY

There is no doubt that pressure-cooking can present safety issues. So can cooking on the stovetop, but you don't often hear about adults who shrink from that because it makes them nervous. A UL-certified pressure cooker such as the Instant Pot must be able to withstand many times its working pressure without leaking. So there is nothing to be afraid of—but there *are* some things to keep in mind:

- **Take the steam seriously:** Using quick release to vent the steam from the Instant Pot releases a serious stream of scorching hot vapor. It's quite impressive—from a safe distance. Use a long wooden spoon and not your hand to release the valve. And keep every part of your body away from the vent while the steam is released.

- **Remember that the inner pot is hot:** Even once the pressure is released, the inner pot and the food inside will still be very hot. Use oven mitts when handling the inner pot.

- **Read the manual:** While you will become more familiar with the Instant Pot as you use it, reading the manual provides important safety precautions.

- **Do not use your Instant Pot as a pressure canner to create shelf-stable jarred food:** While some pressure cookers may be used for this (and some models of the Instant Pot have a Sterilize function that can be used to purify empty jars or cans), pressure canning is not a safe and approved use of the Instant Pot. While the Instant Pot Max offers a canning function, as of this writing it is not proven to meet widely accepted canning safety standards and therefore I cannot recommend it. (See Meet Max, page 7.) Check with the National Center for Home Food Preservation (https://nchfp.uga.edu) for the latest information.

- **Consider the size:** As noted on page 2, but as also bears repeating, the recipes in this book were developed using a 6-quart Instant Pot. The recipes may be used in other sizes (see 3-Quart and 8-Quart Models, page 2), but be careful not to overfill the inner pot—never more than half full for grains, legumes, and other foods that expand during cooking, and never more than two-thirds full for other foods such as meats, soups, and stews.

PRESSURE-COOKING TIPS AND TIDBITS

- Placing a wet towel on the lid speeds up cooling when using natural release, a handy trick to have at your disposal when developing your own recipes. Keep in mind that the recipes in this book that use natural release take into account the cooling time as part of the cooking process, so speeding up the natural-release process could result in undercooked food.

- Different types of beans, rice, and grains cook at different rates (see the charts on pages 268–271). Even two batches of the same type of bean may cook more or less quickly depending on how long the beans were stored at the supermarket or at home. For this reason and because of many other variables, it is not possible to issue one universal, true cooking time for foods—you may find yourself needing to adjust cooking times to your circumstances. My simple advice on this topic: Remember that it is not possible to un-cook overdone food, but you can always cook underdone food a bit more by resealing the Instant Pot and pressure-cooking or cooking with the lid off using the Sauté function.

BEEF BARBACOA TACOS

TOTAL TIME: 1 hour **ACTIVE TIME:** 10 minutes **YIELD:** Serves 6

Salty, spicy, and slightly tangy, this dish delivers flavor on multiple levels. The tender shredded beef showcases the power of the pressure cooker to turn out in just an hour a meal that would ordinarily take hours of slow cooking.

¼ cup apple cider vinegar

2 tablespoons freshly squeezed lime juice

3 cloves garlic, minced

1 chipotle chile in adobo, minced

2 teaspoons ground cumin

2 teaspoons dried oregano

1 teaspoon salt

½ teaspoon freshly ground black pepper

¼ teaspoon ground cloves

2 tablespoons vegetable oil

2½ pounds boneless beef chuck roast, trimmed of most fat and cut into large chunks

½ cup reduced-salt chicken broth or All-Purpose Chicken Stock (page 88)

2 bay leaves

Small (6-inch) corn tortillas, for serving

Salsa or pico de gallo, for serving

Cotija cheese, for serving

1 Whisk together the vinegar, lime juice, garlic, chipotle, cumin, oregano, salt, pepper, and cloves in a medium bowl. Set aside.

2 Press Sauté and use the Sauté or Adjust button to select the highest temperature ("More"). Place the vegetable oil in the inner pot. Wait until the display reads

"Hot," about 5 minutes, then add the beef. Cook with the lid off, turning the beef every 2 minutes, until the beef is browned on most sides, about 8 minutes.

3 Add the vinegar sauce and the chicken broth (be careful—steam may whoosh up!), and then the bay leaves. Stir to combine.

4 Close and lock the lid. Set the valve to Sealing. Press Cancel, then press Manual or Pressure Cook and use the Pressure or Pressure Level button to select High Pressure. Use the – or + button to set the time to 30 minutes.

5 When the cooking cycle ends, press Cancel. Allow the appliance to cool and release pressure naturally, about 20 minutes. (The pressure is released when the small metal float valve next to the pressure-release valve sinks back into the lid and the lid is no longer locked.)

6 Remove the lid. Discard the bay leaves. Use tongs or a large spoon to remove the beef from the inner pot and place it on a cutting board. Shred the beef using two forks: Use one fork to pull off a chunk and then use two forks to shred that piece, holding down the meat with one fork and pulling at it with the other. Repeat with the remaining beef.

7 Serve the beef hot, piled into corn tortillas and topped with salsa and a sprinkling of Cotija cheese, if desired.

Beef Barbacoa and its juices will keep, in an airtight container in the refrigerator, for up to 4 days. To reheat, preheat the oven to 350°F and place the beef in a shallow baking dish with enough of the juices to reach a depth of about ¼ inch. Cover the baking dish tightly with aluminum foil and bake until hot, about 15 minutes.

PINEAPPLE SKIRT STEAK

TOTAL TIME: 25 minutes **ACTIVE TIME:** 5 minutes **YIELD:** Serves 4

Pair this quick dish with some vegetables and rice and dinner is set. The bright flavor of the sweet-tart pineapple and saltiness of the soy sauce combine to make your taste buds stand up and take notice. Getting so much flavor from so few ingredients can make this dish a go-to: Prepare it once and you'll bookmark it for those occasions when you want something impressive but simple.

¾ cup pineapple juice or pineapple juice blend

¼ cup soy sauce

½ teaspoon freshly ground black pepper

1½ pounds skirt steak, sliced about ¼ inch thick against the grain (see Note)

2 scallions, green parts only, thinly sliced, for garnish

---

1 Place the pineapple juice, soy sauce, and pepper in the inner pot and stir to combine. Add the steak and stir to coat it with the sauce. Close and lock the lid. Set the valve to Sealing. Press Manual or Pressure Cook and use the Pressure or Pressure Level button to select High Pressure. Use the – or + button to set the time to 12 minutes.

2 When the cooking cycle ends, carefully use a wooden spoon to release the pressure by turning the pressure-release valve to Venting. (The pressure is released when the small metal float valve next to the pressure-release valve sinks back into the lid and the lid is no longer locked.)

3 Press Cancel and remove the lid. Remove the steak from the inner pot.

4 Serve warm, drizzled with a spoonful of the sauce and garnished with scallions.

Pineapple Skirt Steak and cooking liquid will keep, in an airtight container in the refrigerator, for up to 4 days. To reheat, place the steak in a pot, add cooking liquid to cover the bottom, and warm on the stovetop over medium-low heat, stirring occasionally, for about 5 minutes.

Note: To cut against the grain, slice perpendicular to the muscle fibers running through the steak.

PRESSURE-COOKER BEEF STEW

The Instant Pot and beef stew make a lovely couple. Tough beef that typically requires hours of cooking quickly becomes fork-tender in the pressure cooker. A butternut squash version (see below) gets a touch of sweetness and a streak of brilliant orange from the squash. A meat-and-potatoes version goes back to the basics for a satisfying swipe at hunger (see page 37). An incarnation with Thai spices and coconut milk (see page 36) takes the stew in an unexpected direction. In all cases, serve with a salad and rice or a crusty baguette for sopping up the liquid.

1 BEEF AND BUTTERNUT SQUASH STEW DF

TOTAL TIME: 1 hour 15 minutes

ACTIVE TIME: 20 minutes

YIELD: Serves 6

---

3 tablespoons all-purpose flour

1/2 teaspoon salt, plus extra as needed

1/2 teaspoon freshly ground black pepper, plus extra as needed

2 pounds boneless beef for stewing, such as chuck, cut into 2-inch cubes

3 tablespoons extra-virgin olive oil

1 small white or yellow onion, chopped

1/2 teaspoon finely chopped fresh rosemary leaves (or 1/4 teaspoon dried rosemary)

1/2 teaspoon chopped fresh thyme leaves (or 1/4 teaspoon dried thyme)

1/2 cup reduced-salt chicken broth or All-Purpose Chicken Stock (page 88)

1 small butternut squash (about 1 pound), peeled, seeded, and cut into 1-inch cubes

1 can (14 1/2 ounces) diced tomatoes with their juices

1/2 teaspoon Worcestershire sauce

2 tablespoons chopped fresh Italian (flat-leaf) parsley leaves

---

1 Place the flour, salt, and pepper in a large bowl and stir to combine. Add the beef and toss with the flour mixture until the beef is evenly coated. Set aside.

2 Press Sauté and use the Sauté or Adjust button to select the middle temperature ("Normal"). Place 1 tablespoon of the olive oil in the inner pot, wait about 2 minutes for it to warm, then add the onion, rosemary, and thyme. Cook with the lid off, stirring occasionally until the onion softens slightly, about 5 minutes. Use a large spoon to remove the onion to a bowl; set it aside.

3 Place the remaining 2 tablespoons of the olive oil in the inner pot, wait about 1 minute for it to warm, and then add half of the beef. Cook with the lid off, turning the beef occasionally, until it is browned on most sides, about 5 minutes. Transfer the browned beef to a plate and set aside. Repeat with the remaining beef.

4 Place the chicken broth in the inner pot and use a silicone spatula or wooden spoon to scrape the bottom of the inner pot until most of the brown bits are released, about 1 minute. Add the reserved onion, browned beef, squash, tomatoes, and Worcestershire sauce and stir to combine.

5 Close and lock the lid. Set the valve to Sealing. Press Cancel, then press Manual or Pressure Cook and use the Pressure or Pressure Level button to select High Pressure. Use the – or + button to set the time to 20 minutes.

6 When the cooking cycle ends, press Cancel. Allow the appliance to cool and release pressure naturally, about 30 minutes. (The pressure is released when the small metal float valve next to the pressure-release valve sinks back into the lid and the lid is no longer locked.)

7 Remove the lid and taste the stew for seasoning, adding salt and pepper as needed. Serve hot, garnished with parsley.

Beef and Butternut Squash Stew will keep, in an airtight container in the refrigerator, for up to 4 days. To reheat, place it in a pot and warm on the stovetop over medium heat, stirring occasionally, until hot, about 5 minutes.

② THAI-SPICED BEEF STEW DF

TOTAL TIME: 1 hour 15 minutes

ACTIVE TIME: 20 minutes

YIELD: Serves 6

---

3 tablespoons all-purpose flour

½ teaspoon salt, plus extra as needed

½ teaspoon freshly ground black pepper,
  plus extra as needed

2 pounds boneless beef for stewing,
  such as chuck, cut into 2-inch cubes

3 tablespoons neutral-flavored vegetable oil,
  such as canola or peanut

1 small white or yellow onion, chopped

1 cup coconut milk

¼ cup Thai red curry paste

1 tablespoon peeled and finely grated
  fresh ginger

Juice of 1 small lime

2 tablespoons water

1 tablespoon fish sauce

2 teaspoons sugar

4 medium carrots, peeled and cut into chunks

2 tablespoons chopped fresh cilantro leaves,
  for garnish

---

1 Place the flour, salt, and pepper in a large bowl and stir to combine. Add the beef and toss with the flour mixture until the beef is evenly coated. Set aside.

2 Press Sauté and select the middle temperature. Place 1 tablespoon of the vegetable oil in the inner pot, wait about 2 minutes for it to warm, then add the onion. Cook with the lid off, stirring occasionally, until the onion softens slightly. Remove the onion to a bowl; set it aside.

3 Place the remaining oil in the inner pot, wait about 1 minute for it to warm, and then add half of the beef. Cook with the lid off, turning the beef occasionally, until it is browned on most sides, about 5 minutes. Transfer the browned beef to a plate and set aside. Repeat with the remaining beef.

4 Place the coconut milk, curry paste, ginger, lime juice, water, fish sauce, and sugar in the inner pot and use a silicone spatula or wooden spoon to scrape the bottom of the inner pot until most of the brown bits are released, about 1 minute. Add the reserved onion, browned beef, and carrots and stir to combine.

5 Close and lock the lid. Set the valve to Sealing. Press Cancel, then select High Pressure and set the time to 20 minutes.

6 When the cooking cycle ends, press Cancel. Release pressure naturally, about 30 minutes.

7 Remove the lid and taste the stew for seasoning, adding salt and pepper as needed. Serve hot, garnished with cilantro.

Thai-Spiced Beef Stew will keep, in an airtight container in the refrigerator, for up to 4 days.

③ MEAT AND POTATOES BEEF STEW DF

TOTAL TIME: 1 hour 15 minutes
ACTIVE TIME: 20 minutes
YIELD: Serves 6

---

3 tablespoons all-purpose flour

1/2 teaspoon salt, plus extra as needed

1/2 teaspoon freshly ground black pepper, plus extra as needed

2 pounds boneless beef for stewing, such as chuck, cut into 2-inch cubes

3 tablespoons extra-virgin olive oil

1 small white or yellow onion, chopped

1/2 teaspoon finely chopped fresh rosemary leaves (or 1/4 teaspoon dried rosemary)

1/2 teaspoon chopped fresh thyme leaves (or 1/4 teaspoon dried thyme)

1/4 teaspoon dried oregano

Pinch of cayenne pepper

1 tablespoon balsamic vinegar

2 cups reduced-salt beef broth or All-Purpose Beef Stock (page 90)

3 unpeeled medium red potatoes (about 1 pound total), cut into 1-inch cubes

1/2 teaspoon Worcestershire sauce

Chopped fresh Italian (flat-leaf) parsley leaves, for garnish

---

1 Place the flour, salt, and pepper in a large bowl and stir to combine. Add the beef and toss with the flour mixture until the beef is evenly coated. Set aside.

2 Press Sauté and select the middle temperature. Place 1 tablespoon of the oil in the inner pot, wait about 2 minutes for the oil to heat, then add the onion, rosemary, thyme, oregano, cayenne pepper, and balsamic vinegar. Cook with the lid off, stirring occasionally, until the onion softens slightly. Remove the onion to a bowl; set it aside.

3 Place the remaining oil in the inner pot, wait about 1 minute for it to warm, and then add half of the beef. Cook with the lid off, turning the beef occasionally, until it is browned on most sides, about 5 minutes. Transfer the browned beef to a plate and set aside. Repeat with the remaining beef.

4 Place the beef broth in the inner pot and use a silicone spatula or wooden spoon to scrape the bottom of the inner pot until most of the brown bits are released, about 1 minute. Add the reserved onion, browned beef, potatoes, and Worcestershire sauce and stir to combine.

5 Close and lock the lid. Set the valve to Sealing. Press Cancel, then select High Pressure and set the time to 20 minutes.

6 When the cooking cycle ends, press Cancel. Release pressure naturally, about 30 minutes.

7 Remove the lid and taste the stew for seasoning, adding salt and pepper as needed. Serve hot, garnished with parsley.

Meat and Potatoes Beef Stew will keep, in an airtight container in the refrigerator, for up to 4 days.

MORE FLAVORING AND SERVING IDEAS FOR BEEF STEW

- Omit other herbs and use ground cumin, ground coriander, and finely chopped chipotle in adobo and serve with corn tortillas.

- Add chopped-up bacon with the onion in step 2.

- Reduce the amount of meat and add cooked beans to the finished dish.

- Add frozen peas or frozen mixed vegetables to any variation of stew just after opening the lid. Use the Sauté function and cook with the lid open to heat the vegetables until warm—just a few minutes.

- Substitute sweet potato or yam in Beef and Butternut Squash Stew. Or substitute either in place of the potatoes in Meat and Potatoes Beef Stew.

- Add chunky, natural peanut butter to Thai-Spiced Beef Stew or Meat and Potatoes Beef Stew and garnish with peanuts.

- Add caraway seeds, sweet paprika, and chopped bell peppers to Meat and Potatoes Beef Stew for a Hungarian goulash approximation.

- Swap out half the beef broth in Meat and Potatoes Beef Stew for beer—a stout or dark lager is ideal. Cook for a few minutes with the lid off to allow the alcohol to evaporate.

- Top Meat and Potatoes Beef Stew with cheese when serving. Try shredded sharp Cheddar, blue cheese, or Gruyère.

CUMIN-SPICED PORK SIRLOIN WITH AVOCADO SALSA

TOTAL TIME: 45 minutes   **ACTIVE TIME:** 10 minutes   **YIELD:** Serves 6

Pork sirloin turns out tender and sliceable in this recipe, which creates a sauce for the meat as it cooks. If you serve the pork with rice, save some sauce for drizzling over it. The avocado salsa contributes not only flavor—the mild, buttery avocado pairs well with the acidity of the tomatoes—but color, too, with its bright red and green.

FOR THE AVOCADO SALSA

Juice of 1 small lime

1 small clove garlic, minced

2 medium avocados, pitted, peeled, and diced

1 cup grape tomatoes (about 14 tomatoes), quartered

Salt and freshly ground black pepper

FOR THE CUMIN-SPICED PORK SIRLOIN

2 pounds boneless pork sirloin

1 teaspoon ground cumin

1 teaspoon salt

1 teaspoon freshly ground black pepper

2 tablespoons neutral-flavored vegetable oil, such as canola or peanut

1 cup water

Finely grated zest and juice of 2 small limes

2 cloves garlic, peeled and whole

1 Make the salsa: Place the lime juice and minced garlic in a small bowl. Add the avocado and toss to coat. Add the tomatoes and a pinch each of salt and pepper. Taste and adjust the seasoning, adding more salt and pepper as needed.

2 Make the pork: Rub the pork all over with the cumin, salt, and pepper.

3 Press Sauté and use the Sauté or Adjust button to select the highest temperature ("More"). Place the vegetable oil in the inner pot. Wait until the display reads "Hot," about 5 minutes, then add the pork. Cook with the lid off, turning the pork every 2 minutes, until it is browned on most sides, about 8 minutes.

4 Pour the water into the inner pot (be careful—steam may whoosh up!). Add the lime zest, lime juice, and garlic.

5 Close and lock the lid. Set the valve to Sealing. Press Cancel, then press Manual or Pressure Cook and use the Pressure or Pressure Level button to select High Pressure. Use the - or + button to set the time to 20 minutes.

6 When the cooking cycle ends, press Cancel. Allow the appliance to cool and release pressure naturally, about 15 minutes. (The pressure is released when the small metal float valve next to the pressure-release valve sinks back into the lid and the lid is no longer locked.)

7 Remove the lid. Use tongs to remove the pork from the inner pot and place it on a cutting board. Use a chef's knife to cut the pork crosswise into 1/2-inch slices, then transfer them to a serving platter. Spoon some of the cooking liquid over the pork, and serve hot, accompanied by the salsa.

Avocado Salsa will keep, in an airtight container in the refrigerator, for up to 2 days.

Cumin-Spiced Pork Sirloin and its juices will keep, in an airtight container in the refrigerator, for up to 4 days. To reheat, preheat the oven to 350°F and place the pork in a shallow baking dish with enough of the juices to reach a depth of about 1/4 inch. Cover the baking dish tightly with aluminum foil and bake until hot, about 15 minutes.

CARAMELIZED ONIONS

TOTAL TIME: 1 hour 15 minutes   **ACTIVE TIME:** 15 minutes   **YIELD:** Makes about 1½ cups

V

Caramelized onions seem like a little bit of kitchen alchemy. In goes something with a sharp, biting flavor and out comes something sweet and mellow. Typically, caramelizing onions requires a lot of stirring on the stovetop under a watchful eye. But the Instant Pot makes most of the cooking hands-off. There's another helper here, too: The baking soda in this recipe increases the pH of the onions and allows them to brown more readily. Serve these onions as a side dish with steak or chicken, place them atop a hamburger, or use them to turn a "baked" potato (see page 100) into something out of the ordinary.

2 tablespoons unsalted butter

4 medium white or yellow onions (about 2 pounds), thinly sliced

¼ teaspoon baking soda

Salt and freshly ground black pepper

1 Press Sauté and use the Sauté or Adjust button to select the middle temperature ("Normal"). Place the butter in the inner pot, wait about 1 minute for the butter to melt, then add the onions, baking soda, a pinch of salt, and a pinch of pepper. Cook with the lid off, stirring occasionally until the onions soften slightly and begin to release liquid, about 5 minutes.

2 Close and lock the lid. Make sure the valve is set to Sealing. Press Cancel, then press Manual or Pressure Cook and use the Pressure or Pressure Level button to select High Pressure. Use the − or + button to set the time to 40 minutes.

3 When the cooking cycle ends, carefully use a wooden spoon to release the pressure by turning the pressure-release valve to Venting. (The pressure is released when the small metal float valve next to the pressure-release valve sinks back into the lid and the lid is no longer locked.)

4 Press Cancel, then press Sauté and use the Sauté or Adjust button to select the middle temperature ("Normal"). Cook with the lid off, stirring occasionally, until most of the liquid has evaporated and the remaining liquid is thick, about 10 minutes. As more liquid evaporates, you will need to stir more frequently to avoid burning the onions. (No need to be too fastidious, though—a little charred onion is good for flavor.)

5 Press Cancel. Taste and adjust the seasoning, adding more salt and pepper as needed. Serve hot.

Caramelized Onions will keep, in an airtight container in the refrigerator, for up to 1 week. To reheat, place them in a small pot, add a splash of water, and warm on the stovetop over medium-low heat, stirring occasionally, for about 5 minutes.

Note: Astute readers may gather that this recipe contains no water. But doesn't the Instant Pot need water in order to reach pressure? Yes. But that water doesn't always have to come from pure H_2O. In this case, the onions—mostly water themselves—contain all the liquid that is necessary for the recipe to work.

Clockwise from top: Spicy Pork Shoulder in Salsa, Teriyaki Pork Shoulder, Barbecue Pork Shoulder

TENDER PRESSURE-COOKER PORK SHOULDER

Sure, we could whip up our own barbecue or teriyaki sauce from scratch. But do we always have the time and inclination? These recipes are my answer to that question. ("No." The answer is "no.") Take note that store-bought sauces generally contain sugars and thickeners that make them a bad match for pressure-cooking as is. That's why there is water in this recipe. It thins out the sauce and helps give the Instant Pot enough liquid to reach pressure. If you wish, you can thicken the sauce at the end by using the Sauté function and cooking with the lid off.

① BARBECUE PORK SHOULDER DF

TOTAL TIME: 1 hour 10 minutes

ACTIVE TIME: 10 minutes

YIELD: Serves 8

---

1 tablespoon neutral-flavored vegetable oil, such as canola or peanut

3 pounds bone-in pork shoulder

½ cup water

¾ cup store-bought barbecue sauce

8 crusty rolls, split open, for serving (optional)

Coleslaw, for serving (optional)

---

1 Press Sauté and use the Sauté or Adjust button to select the highest temperature ("More"). Place the vegetable oil in the inner pot. Wait until the display reads "Hot," about 5 minutes, then add the pork. Cook with the lid off, turning the pork every 2 minutes, until the pork is browned on most sides, about 8 minutes.

2 Add the water (be careful—steam may whoosh up!), then pour the barbecue sauce over the meat and spread it around the meat. Close and lock the lid. Set the valve to Sealing. Press Cancel, then press Manual or Pressure Cook and use the Pressure or Pressure Level button to select High Pressure. Use the – or + button to set the time to 25 minutes.

3 When the cooking cycle ends, press Cancel. Allow the appliance to cool and release pressure naturally, about 15 minutes. (The pressure is released when the small metal float valve next to the pressure-release valve sinks back into the lid and the lid is no longer locked.)

4 Remove the lid. Remove the pork from the inner pot and place it on a cutting board. Slice the pork thin, working around the bone, spoon some of the liquid from the inner pot over the pork, and serve hot, piled on rolls and topped with coleslaw, if you wish.

Barbecue Pork Shoulder and its cooking juices will keep, in an airtight container in the refrigerator, for up to 4 days. To reheat, preheat the oven to 350°F and place the pork in a shallow baking dish with enough of the juices to reach a depth of about ¼ inch. Cover the baking dish tightly with aluminum foil and bake until hot, about 15 minutes.

2 TERIYAKI PORK SHOULDER DF

TOTAL TIME: 1 hour 10 minutes
ACTIVE TIME: 10 minutes
YIELD: Serves 8

Replace the barbecue sauce with store-bought teriyaki sauce. Serve with lightly sautéed baby spinach and fresh pineapple rings.

3 SPICY PORK SHOULDER IN SALSA DF

TOTAL TIME: 1 hour 10 minutes
ACTIVE TIME: 10 minutes
YIELD: Serves 8

Replace the barbecue sauce with 1½ cups jarred salsa. Omit the water. Serve with Cilantro-Lime White Rice (page 212) and black beans.

PINTO BEANS WITH CHORIZO

TOTAL TIME: 1 hour 15 minutes   **ACTIVE TIME:** 15 minutes   **YIELD:** Serves 6

This dish uses sausage as a shortcut for infusing flavor into the beans. While chorizo is available in both fresh and dried forms, the dried (Spanish) form is what we're after here. Smoky and garlicky but not usually too hot, it lends flavor to the whole dish. As easy as the beans are to prepare, when they are spooned onto corn tortillas and topped with crunchy lettuce and salty cheese, it all tastes like no effort was spared.

1 tablespoon neutral-flavored vegetable oil, such as canola or peanut

4 ounces dried chorizo, quartered lengthwise and thinly sliced

1 medium white or yellow onion, chopped

3 cloves garlic, chopped

2 cups dried pinto beans, rinsed, drained, and picked over to remove debris

2 bay leaves

½ teaspoon freshly ground black pepper

3 cups reduced-salt chicken broth or All-Purpose Chicken Stock (page 88)

1 can (14½ ounces) diced tomatoes, drained

Small (6-inch) corn tortillas, for serving

Shredded lettuce, for serving

Crumbled añejo cheese or freshly grated Pecorino Romano cheese, for garnish (see Note)

1 Press Sauté and use the Sauté or Adjust button to select the lowest temperature ("Less"). Place the vegetable oil in the inner pot, wait about 1 minute for it to warm, then add the chorizo. Cook with the lid off, stirring occasionally, until the chorizo releases some fat and becomes crispy, about 5 minutes.

2 Add the onion and garlic and cook with the lid off until the onions are fragrant, about 2 minutes.

3 Place the beans, bay leaves, and pepper in the inner pot. Wait a moment and then pour in the broth. (Adding the beans first lets the temperature in the inner pot cool down a bit so that steam doesn't whoosh up when the broth is added.) Close and lock the lid. Set the valve to Sealing. Press Cancel, then press Manual or Pressure Cook and use the Pressure or Pressure Level button to select High Pressure. Use the – or + button to set the time to 35 minutes.

4 When the cooking cycle ends, press Cancel. Allow the appliance to cool and release pressure naturally, about 15 minutes. (The pressure is released when the small metal float valve next to the pressure-release valve sinks back into the lid and the lid is no longer locked.)

5 Remove the lid. Discard the bay leaves. Add the diced tomatoes. Press Cancel, then press Sauté and use the Adjust button to select the middle temperature ("Normal").

The liquid will bubble vigorously. Cook with the lid off until the beans are tender, about 10 minutes.

6 Serve the beans hot, piled in corn tortillas, topped with shredded lettuce, and garnished with cheese.

Pinto Beans with Chorizo will keep, in an airtight container in the refrigerator, for up to 4 days. To reheat, place the beans in a pot and warm on the stovetop over medium heat, stirring occasionally, for about 5 minutes.

Note: *Añejo* means "mature" in Spanish and refers to a crumbly, salty aged cheese often available in supermarkets with a good selection of Mexican products. If you can't find it, worry not; Pecorino Romano adds a similar salty bite.

FRAGRANT LAMB AND CHICKPEA STEW

TOTAL TIME: 1 hour 30 minutes   **ACTIVE TIME:** 15 minutes   **YIELD:** Serves 8

Lamb isn't usually in my dinner rotation, which is part of what makes this recipe so special. The other parts are that it comes together so quickly in the Instant Pot and uses spices we typically associate with sweet dishes—cinnamon, cloves—to lend an exotic perfume to the dish and give the flavor a big boost.

---

1 tablespoon ground cumin

1 tablespoon ground coriander

¼ teaspoon ground cloves

Generous pinch of cayenne pepper

¼ teaspoon salt, plus extra as needed

¼ teaspoon freshly ground black pepper, plus extra as needed

2 pounds boneless lamb for stew, such as shoulder, cut into 2-inch cubes

1 tablespoon neutral-flavored vegetable oil, such as canola or peanut

2 medium white or yellow onions, chopped

2 cloves garlic, finely chopped

1 can (28 ounces) diced tomatoes with their juices

¾ cup reduced-salt chicken broth or All-Purpose Chicken Stock (page 88)

1 cinnamon stick, about 3 inches

½ cup dried chickpeas, rinsed, drained, and picked over to remove debris

Finely chopped fresh cilantro, large stems removed, for garnish

---

1 In a large bowl, combine the cumin, coriander, cloves, cayenne pepper, salt, and pepper. Add the lamb and toss to coat it evenly with the spices. Set aside.

2 Press Sauté and use the Sauté or Adjust button to select the middle temperature ("Normal"). Place 1 tablespoon of the vegetable oil in the inner pot, wait about 1 minute for it to warm, then add the onions and garlic. Cook with the lid off, stirring occasionally, until the onions soften slightly, about 5 minutes.

3 Add the tomatoes, chicken broth, cinnamon stick, chickpeas, and lamb and stir to distribute evenly.

4 Close and lock the lid. Set the valve to Sealing. Press Cancel, then press Manual or Pressure Cook and use the Pressure or Pressure Level button to select High Pressure. Use the – or + button to set the time to 45 minutes.

5 When the cooking cycle ends, press Cancel. Allow the appliance to cool and release pressure naturally, about 30 minutes. (The pressure is released when the small metal float valve next to the pressure-release valve sinks back into the lid and the lid is no longer locked.)

6 Remove the lid. Discard the cinnamon stick and taste the stew for seasoning, adding salt and pepper as needed. Serve hot with a generous portion of the broth, garnished with cilantro.

Fragrant Lamb and Chickpea Stew will keep, in an airtight container in the refrigerator, for up to 4 days. To reheat, place it in a pot and warm on the stovetop over medium heat, stirring occasionally, until hot, about 5 minutes.

NO-STIR POLENTA

1·2·3

Once you have this basic method down, it doesn't take much to dress it up with some sun-dried tomatoes and Parmesan cheese, chanterelle mushrooms, or a piquant Gorgonzola (see page 53). Although you may find some cornmeal specially labeled for use in polenta, any medium-grind cornmeal will do. Polenta refers to the finished dish, not the cornmeal with which it's made. Avoid anything labeled instant or precooked polenta, or finely ground cornmeal that has the consistency of wheat flour.

Master Method

30

TOTAL TIME: 25 minutes
ACTIVE TIME: 5 minutes
YIELD: Serves 4

2 tablespoons unsalted butter

1 cup medium-grind cornmeal

4 cups reduced-salt chicken broth or
    All-Purpose Chicken Stock (page 88)

Salted butter, for serving

1 Press Sauté and use the Sauté or Adjust button to select the middle temperature ("Normal"). Place the unsalted butter in the inner pot, wait about 1 minute for the butter to melt, then add the cornmeal. Cook with the lid off, stirring frequently, until the cornmeal is evenly coated in the butter, about 1 minute.

2 Add the chicken broth and stir to combine with the cornmeal, scraping the inner pot so that no cornmeal sticks to the bottom. Close and lock the lid. Set the valve to Sealing. Press Cancel, then press Manual or Pressure Cook and use the Pressure or Pressure Level button to select High Pressure. Use the – or + button to set the time to 8 minutes.

3 When the cooking cycle ends, press Cancel. Allow the appliance to cool and release pressure naturally, about 15 minutes. (The pressure is released when the small metal float valve next to the pressure-release valve sinks back into the lid and the lid is no longer locked.)

4 Remove the lid, stir the polenta to incorporate any unabsorbed broth, spoon into four individual bowls or a large serving bowl, and serve hot topped with salted butter.

No-Stir Polenta will keep, in an airtight container in the refrigerator, for up to 3 days. To reheat it, place the polenta in a pot, add water or chicken broth (you'll want ¼ cup liquid for each cup of polenta), and use a potato masher to break up any chunks. Warm on the stovetop over medium-low heat, mashing occasionally, until heated through, about 5 minutes.

1 SUN-DRIED TOMATO AND PARMESAN POLENTA 30

TOTAL TIME: 25 minutes
ACTIVE TIME: 5 minutes
YIELD: Serves 4

After removing the lid and stirring the polenta, add ¼ cup chopped sun-dried tomatoes (in oil, drained). Stir ¼ cup freshly grated Parmesan cheese into the polenta just before serving hot.

2 GORGONZOLA POLENTA 30

TOTAL TIME: 25 minutes
ACTIVE TIME: 5 minutes
YIELD: Serves 4

Replace half of the chicken broth with water. After removing the lid and stirring the polenta, add 4 ounces crumbled Gorgonzola (about 1 cup) and stir to distribute the cheese just before serving hot.

3 CHANTERELLE AND PARMESAN POLENTA 30

TOTAL TIME: 25 minutes
ACTIVE TIME: 5 minutes
YIELD: Serves 4

While the polenta cooks, soak ½ ounce dried chanterelle mushrooms in 1 cup warm water for 20 minutes. Remove the mushrooms, place them in a colander, and rinse them under running water, using your fingers to toss them occasionally to make sure they are thoroughly rinsed. Finely chop the mushrooms and stir them into the polenta after the lid is removed. Stir ½ cup freshly grated Parmesan cheese into the polenta just before serving hot.

MORE FLAVORING AND SERVING IDEAS FOR POLENTA

- Stir in a generous knob of unsalted butter or fruity extra-virgin olive oil just after the lid is removed.

- Stir in heavy (whipping) cream just after the lid is removed, then replace the lid and allow the cream to warm before serving.

- Serve the polenta with crumbled goat cheese and a drizzle of honey.

- Serve with a spoonful of Faux-Roasted Garlic (page 59) stirred in.

- Drain jarred, roasted red peppers, chop them, and then add them just after the lid is removed. Replace the lid and allow the peppers to warm before serving.

- Serve with sweet or spicy Italian sausage and tomato sauce.

- If you have some white truffles just, you know, lying around, those will do nicely shaved thin and served atop the polenta.

- Add chopped walnuts to Gorgonzola Polenta (page 53) just after the lid is removed.

- Substitute dried porcini or shiitake mushrooms for the dried chanterelle mushrooms.

- Pan-fry (or sauté in the Instant Pot) the leftovers in butter: Make patties out of the chilled polenta. Cook with melted butter until browned on one side and then flip to brown the other side.

NO-STIR RISOTTO

1·2·3

This creamy, comforting Italian rice dish conjures up images of nearly endless stirring, but happily the Instant Pot relieves you of that duty. That's right, you get all the flavor (and bragging rights) of risotto without the incessant stirring. Serve this risotto as is or prepare it three different ways: with lemon and peas for a bright, springlike flavor (see page 57), with mushrooms for earthy overtones (see page 57), or with roasted tomatoes for a concentrated taste of summer (see page 58).

Master Method

30

TOTAL TIME: 20 minutes
ACTIVE TIME: 5 minutes
YIELD: Serves 8

¼ cup (½ stick) salted butter

2 cups arborio rice

4 cups reduced-salt chicken broth or All-Purpose Chicken Stock (page 88), plus extra as needed

1 Press Sauté and use the Sauté or Adjust button to select the middle temperature ("Normal"). Place the butter in the inner pot, wait about 1 minute for it to melt, then add the rice. Cook with the lid off, stirring occasionally, until the grains of rice are opaque and well coated in butter, about 4 minutes.

2 Add the chicken broth and stir to combine with the risotto, scraping the pot so that no risotto sticks to the bottom. Close and lock the lid. Set the valve to Sealing. Press Cancel, then press Manual or Pressure Cook and use the Pressure or Pressure Level button to select High Pressure. Use the – or + button to set the time to 7 minutes.

3 When the cooking cycle ends, carefully use a wooden spoon to release the pressure by turning the pressure-release valve to Venting. (The pressure is released when the small metal float valve next to the pressure-release valve sinks back into the lid and the lid is no longer locked.)

4 Press Cancel and remove the lid. Stir the risotto thoroughly. (If the risotto is too thick, add about 1 tablespoon of water or

Clockwise from top: Mushroom Risotto, Roasted Tomato Risotto, Risotto with Lemon and Peas

broth and stir for 5 seconds. Repeat as desired.) Serve hot.

No-Stir Risotto will keep, in an airtight container in the refrigerator, for up to 3 days. Risotto does not reheat particularly well, though. Your best bet is placing it in a pot with a generous splash of chicken broth. Warm the pot on the stovetop over medium-low heat while stirring occasionally for about 5 minutes, adding more broth as needed to give the risotto a loose and creamy texture.

1 RISOTTO WITH LEMON AND PEAS 30

TOTAL TIME: 20 minutes
ACTIVE TIME: 5 minutes
YIELD: Serves 8

Add the finely grated zest of 2 small lemons to the melted butter in step 1, before adding the rice. After removing the lid, stir in 1 cup frozen peas and stir frequently until the peas are warmed through, about 2 minutes. (If the risotto is too thick, add about 1 tablespoon of water or broth and stir for 5 seconds. Repeat as desired.) Serve hot.

2 MUSHROOM RISOTTO 30

TOTAL TIME: 30 minutes
ACTIVE TIME: 15 minutes
YIELD: Serves 8

1 Start by pressing Sauté and using the Adjust button to select the middle temperature ("Normal"). Place 2 tablespoons unsalted butter in the inner pot, wait about 1 minute for the butter to melt, then add 8 ounces sliced white mushrooms. Cook, stirring frequently, until the mushrooms are softened, about 10 minutes. Transfer the mushrooms to a bowl, and set them aside at room temperature.

2 Wearing oven mitts, remove the inner pot (be careful—it's hot!), and pour any cooking liquid into a large measuring cup. Add enough chicken broth to the cooking liquid to equal 4 cups, and set it aside. (If your measuring cup has just a 2-cup capacity, add enough broth to the cooking liquid to equal 2 cups, pour that into a large bowl, and then measure another 2 cups broth into the bowl—you want a total of 4 cups liquid.)

3 Return the inner pot to the appliance, and proceed with the Master Method from step 1. In step 2, replace the chicken broth with the reserved cooking liquid mixture. After removing the lid in step 4, add the reserved mushrooms and stir frequently until they are warmed through, about 1 minute. (If the risotto is too thick, add about 1 tablespoon of water or broth and stir for 5 seconds. Repeat as desired.) Add finely chopped Italian (flat-leaf) parsley leaves just before serving hot.

③ ROASTED TOMATO RISOTTO ③⓪

TOTAL TIME: 20 minutes
ACTIVE TIME: 5 minutes
YIELD: Serves 8

In step 1, substitute ¼ cup extra-virgin olive oil for the butter and wait about 15 seconds for the oil to warm before adding the rice. After removing the lid in step 4, add 1 cup drained, diced fire-roasted tomatoes (from one 14½-ounce can) and ¼ cup freshly grated Parmesan cheese and stir thoroughly until the tomatoes are warmed through, about 1 minute. Add thinly sliced ribbons of fresh basil just before serving hot.

MORE FLAVORING AND SERVING IDEAS FOR RISOTTO

- Serve with freshly grated Parmesan cheese.

- Serve with Caramelized Onions (page 42).

- Serve with a spoonful of Faux-Roasted Garlic (page 59) stirred in.

- Crush a few threads of saffron between your fingers and add them to the inner pot with the rice in the Master Method.

- Add cooked crab or lobster meat to the Master Method recipe just before serving.

- Is everything better with bacon? Risotto certainly can be. After opening the lid, fold in cooked, chopped bacon.

- Turn leftover risotto into risotto cakes: For each 3 cups cooked risotto, mix in 1 egg yolk and ½ cup breadcrumbs. Form the mixture into 12 balls, then flatten the balls into 2-inch pucks. Pan-fry with oil in a skillet until golden brown, about 3 minutes on each side.

FAUX-ROASTED GARLIC

TOTAL TIME: 30 minutes   **ACTIVE TIME:** 5 minutes   **YIELD:** 4 bulbs garlic

The Instant Pot makes quick work of garlic here, turning the raw product into a creamy and just barely sweet spread that pairs beautifully with an extra-virgin olive oil. It deserves to find a home on a good, crusty loaf of bread. But don't stop there. You can stir it into soup or cooked rice, spread it on toasted bread, or toss it with pasta and Parmesan. I will stop there because I'm making myself hungry.

4 large bulbs garlic

1 cup water

¼ cup extra-virgin olive oil,
   plus extra as needed

Salt and freshly ground black pepper

1 Slice the top off each garlic bulb, just enough to expose the cloves while leaving the bulb and most of the papery skin intact.

2 Place the steaming rack in the inner pot, pour in the water, and then place the garlic on the steaming rack.

3 Close and lock the lid. Set the valve to Sealing. Press Manual or Pressure Cook and use the Pressure or Pressure Level button to select High Pressure. Use the – or + button to set the time to 5 minutes.

4 When the cooking cycle ends, press Cancel. Allow the appliance to cool and release pressure naturally, about 15 minutes. (The pressure is released when the small metal float valve next to the pressure-release valve sinks back into the lid and the lid is no longer locked.)

5 Remove the lid. Use tongs to carefully remove the garlic bulbs. When the garlic is cool enough to handle, squeeze it into a ramekin, discarding the skins. Add the olive oil, a pinch of salt, and a pinch of pepper, and mash with a fork until a smooth paste forms. Serve warm or at room temperature.

Faux-Roasted Garlic will keep, in an airtight container in the refrigerator, for up to 3 days.

Clockwise from top: Wheat Berry Salad with Citrus Dressing and Feta, Wheat Berries with Yogurt and Honey, Herbed Wheat Berry Tabbouleh

WONDERFUL WHEAT BERRIES

1·2·3

While wheat berries may not be a pantry staple for everyone, they might just become one in your household, stashed in the cupboard until called upon for recipes such as these. Ordinarily, they require presoaking or take a long time to cook, but this is not a problem with the Instant Pot. The nutty and very slightly sweet berries are excellent mixed into salads (see page 62), in a crunchy tabbouleh (see page 62), and stirred into your morning yogurt (see page 63).

Master Method

V VN DF X2 60

TOTAL TIME: 45 minutes
ACTIVE TIME: 5 minutes
YIELD: Makes about 3 cups

1¼ cup wheat berries (see Note)

3 cups water

1 teaspoon salt

1 Place the wheat berries, water, and salt in the inner pot. Close and lock the lid. Make sure the valve is set to Sealing. Press Manual or Pressure Cook and use the Pressure or Pressure Level button to select High Pressure. Use the – or + button to set the time to 30 minutes.

2 When the cooking cycle ends, carefully use a wooden spoon to release the pressure by turning the pressure-release valve to Venting. (The pressure is released when the small metal float valve next to the pressure-release valve sinks back into the lid and the lid is no longer locked.)

3 Press Cancel and remove the lid. Wearing oven mitts, remove the inner pot (be careful—it's hot!) and drain the wheat berries through a colander.

Wonderful Wheat Berries will keep, in an airtight container in the refrigerator, for up to 1 week.

Note: Wheat berries are available at some supermarkets and many natural foods stores.

1 WHEAT BERRY SALAD WITH CITRUS DRESSING AND FETA V X2 60

TOTAL TIME: 45 minutes

ACTIVE TIME: 15 minutes

YIELD: Serves 8

---

1 tablespoon freshly squeezed lemon juice

5 tablespoons extra-virgin olive oil

½ small white or yellow onion, thinly sliced

3 cups cooked wheat berries (see page 61), warm or at room temperature

1 cup diced feta cheese (about 4 ounces)

1 small cucumber, peeled, seeded, and finely chopped

1 teaspoon ground cumin

1 small bunch fresh dill (about 1 ounce), large stems removed, finely chopped

---

1 Make the dressing: Place the lemon juice and olive oil in a Mason jar with a lid (or an airtight container) and shake to combine them. Place the onion in a small bowl and pour the dressing over the onion. Allow the onion to soak in the dressing at room temperature for 30 minutes.

2 Place the cooked wheat berries in a large serving bowl. Add the onion, dressing, feta, cucumber, cumin, and dill to the bowl. Stir to evenly distribute everything. Serve warm or at room temperature.

Wheat Berry Salad with Citrus Dressing and Feta will keep, in an airtight container in the refrigerator, for up to 2 days. Serve leftovers chilled.

2 HERBED WHEAT BERRY TABBOULEH V VN DF X2 30

TOTAL TIME: 15 minutes

ACTIVE TIME: 15 minutes

YIELD: Serves 6

---

1 tablespoon freshly squeezed lemon juice

¼ cup extra-virgin olive oil

¾ teaspoon salt, plus extra as needed

¾ teaspoon freshly ground black pepper, plus extra as needed

3 cups cooked wheat berries (see page 61), warm or at room temperature

1 small bunch scallions, finely chopped

1 sprig fresh mint, stems removed, leaves chopped

1 small bunch Italian (flat-leaf) parsley, stems removed, leaves chopped

1 medium cucumber, unpeeled, seeded, and chopped

2 cups cherry tomatoes, halved

---

1 Make the dressing: Place the lemon juice, olive oil, salt, and pepper in a Mason jar with a lid (or an airtight container) and shake to combine them.

2 Place the cooked wheat berries in a large serving bowl and pour the dressing over them.

3 Add the scallions, mint, parsley, cucumber, and tomatoes to the bowl. Stir to evenly distribute everything. Taste and adjust seasoning, adding salt and pepper as needed. Serve warm, at room temperature, or chilled.

Herbed Wheat Berry Tabbouleh will keep, in an airtight container in the refrigerator, for up to 3 days. Serve leftovers chilled or at room temperature.

3 WHEAT BERRIES WITH YOGURT AND HONEY

V X2 60

TOTAL TIME: 5 minutes
ACTIVE TIME: 5 minutes
YIELD: Serves 1

½ cup cooked wheat berries (see page 61), warm or cold

2 tablespoons honey, warmed (see Note)

¼ cup plain yogurt (see page 226)

Fresh raspberries and/or blueberries, for serving

---

1 Place the wheat berries in a small bowl and stir in 1 tablespoon of honey, making sure the honey is evenly distributed.

2 Pour the yogurt over the wheat berries and lightly stir to coat some of the wheat berries on the bottom with the yogurt. (It's okay if much of the yogurt remains on top.)

3 Drizzle the remaining 1 tablespoon of honey over the wheat berries and yogurt, top with the berries, and serve.

Note: To warm the honey, set the honey jar in a bowl of very warm water for about 10 minutes; this will make the honey more fluid and easier to spread.

Clockwise from top: Quick Chorizo and Tortilla Chip Chili, Quick White Bean and Turkey Chili, Quick Taco-Style Chili

QUICK CHILI

1·2·3

We're going to make chili quickly here, which means we're not even going to wait for the beans to cook in the Instant Pot. These recipes use beans that are already cooked, whether from your Instant Pot the day before (see page 70) or from a can. Try a white bean and turkey chili with a classic flavor (see below), a sausage-based chili with a pleasant chew from the addition of tortilla chips (see page 66), or a taco-inspired chili (see page 68). Either way, pressure-cooking the chili produces a slow-cooked taste in a fraction of the time.

Master Method

1 QUICK WHITE BEAN AND TURKEY CHILI

X2 60

TOTAL TIME: 45 minutes

ACTIVE TIME: 10 minutes

YIELD: Serves 6

1 tablespoon neutral-flavored vegetable oil, such as canola or peanut

1 medium green bell pepper, stemmed, seeded, and chopped

1 medium white or yellow onion, chopped

2 large stalks celery, leaves discarded, chopped

1 clove garlic, finely chopped

1 pound ground turkey

2 tablespoons chili powder

1 teaspoon salt, plus extra as needed

1/4 teaspoon freshly ground black pepper, plus extra as needed

1/2 teaspoon dried oregano

3 tablespoons tomato paste

1 can (14 1/2 ounces) diced tomatoes with their juices

1 can (15 ounces) white beans, such as great northern or white kidney, drained and rinsed

1 cup shredded Cheddar cheese, for garnish

2 scallions, trimmed and thinly sliced, for garnish

1 Press Sauté and use the Sauté or Adjust button to select the middle temperature ("Normal"). Place the vegetable oil in the inner pot, wait about 1 minute for it to warm, then add the bell pepper, onion, celery, and garlic. Cook with the lid off, stirring occasionally, until the onion softens slightly, about 5 minutes.

2 Add the turkey and use a wooden spoon or silicone spatula to break it up into small pieces as it cooks. Cook the turkey until it is no longer pink, about 5 minutes.

3 Add the chili powder, salt, pepper, oregano, tomato paste, and diced tomatoes with their juices and stir until everything is evenly mixed.

4 Close and lock the lid. Set the valve to Sealing. Press Cancel, then press Manual or Pressure Cook and use the Pressure or Pressure Level button to select High Pressure. Use the – or + button to set the time to 20 minutes.

5 When the cooking cycle ends, carefully use a wooden spoon to release the pressure by turning the pressure-release valve to Venting. (The pressure is released when the small metal float valve next to the pressure-release valve sinks back into the lid and the lid is no longer locked.)

6 Press Cancel and remove the lid. Add the beans, stirring to distribute them evenly, then close and lock the lid to allow the residual heat to warm the beans, about 5 minutes.

7 Taste and adjust the seasoning, adding more salt and pepper as needed. Serve the chili hot, garnished with the shredded Cheddar and scallions.

Quick White Bean and Turkey Chili will keep, in an airtight container in the refrigerator, for up to 4 days. To reheat, place it in a pot and warm on the stovetop over medium heat, stirring occasionally, until hot, about 5 minutes.

② QUICK CHORIZO AND TORTILLA CHIP CHILI

X2 60

TOTAL TIME: 45 minutes
ACTIVE TIME: 10 minutes
YIELD: Serves 6

1 tablespoon neutral-flavored vegetable oil, such as canola or peanut

1 medium green bell pepper, stemmed, seeded, and chopped

1 medium white or yellow onion, chopped

2 large stalks celery, leaves discarded, chopped

1 clove garlic, finely chopped

1 pound Mexican chorizo, removed from its casings (see Note)

1 tablespoon chili powder

1/4 teaspoon freshly ground black pepper, plus extra as needed

1/2 teaspoon dried oregano

3 tablespoons tomato paste

1 can (14 1/2 ounces) diced tomatoes with their juices

2 ounces tortilla chips (about 30 chips)

1 can (15 ounces) black beans, drained and rinsed

Pico de gallo, for serving

Crema Mexicana or sour cream, for serving

---

1 Press Sauté and select the middle temperature. Place the vegetable oil in the inner pot, wait about 1 minute for it to warm, then add the bell pepper, onion, celery, and garlic. Cook with the lid off, stirring occasionally, until the onion softens slightly, about 5 minutes.

2 Add the chorizo and cook, stirring occasionally to break it up into small pieces, until it is no longer pink, about 5 minutes.

3 Add the chili powder, pepper, oregano, tomato paste, diced tomatoes, and tortilla chips, stirring to submerge and break up the chips.

4 Close and lock the lid. Set the valve to Sealing. Press Cancel, then select High Pressure. Set the time to 20 minutes.

5 When the cooking cycle ends, carefully use a wooden spoon to release the pressure.

6 Press Cancel and remove the lid. Add the beans, stirring to distribute them evenly, then close and lock the lid to allow the residual heat to warm the beans, about 5 minutes.

7 Taste and adjust the seasoning, adding more salt and pepper as needed. Serve the chili hot, with the pico de gallo and crema Mexicana.

Quick Chorizo and Tortilla Chip Chili will keep, in an airtight container in the refrigerator, for up to 4 days.

Note: Mexican-style chorizo is the kind made with uncooked, ground meat; you want that instead of the dried Spanish version here.

3 QUICK TACO-STYLE CHILI DF X2 60

TOTAL TIME: 45 minutes
ACTIVE TIME: 10 minutes
YIELD: Serves 6

---

1 tablespoon neutral-flavored vegetable oil, such as canola or peanut

1 medium green bell pepper, stemmed, seeded, and chopped

1 medium white or yellow onion, chopped

2 large stalks celery, leaves discarded, chopped

1 clove garlic, finely chopped

1 pound ground turkey or beef

1 package (1 ounce) taco seasoning mix (see box, page 69)

3 tablespoons tomato paste

1 can (14½ ounces) diced tomatoes with their juices

1 can (15 ounces) pinto beans, drained and rinsed

Salt and freshly ground black pepper

Small cubes of avocado, for garnish

Chopped fresh cilantro leaves, for garnish

---

1 Press Sauté and select the middle temperature. Place the vegetable oil in the inner pot, wait about 1 minute for the oil to warm, then add the bell pepper, onion, celery, and garlic. Cook with the lid off, stirring occasionally, until the onion softens slightly, about 5 minutes.

2 Add the turkey and cook, stirring occasionally to break it up into small pieces, until it is no longer pink, about 5 minutes.

3 Add the taco seasoning, tomato paste, and diced tomatoes, stirring to combine.

4 Close and lock the lid. Set the valve to Sealing. Press Cancel, then select High Pressure. Set the time to 20 minutes.

5 When the cooking cycle ends, carefully use a wooden spoon to release the pressure.

6 Press Cancel and remove the lid. Add the beans, stirring to distribute them evenly, then close and lock the lid to allow the residual heat to warm the beans, about 5 minutes.

7 Taste and adjust the seasoning, adding salt and pepper as needed. Serve the chili hot, garnished with the avocado and cilantro.

Quick Taco-Style Chili will keep, in an airtight container in the refrigerator, for up to 4 days.

MORE FLAVORING AND SERVING IDEAS FOR QUICK CHILI

- Add leftover Sweet Potatoes with Parsley and Balsamic Vinegar (page 253) to any variety of chili.

- Use vegetarian crumbles instead of ground beef or turkey.

- Serve with cooked rigatoni or elbow pasta and top with shredded cheese.

- Top with Crème Fraîche (page 233).

- When adding the beans to Quick White Bean and Turkey Chili, add 2 tablespoons peanut butter and ¼ cup coconut milk. Taste and then add more if desired.

- When adding the beans to Quick White Bean and Turkey Chili, add raisins too.

- In Quick White Bean and Turkey Chili, reduce the chili powder to 1 tablespoon and add 2 teaspoons ground cumin and 1 chopped chipotle in adobo.

- Make your own taco seasoning for Quick Taco-Style Chili (feel free to customize to your own taste): Combine 2 teaspoons chili powder, 1 teaspoon ground cumin, ½ teaspoon sweet paprika, ½ teaspoon salt, ½ teaspoon freshly ground black pepper, ¼ teaspoon garlic powder, ¼ teaspoon onion powder, ¼ teaspoon dried oregano, and a pinch of cayenne pepper.

- Serve Quick Taco-Style Chili in small tostada bowls.

SUPER SIMPLE BEANS  1·2·3

As a kid, you never really picture yourself all grown up and saying this, but here we are: I am really excited about beans. The Instant Pot did that to me. And I want you to be excited about beans, too. Now that beans don't require presoaking and planning, I am much more likely to have them for dinner, which is good for my diet and my budget.

Beans are extraordinarily versatile. Enjoy black beans as a dip for tortilla chips (see page 71), turn white beans into a spreadable hummus (see page 72), and enjoy lima beans and spinach with bow-tie pasta for an easy boost in nutrition and taste (see page 72). In all cases, the beans can be prepared one day and then the final dish prepared on another. For more bean cookery tidbits, see the box on page 73.

Master Method

V VN DF X2

TOTAL TIME: About 1 hour 15 minutes (varies according to bean type)

ACTIVE TIME: 10 minutes

YIELD: Makes about 2½ cups

---

1 cup dried black beans, white kidney beans, or lima beans, rinsed, drained, and picked over to remove debris

½ teaspoon salt

5 cups water

---

1 Place the beans, salt, and water in the inner pot. Close and lock the lid. Set the valve to Sealing. Press Manual or Pressure Cook and use the Pressure or Pressure Level button to select High Pressure. Use the – or + button to set the time to 25 minutes for black beans or lima beans, or 40 minutes for white kidney beans.

2 When the cooking cycle ends, press Cancel. Allow the appliance to cool and release pressure naturally, about 30 minutes. (The pressure is released when the small metal float valve next to the pressure-release valve sinks back into the lid and the lid is no longer locked.)

3 Remove the lid. Bite into a bean. It should offer a slight resistance to the tooth but should have no hard spots. If it is not soft enough, press Sauté and use the Adjust button to select the middle temperature ("Normal"). Cook with the lid off, stirring occasionally, and allow the liquid to come to a boil, about 5 minutes. After the liquid has boiled, taste a bean every 5 minutes until cooked and then press Cancel.

4 Wearing oven mitts, remove the inner pot (be careful—it's hot!) and drain the beans through a colander.

Super Simple Beans will keep, in an airtight container in the refrigerator, for up to 5 days. Serve warm, chilled, or at room temperature.

① BLACK BEAN DIP

TOTAL TIME: 20 minutes
ACTIVE TIME: 20 minutes
YIELD: Makes about 3 cups

¼ cup extra-virgin olive oil

1 small white or yellow onion, chopped

2 cloves garlic, chopped

2½ cups cooked black beans (see page 70)

½ teaspoon salt, plus extra as needed

½ teaspoon ground cumin

1 teaspoon chili powder

2 tablespoons freshly squeezed lime juice

¼ cup water, plus extra as needed

Chopped fresh cilantro, large stems removed, for garnish

Tortilla chips, for serving

---

1 Press Sauté and use the Sauté or Adjust button to select the lowest temperature ("Less"). Place the olive oil in the inner pot, wait about 1 minute for it to warm, then add the onion and garlic. Cook with the lid off, stirring occasionally, until the onion is very soft, about 15 minutes.

2 Press Cancel and use a large spoon to transfer the onion mixture to the bowl of a food processor. Add the black beans, salt, cumin, chili powder, lime juice, and water and pulse until smooth, about 20 short pulses. Stop processing and use a rubber spatula to scrape down the sides of the bowl if necessary to distribute everything evenly.

3 Taste and adjust the seasoning, adding more salt as needed. Transfer the bean dip to a serving bowl. Garnish with cilantro and serve warm or at room temperature with tortilla chips.

Black Bean Dip will keep, in an airtight container in the refrigerator, for up to 5 days. Serve chilled or at room temperature.

2 WHITE BEAN HUMMUS V VN DF X2 30

TOTAL TIME: 5 minutes

ACTIVE TIME: 5 minutes

YIELD: Makes about 2 cups

2½ cups cooked white kidney beans
(see page 70)

¼ cup extra-virgin olive oil

1 small clove garlic

Pinch of salt, plus extra as needed

¼ teaspoon freshly ground black pepper,
plus extra as needed

1 teaspoon ground cumin, plus extra for garnish

¼ teaspoon ground ginger

Crackers, for serving

---

1 Place the beans, olive oil, garlic, salt, pepper, cumin, and ginger in the bowl of a food processor and pulse until smooth, about 15 short pulses. Stop processing and use a rubber spatula to scrape down the sides of the bowl if necessary to distribute everything evenly.

2 Taste and adjust the seasoning, adding more salt as needed. Transfer the hummus to a serving bowl. Garnish with a dusting of cumin and serve warm or at room temperature with crackers.

White Bean Hummus will keep, in an airtight container in the refrigerator, for up to 5 days. Serve chilled or at room temperature.

3 FARFALLE WITH CREAMY LIMA BEANS AND SPINACH 30

TOTAL TIME: 10 minutes

ACTIVE TIME: 10 minutes

YIELD: Serves 8

---

2 tablespoons extra-virgin olive oil

2 cloves garlic, finely chopped

¼ teaspoon crushed red pepper flakes

5 ounces baby spinach

2½ cups cooked lima beans (see page 70)

1 cup reduced-salt chicken broth or
All-Purpose Chicken Stock (page 88)

¼ teaspoon salt, plus extra as needed

¼ teaspoon freshly ground black pepper,
plus extra as needed

1 pound farfalle (bow-tie) pasta, cooked al dente

¼ cup freshly grated Parmesan cheese

---

1 Press Sauté and use the Sauté or Adjust button to select the middle temperature ("Normal"). Place the olive oil in the inner pot, wait about 1 minute for it to warm up, then add the garlic and red pepper flakes. Cook with the lid off, stirring occasionally, until the garlic is fragrant but not browned, about 1 minute.

2 Add the spinach, half the beans, and the chicken broth, salt, and pepper. Cook with the lid off, stirring occasionally, until the spinach is wilted and the beans have softened, about 3 minutes.

3 In a medium bowl, use a potato masher or immersion blender to puree the remaining beans. Add the cooked pasta to the inner pot and then add the mashed beans, stirring to coat the pasta with the bean puree. Press Cancel and add the Parmesan. Stir to distribute evenly until the pasta and beans are warmed through, about 2 minutes. Taste and adjust the seasoning, adding more salt and pepper as needed.

4 Use a large spoon to scoop the pasta into a large serving bowl.

Farfalle with Creamy Lima Beans and Spinach will keep, in an airtight container in the refrigerator, for up to 3 days. To reheat, place in a pot on the stovetop over medium-low heat, cover, and stir occasionally until hot, about 5 minutes.

SPILLING THE BEANS

I am going to reveal a secret: When it comes to making beans in the Instant Pot, there is no single magic cooking time to rule them all. Most dried beans take between 20 minutes and 40 minutes of cooking time at high pressure. Smaller legumes such as lentils may take as little as 15 minutes. All that said, I can give you a few certainties:

• Pressure-cooking beans in the Instant Pot eliminates the need for presoaking.

• Slightly undercooking works better than overcooking; you cannot un-cook something, but you can always cook it a little bit more either by sealing the lid again and pressure-cooking once more or by removing the lid and using the Sauté function.

• Many variables go into timing, including how long the beans have been sitting on the supermarket shelf, the specific type of bean, and the size of the bean. For the fastest-cooking beans, it pays to buy from a store with a lot of product turnover, which will give you fresher beans.

• Jotting down notes of the cooking times that work for you will help you develop a sense of timing for the beans you make the most.

• One last certainty: No matter the kind of bean, it cooks more quickly in the Instant Pot.

MORE FLAVORING AND SERVING IDEAS FOR BEANS

- Toss just about any kind of cooked bean—black or pinto work particularly well—with fresh corn kernels, chopped avocado, chopped tomatoes, and lime juice for a colorful and flavorful side dish.

- Whisk together 3 parts extra-virgin olive oil, 1 part vinegar, and a dab of Dijon mustard. Thinly slice shallots and marinate them in the vinaigrette while the beans cook. Toss the cooked beans—lima or white kidney beans work particularly nicely—with the marinated shallots and vinaigrette.

- For a quick and complete meal, toss cooked beans with rice and jarred salsa. Top with shredded cheese.

- Mash cooked beans with a fork and spread on a thick slice of whole-wheat toast before layering with sliced avocado.

- Toss cooked beans—black beans offer a pleasing color contrast—with Sweet Potatoes with Parsley and Balsamic Vinegar (page 253).

- Sauté chopped bacon, finely chopped jalapeño, and chopped onion until the bacon is crisp and onion is soft. Add cooked beans and cooked rice and continue cooking until heated through.

- Toss cooked beans with crumbled feta, finely chopped fresh Italian (flat-leaf) parsley, olive oil, and lemon juice.

- Place a flour tortilla on a preheated waffle iron. Place cooked beans and cheese on the flour tortilla, leaving a 1-inch margin at the edge. Top with a second flour tortilla, close the waffle iron, and waffle until the cheese has melted, about 3 minutes.

- Toss cooked beans—I especially like kidney beans here—with high-quality canned, oil-packed tuna and chopped red, orange, or yellow bell pepper.

BEYOND BASIC BLACK BEAN SOUP

TOTAL TIME: 1 hour 15 minutes   **ACTIVE TIME:** 15 minutes   **YIELD:** Serves 6

Everyone needs something in basic black, right? But there's no need to be boring. I'm talking about beans, naturally. Dried black beans make a good, inexpensive pantry staple, especially when the Instant Pot eliminates the need for presoaking them. A few elements take this beyond basic: Don't skimp on the lime juice, pico de gallo, or tortilla chips here, which provide important zing, color, and crunch. When it comes to the pico de gallo, grab some ready-made from the supermarket or make your own from your favorite recipe. And if you happen to have more tortilla chips on hand for dipping, I bet no one will turn them down.

2 tablespoons extra-virgin olive oil

1 clove garlic, minced

1 medium white or yellow onion, coarsely chopped

2 stalks celery, leaves discarded, coarsely chopped

2 medium carrots, peeled and coarsely chopped

1 pound dried black beans, rinsed, drained, and picked over to remove debris

1 tablespoon chili powder

2 bay leaves

1 teaspoon ground cumin

1 teaspoon dried oregano

4 cups reduced-salt chicken broth or All-Purpose Chicken Stock (page 88)

1 cup water

1 medium lime, cut into wedges

Pico de gallo, for garnish (store-bought or homemade)

Crumbled tortilla chips, for garnish

1 Press Sauté and use the Sauté or Adjust button to select the lowest temperature ("Less"). Place the olive oil in the inner pot, wait about 1 minute for it to warm, then add the garlic, onion, celery, and carrots. Cook with the lid off, stirring occasionally, until the onion softens slightly, about 5 minutes.

2 Add the beans, followed by the chili powder, bay leaves, cumin, and oregano. Stir to combine, then add the chicken broth and water.

3 Close and lock the lid. Set the valve to Sealing. Press Cancel, then press Manual or Pressure Cook and use the Pressure or Pressure Level button to select High Pressure. Use the – or + button to set the time to 30 minutes.

4 When the cooking cycle ends, press Cancel. Allow the appliance to cool and release pressure naturally, about 30 minutes. (The pressure is released when the small metal float valve next to the pressure-release valve sinks back into the lid and the lid is no longer locked.)

5 Taste to make sure the beans are cooked: They should not be mushy but should yield easily to the tooth. If they are not soft enough, press Sauté, use the Adjust button to select the middle temperature ("Normal"), and continue cooking with the lid off, adding water as necessary to prevent the soup from drying out and checking on the beans every 5 minutes until they are soft enough.

6 Discard the bay leaves. Divide the soup among 6 bowls and serve with a squeeze from a lime wedge and garnished with pico de gallo and crumbled tortilla chips.

Beyond Basic Black Bean Soup will keep, in an airtight container in the refrigerator, for up to 5 days. To reheat, place the soup in a pot and warm on the stovetop over medium heat, stirring occasionally, for about 5 minutes.

SMOKY POTATO AND KALE SOUP

TOTAL TIME: 25 minutes   **ACTIVE TIME:** 15 minutes   **YIELD:** Serves 6

This vegetarian soup gets a flavor boost from canned chipotle peppers in adobo, which provide a smokiness as well as some heat. Pressure-cooking the potatoes gives them a head start, while adding the kale at the end ensures it does not fall apart.

1 cup water

1½ pounds baby potatoes (about 15 potatoes), unpeeled, quartered

1 tablespoon extra-virgin olive oil

1 small white or yellow onion, finely chopped

2 cloves garlic, minced

Pinch of salt, plus extra for serving

Pinch of freshly ground black pepper, plus extra for serving

6 cups reduced-salt vegetable broth

1 tablespoon chili powder

½ teaspoon dried oregano

½ teaspoon minced canned chipotle chiles in adobo

8 ounces flat-leaf or curly-leaf kale, stems removed, leaves sliced crosswise into ¼-inch ribbons

Crème Fraîche (page 233) or sour cream, for serving

1 Place the water and the potatoes in the inner pot. Close and lock the lid. Set the valve to Sealing. Press Manual or Pressure Cook and use the Pressure or Pressure Level button to select High Pressure. Use the – or + button to set the time to 1 minute.

2 When the cooking cycle ends, carefully use a wooden spoon to release the pressure by turning the pressure-release valve to Venting. (The pressure is released when the small metal float valve next to the pressure-release valve sinks back into the lid and the lid is no longer locked.)

3 Remove the lid. Wearing oven mitts, remove the inner pot (be careful—it's hot!), drain the potatoes through a colander, and set them aside until step 6. Return the inner pot to the appliance.

4 Press Cancel, then press Sauté and use the Sauté or Adjust button to select the lowest temperature ("Less"). Place the olive oil in the inner pot, wait about 1 minute for it to warm, then add the onion, garlic, and a pinch each of salt and pepper. Cook with the lid off, stirring occasionally, until the onion softens slightly, about 5 minutes.

5 Add the broth, chili powder, oregano, and chipotle and stir to combine. Press Cancel, then press Sauté and use the Sauté or Adjust button to select the middle temperature ("Normal").

6 Allow the soup to come to a simmer, about 5 minutes. Add the kale and reserved potatoes, stir to submerge the kale, and cook with the lid off until a steak knife easily pierces a potato and the kale is soft, about 5 minutes.

7 Serve hot, garnished with a dollop of crème fraîche and a dash of salt and pepper.

Smoky Potato and Kale Soup will keep, in an airtight container in the refrigerator, for up to 5 days. To reheat, place the soup in a pot and warm on the stovetop over medium heat, stirring occasionally, for about 5 minutes.

HARD-BOILED EGGS

TOTAL TIME: 15 minutes   **ACTIVE TIME:** 5 minutes   **YIELD:** 6 eggs

Hard-boiling eggs consistently and easily can be a hard problem to crack. But the Instant Pot lets you take care of it with the push of a button, giving you eggs that cook and peel beautifully. One thing to consider: Old eggs will peel better. (That's not just me or the Internet telling you that; that's straight from the American Egg Board.) This method produces eggs with a firm and fully cooked yolk. If you find the yolk *too* firm for your liking, the answer may be to reduce the cooking time by as little as 1 minute.

1 cup water

6 large eggs

1 Place the steaming rack in the inner pot, then pour in the water. Place the eggs directly on the steaming rack. (For easier removal of the finished eggs, you may also want to use a silicone or collapsible metal steamer basket.)

2 Close and lock the lid. Set the valve to Sealing. Press Manual or Pressure Cook and use the Pressure or Pressure Level button to select High Pressure. Use the – or + button to set the time to 5 minutes.

3 When the cooking cycle ends, wait 5 minutes and then carefully use a wooden spoon to release the pressure by turning the pressure-release valve to Venting. (The pressure is released when the small metal float valve next to the pressure-release valve sinks back into the lid and the lid is no longer locked.)

4 Press Cancel and remove the lid. Transfer the eggs to a medium bowl of cold water with ice. Allow the eggs to cool 5 minutes in the ice water before removing them. Serve warm, or refrigerate the eggs and serve them chilled.

Hard-Boiled Eggs will keep, unpeeled, in the refrigerator for up to 1 week.

BACON, CORN, AND POTATO CHOWDER

TOTAL TIME: 40 minutes   **ACTIVE TIME:** 20 minutes   **YIELD:** Serves 6

Ask me how much fresh corn I eat in August and I will answer, "a lot." But summer isn't exactly chowder weather. And when colder temperatures come, I turn to frozen corn, preserved at the peak of the season and a much better bet for flavor and convenience in winter. A crusty baguette complements the chowder well and helps you get every last drop from the bowl.

---

4 slices bacon, halved crosswise to yield 8 short strips

1 small white or yellow onion, finely chopped

1 stalk celery, leaves discarded, coarsely chopped

1 pound unpeeled red potatoes, cut into ¾-inch cubes

2 bay leaves

2 cups reduced-salt chicken broth or All-Purpose Chicken Stock (page 88)

3 cups (from one 16-ounce bag) frozen corn kernels

1 teaspoon chopped fresh thyme leaves

½ teaspoon salt

¼ teaspoon freshly ground black pepper

1½ cups whole milk

¼ teaspoon hot sauce

---

1 Line the bottom of the inner pot with the bacon. Press Sauté and use the Sauté or Adjust button to select the middle temperature ("Normal"). Cook with the lid off and use a silicone spatula or wooden spoon to move the bacon around occasionally so that it cooks evenly. Cook until the bacon is crisp, about 6 minutes.

2 Remove the bacon, leaving behind the fat. Allow the bacon to drain on a paper towel-lined plate until step 7.

3 With the Sauté function and middle temperature ("Normal") still selected, add the onion and celery to the bacon fat. Cook with the lid off, stirring occasionally, until the onion and celery soften, about 5 minutes.

4 Add the potatoes and bay leaves. Wait a moment and then pour in the broth. (Adding the potatoes first lets the temperature in the inner pot cool down a bit so that steam doesn't whoosh up when the broth is added.) Close and lock the lid. Set the valve to Sealing. Press Cancel, then press Manual or Pressure Cook and use the Pressure or Pressure Level button to select High Pressure. Use the – or + button to set the time to 1 minute.

5 When the cooking cycle ends, carefully use a wooden spoon to release the pressure by turning the pressure-release valve to Venting. (The pressure is released when the small metal float valve next to the pressure-release valve sinks back into the lid and the lid is no longer locked.)

6 Remove the lid. Discard the bay leaves. Add the corn, thyme, salt, pepper, milk, and hot sauce. Press Cancel, then press Sauté and use the Sauté or Adjust button to select the lowest temperature ("Less"). Cook with the lid off, stirring occasionally, until the chowder is hot, about 5 minutes.

7 Chop the bacon. Add half of the bacon to the chowder and stir to distribute it; reserve the rest to use as a garnish.

8 Serve the chowder hot, garnished with the reserved bacon.

Bacon, Corn, and Potato Chowder will keep, in an airtight container in the refrigerator, for up to 3 days. To reheat, place the chowder in a pot and warm on the stovetop over medium heat, stirring occasionally, for about 5 minutes.

WINTER SQUASH SOUP

1·2·3

Winter squash makes a brightly colored soup in no time when paired with the high pressure of the Instant Pot, which cooks the dense squash quickly. Try a pleasantly sweet soup made with striped Delicata squash and nutty crème fraîche (see below), add curry powder to squash soup for warm, spicy notes (see page 85), or try ginger and sriracha to give winter squash an edge of heat (see page 86).

Master Method

1 DELICATA SQUASH SOUP WITH CRÈME FRAÎCHE 60

TOTAL TIME: 1 hour
ACTIVE TIME: 10 minutes
YIELD: Serves 6

---

2 tablespoons unsalted butter

1 small white or yellow onion, chopped

4 cups reduced-salt chicken broth or All-Purpose Chicken Stock (page 88)

3 Delicata squash (about 3 pounds total), peeled, seeded, and cut into 1-inch cubes (see Note)

¼ teaspoon dried thyme

¼ teaspoon salt, plus extra as needed

¼ teaspoon freshly ground black pepper, plus extra as needed

Pinch of freshly grated nutmeg

Pinch of cayenne pepper

1 cup Crème Fraîche (page 233) plus extra for garnish

Toasted pumpkin seeds, for garnish

---

1 Press Sauté and use the Sauté or Adjust button to select the middle temperature ("Normal"). Place the butter in the inner pot, wait about 1 minute for it to melt, then add the onion. Cook with the lid off, stirring occasionally, until the onion softens slightly, about 5 minutes.

2 Add the broth, squash, thyme, salt, black pepper, nutmeg, and cayenne pepper. Stir to combine.

From left to right: Delicata Squash Soup with Crème Fraîche, Curried Squash Soup, Gingered Sriracha Squash Soup

3 Close and lock the lid. Set the valve to Sealing. Press Cancel, then press Manual or Pressure Cook and use the Pressure or Pressure Level button to select High Pressure. Use the – or + button to set the time to 10 minutes.

4 When the cooking cycle ends, press Cancel. Allow the appliance to cool and release pressure naturally, about 30 minutes. (The pressure is released when the small metal float valve next to the pressure-release valve sinks back into the lid and the lid is no longer locked.)

5 Remove the lid. Use an immersion blender to puree the soup, or transfer the soup to a blender and puree it. (If using a blender, you may need to puree the soup in batches. Take care when pureeing the hot soup and do not overfill your blender.) Return the pureed soup to the inner pot.

6 Add 1 cup crème fraîche and stir to incorporate it. Taste and add more salt and pepper as needed. Serve hot, garnished with pumpkin seeds and additional crème fraîche.

Delicata Squash Soup with Crème Fraîche will keep, in an airtight container in the refrigerator, for up to 3 days. To reheat, place it in a pot and warm over medium heat, stirring occasionally, until hot, about 5 minutes.

Note: The peel on Delicata squash is edible. If you have a powerful blender, you can leave the skin on. Otherwise, and especially if using an immersion blender, peel the squash to ensure a silky, smooth soup.

② CURRIED SQUASH SOUP DF 60

TOTAL TIME: 1 hour
ACTIVE TIME: 10 minutes
YIELD: Serves 6

---

2 tablespoons neutral-flavored vegetable oil, such as canola or peanut

1 small white or yellow onion, chopped

4 cups reduced-salt chicken broth or All-Purpose Chicken Stock (page 88)

1 medium butternut squash (about 2 pounds), peeled, seeded, and cut into 1-inch cubes

¼ teaspoon salt, plus extra as needed

¼ teaspoon freshly ground black pepper, plus extra as needed

2 tablespoons tightly packed brown sugar, plus extra as needed

1 tablespoon curry powder

1 cup coconut milk

Chopped fresh cilantro leaves, for garnish

---

1 Press Sauté and select the middle temperature. Place the vegetable oil in the inner pot, wait about 1 minute for it to heat, then add the onion. Cook with the lid off, stirring occasionally, until the onion softens slightly, about 5 minutes.

2 Add the broth, followed by the squash, salt, pepper, brown sugar, and curry powder and stir to combine.

3 Close and lock the lid. Set the valve to Sealing. Press Cancel, then select High Pressure. Set the time to 10 minutes.

4 When the cooking cycle ends, press Cancel. Release pressure naturally, about 30 minutes.

5 Remove the lid. Use an immersion blender to puree the soup, or transfer the soup to a blender and puree it. Return the pureed soup to the inner pot.

6 Add the coconut milk to the soup and stir to incorporate it. Taste and adjust the seasoning, adding more salt, pepper, or sugar as needed. Serve hot, garnished with cilantro.

Curried Squash Soup will keep, in an airtight container in the refrigerator, for up to 3 days.

3 GINGERED SRIRACHA SQUASH SOUP 60

TOTAL TIME: 1 hour
ACTIVE TIME: 10 minutes
YIELD: Serves 6

---

2 tablespoons unsalted extra-virgin olive oil, plus extra for garnish

1 small white or yellow onion, chopped

2 tablespoons peeled and finely grated fresh ginger

4 cups reduced-salt chicken broth or All-Purpose Chicken Stock (page 88)

1 medium butternut squash (about 2 pounds), peeled, seeded, and cut into 1-inch cubes

¼ teaspoon salt, plus extra as needed

¼ teaspoon freshly ground black pepper, plus extra as needed

Pinch of freshly grated nutmeg

1 teaspoon sriracha, plus extra for garnish

½ teaspoon ground ginger

1 cup heavy (whipping) cream

---

1 Press Sauté and select the middle temperature. Place the olive oil in the inner pot, wait about 1 minute for it to heat, then add the onion and fresh ginger. Cook with the lid off, stirring occasionally, until the onion softens slightly, about 5 minutes.

2 Add the broth, and use a wooden spoon or silicone spatula to scrape up the browned bits at the bottom of the inner pot. Add the squash, salt, pepper, and nutmeg and stir to combine.

3 Close and lock the lid. Set the valve to Sealing. Press Cancel, then select High Pressure. Set the time to 10 minutes.

4 When the cooking cycle ends, press Cancel. Release pressure naturally, about 30 minutes.

5 Remove the lid. Add the sriracha and ground ginger. Use an immersion blender to puree the soup, or transfer the soup to a blender and puree it. Return the pureed soup to the inner pot.

6 Add the heavy cream to the soup and stir to incorporate it. Taste and adjust the seasoning, adding more salt and pepper as needed. Serve hot, drizzled with olive oil and additional sriracha if you like.

Gingered Sriracha Squash Soup will keep, in an airtight container in the refrigerator, for up to 3 days.

ALL-PURPOSE BONE BROTH

I am sometimes guilty of using the terms "stock" and "broth" interchangeably, though for many traditionalists a stock is something made from bones, whereas a broth is something flavored with meat. You can tout these recipes as "stock"—or "bone broth"—but know that supermarket versions (typically referred to as "broth") will certainly work for the recipes in this book where stock is specified.

Commercial broth often comes laden with salt, which is one reason the recipes in this book call for reduced-salt broth when using the store-bought version. While a little salt highlights and rounds out the edges of flavors, too much kills any nuance and overpowers the broth. Because it's easy to add salt later and practically impossible to take it out, these stocks start out lightly salted and form an excellent basic building block for many dishes.

Consider this recipe a template and take advantage of your Instant Pot to turn scraps of food into a savory part of dinner (see Tips, page 90).

1 ALL-PURPOSE CHICKEN STOCK DF

TOTAL TIME: 13 hours 30 minutes (including cooling time)

ACTIVE TIME: 15 minutes

YIELD: Makes about 2 quarts

---

1 tablespoon extra-virgin olive oil

Bones from one (3- to 4-pound) cooked chicken, broken down to fit in inner pot

2 large carrots, cut into chunks

2 large stalks celery, leaves included, cut into chunks

1 medium white or yellow onion, cut into quarters (see Note)

1/2 teaspoon salt

1 tablespoon black peppercorns

2 bay leaves

1 teaspoon apple cider vinegar

8 cups water

---

1 Press Sauté and use the Sauté or Adjust button to select the middle temperature ("Normal"). Place the olive oil in the inner pot. Wait until the display reads "Hot," about 5 minutes, then add the chicken bones. Cook with the lid off, stirring frequently and turning the bones often, until the bones and any meat on them brown slightly, about 10 minutes.

2 Place the carrots, celery, onion, salt, peppercorns, bay leaves, and vinegar in the inner pot. Pour the water into the inner pot, taking care not to fill it more than two-thirds full. (If this means you don't use all the water, that's fine. You'll just have extra-concentrated stock, which you can adjust to taste later, either diluting it with water or using full strength for a more intense flavor.)

3 Close and lock the lid. Set the valve to Sealing. Press Cancel, then press Manual or Pressure Cook and use the Pressure or Pressure Level button to select High Pressure. Use the − or + button to set the time to 40 minutes.

4 When the cooking cycle ends, press Cancel. Allow the appliance to cool and release pressure naturally, about 30 minutes. (The pressure is released when the small metal float valve next to the pressure-release valve sinks back into the lid and the lid is no longer locked.)

5 Remove the lid. Pour the stock through a fine-mesh strainer into a large bowl. Discard everything in the strainer.

6 Fill a sink with cold water and place the bowl of strained stock in it to cool (make sure the bowl sits upright and doesn't wobble or tip). After 1 hour, remove the bowl from the sink, cover it with plastic wrap, and place it in the refrigerator to chill overnight.

7 When the stock has cooled, use a large spoon to scrape off and discard the solid layer of fat that has formed on top.

All-Purpose Chicken Stock will keep, in an airtight container in the refrigerator, for up to 3 days. To reheat, place it in a pot and warm on the stovetop over medium heat, stirring occasionally, until hot, about 5 minutes. Or place single-use portions (2 to 4 cups) of the stock in airtight, freezer-safe containers or zip-top freezer bags and freeze for up to 3 months.

Note: You can leave the skin on the onion. Just trim the root end where the dirt tends to accumulate and make certain the skin is free of dirt.

4- to 6-inch lengths so that they fit in the inner pot. To the spices in step 2, add 2 cloves peeled garlic, 2 sprigs fresh thyme, and 1 small handful fresh Italian (flat-leaf) parsley, stems included. Because of the volume of food in the inner pot, it will take the Instant Pot about 1 hour to release pressure naturally.

③ ALL-PURPOSE PORK STOCK DF

TOTAL TIME: 13 hours 30 minutes (including cooling time)

ACTIVE TIME: 15 minutes

YIELD: Makes about 2 quarts

Use 3 pounds pork bones, cut into 4- to 6-inch lengths. To the spices in step 2, add 2 cloves garlic; 2 small stalks lemongrass (about 8 inches each), slightly smashed with the back of a chef's knife; 1 pinch crushed red pepper flakes; and 1 small handful fresh Italian (flat-leaf) parsley, stems included. Because of the volume of food in the inner pot, it will take the Instant Pot about 1 hour to release pressure naturally.

② ALL-PURPOSE BEEF STOCK DF

TOTAL TIME: 13 hours 30 minutes (including cooling time)

ACTIVE TIME: 15 minutes

YIELD: Makes about 2 quarts

Use 3 pounds beef bones. Because beef bones tend to be larger than chicken bones, ask the butcher to cut them into

BEET AND BLUE CHEESE SALAD

TOTAL TIME: 40 minutes   **ACTIVE TIME:** 10 minutes   **YIELD:** Serves 4

Fresh beets are brilliantly red and sweet, but their one drawback is that they can take a long time to cook. Fortunately, the Instant Pot makes quick work of them. In this salad, the sharp and salty blue cheese plays off the beets' natural sweetness to create a contrasting and tasty flavor combination.

---

1 cup water

4 medium beets (1½ pounds total), trimmed and unpeeled (see Note)

3 tablespoons extra-virgin olive oil

1 tablespoon distilled white vinegar

½ teaspoon Dijon mustard

Pinch of salt, plus extra as needed

Pinch of freshly ground black pepper, plus extra as needed

¼ cup crumbled blue cheese

¼ cup finely chopped fresh Italian (flat-leaf) parsley

---

1 Place the water and beets in the inner pot. Close and lock the lid. Set the valve to Sealing. Press Manual or Pressure Cook and use the Pressure or Pressure Level button to select High Pressure ("More"). Use the – or + button to set the time to 25 minutes.

2 While the beets cook, make the dressing: Place the olive oil, vinegar, mustard, salt, and pepper in a Mason jar with a lid (or an airtight container) and shake to combine. Set aside.

3 When the cooking cycle ends, carefully use a wooden spoon to release the pressure by turning the pressure-release valve to Venting. (The pressure is released when the small metal float valve next to the pressure-release valve sinks back into the lid and the lid is no longer locked.)

4 Press Cancel and remove the lid. Use oven mitts to remove the inner pot (be careful—it's hot!) and drain the beets through a colander. Keep the beets in the colander and run cold water over them until they are cool to the touch, about 3 minutes. Using a dull knife, aluminum foil (see Note), or your fingers (careful, beets will stain!), rub the skin off the beets.

5 Place the beets on a cutting board and chop them into $1/2$-inch cubes. Transfer them to a large serving bowl.

6 Add the dressing and blue cheese and toss to coat. Sprinkle with the parsley and serve warm.

Beet and Blue Cheese Salad will keep, in an airtight container in the refrigerator, for up to 2 days. Serve chilled or at room temperature.

Note: To peel the beets without staining your hands, use aluminum foil. With a small sheet of foil in one hand, hold the beet with the foil and use a ball of foil in the other hand to scrape the skin off.

CHICKPEA SALAD

1·2·3

Chickpeas—a.k.a. garbanzo beans—are versatile and at home in any number of dishes. While they are available canned, they're cheaper and heartier in texture when made from dried. And the Instant Pot makes quick work of them. Try them with kale that has been thinly sliced and marinated to soften a bit while retaining an appealing crunch (see page 95). Or pair them with lemon and dill for a refreshing, citrusy zip (see page 96). Chickpeas can also add protein and texture to a simple romaine, tomato, and Parmesan salad (see page 95) that's an excellent addition to the weeknight dinner table. Or create your own salad, pairing the chickpeas with vegetables and/or greens and the cheese of your choice.

Master Method

V · VN · DF · X2

TOTAL TIME: 1 hour 10 minutes

ACTIVE TIME: 10 minutes

YIELD: Makes about 2½ cups

---

1 cup dried chickpeas, rinsed, drained, and picked over to remove debris

½ teaspoon salt

5 cups water

---

1 Place the chickpeas, salt, and water in the inner pot. Close and lock the lid. Set the valve to Sealing. Press Manual or Pressure Cook and use the Pressure or Pressure Level button to select High Pressure. Use the – or + button to set the time to 35 minutes.

2 When the cooking cycle ends, press Cancel. Allow the appliance to cool and release pressure naturally, about 25 minutes. (The pressure is released when the small metal float valve next to the pressure-release valve sinks back into the lid and the lid is no longer locked.)

3 Remove the lid. Wearing oven mitts, remove the inner pot (be careful—it's hot!) and drain the chickpeas through a colander.

Chickpeas will keep, in an airtight container in the refrigerator, for up to 5 days. Serve chilled or at room temperature.

1 CHICKPEA, KALE, AND MANCHEGO SALAD

V X2 30

TOTAL TIME: 10 minutes

ACTIVE TIME: 5 minutes

YIELD: Serves 8

Juice of 2 small lemons

1 small shallot, finely chopped

2 teaspoons honey

1/4 teaspoon salt

Pinch of cayenne pepper

8 ounces flat-leaf or curly-leaf kale, stems removed, leaves sliced into 1/4-inch ribbons (see Note)

2 1/2 cups cooked chickpeas (see page 94), warm or at room temperature

1/4 cup extra-virgin olive oil

6 ounces Manchego cheese, thinly sliced

---

1 In a large bowl, whisk the lemon juice, shallot, honey, salt, and cayenne pepper. Add the kale to the bowl and toss to coat it evenly with the dressing. Allow the dressed kale to sit for 5 minutes.

2 Add the chickpeas and olive oil to the bowl with the kale and toss thoroughly to coat the kale with oil. Add the cheese and toss just until the cheese is well distributed. Serve at room temperature or chilled.

Chickpea, Kale, and Manchego Salad will keep, in an airtight container in the refrigerator, for up to 2 days. Serve leftovers chilled.

Note: To slice the kale into ribbons: Tear the leaves from the stem. Stack several leaves together and then roll up the leaves tightly like a cigar. Slice crosswise to yield ribbons.

2 CHICKPEAS WITH ROMAINE LETTUCE, TOMATOES, AND PARMESAN

V X2 30

TOTAL TIME: 10 minutes

ACTIVE TIME: 10 minutes

YIELD: Serves 8

1/3 cup extra-virgin olive oil

1 tablespoon balsamic vinegar

Pinch of salt

Pinch of freshly ground black pepper

2 medium romaine lettuce hearts (about 12 ounces total), cut into bite-size pieces

1/2 cup freshly grated Parmesan cheese, plus extra for shaving on top

2 cups cherry tomatoes, halved

2 1/2 cups cooked chickpeas (see page 94), warm or at room temperature

1 Make the dressing: Place the olive oil, vinegar, salt, and pepper in a Mason jar with a lid (or an airtight container) and shake to combine.

2 Place the lettuce in a large bowl and pour the dressing over it. Toss to distribute the dressing evenly. Add the Parmesan and toss to distribute it evenly. Add the tomatoes and chickpeas and toss to distribute them evenly.

3 Divide the salad among 8 individual bowls. Use a vegetable peeler to shave several curls of Parmesan cheese atop each bowl. Serve at room temperature or chilled.

Chickpeas with Romaine Lettuce, Tomatoes, and Parmesan will keep, in an airtight container in the refrigerator, for up to 2 days. Serve leftovers chilled.

③ CHICKPEAS WITH LEMON, FETA, AND FRESH DILL [V] [X2] [30]

TOTAL TIME: 5 minutes
ACTIVE TIME: 5 minutes
YIELD: Serves 8

¼ cup extra-virgin olive oil

Freshly squeezed juice of 1 large lemon

1 teaspoon honey

Pinch of salt

Pinch of freshly ground black pepper

1 medium English cucumber, peeled, quartered, and sliced ¼ inch thick

1 cup diced feta cheese (about 4 ounces)

2½ cups cooked chickpeas (see page 94), warm or at room temperature

1 large bunch fresh dill (about 2 ounces), large stems removed, fronds finely chopped

1 Make the dressing: Place the olive oil, lemon juice, honey, salt, and pepper in a Mason jar with a lid (or an airtight container) and shake to combine.

2 Place the cucumber, feta, chickpeas, and dill in a large bowl and toss to combine. Pour the dressing over the salad and then toss the salad to distribute the dressing. Serve at room temperature or chilled.

Chickpeas with Lemon, Feta, and Fresh Dill will keep, in an airtight container in the refrigerator, for up to 2 days. Serve leftovers chilled.

MORE FLAVORING AND SERVING IDEAS FOR CHICKPEAS

- Make them crispy and crunchy: Toss cooked chickpeas with olive oil, salt, and pepper. (Add garlic powder, ground cumin, or curry powder for a twist.) Place them on a rimmed baking sheet and bake in a preheated 450°F oven, shaking the pan occasionally, until browned, about 30 minutes.

- Toss cooked chickpeas with chopped red bell pepper, olive oil, and salt and pepper for a brightly colored, fresh-tasting salad.

- Place equal parts lightly mashed cooked chickpeas and whole chickpeas on a round pizza dough, drizzled generously with extra-virgin olive oil, and bake the pizza as normal. Just before the pizza is finished, remove it from the oven and top with diced cooked chicken breast and crumbled feta cheese and then cook until the chicken and feta are warm.

- Coarsely mash cooked chickpeas with mayonnaise and diced celery. Use as a stand-in for tuna in a sandwich.

- Tossed with olive oil and lemon juice, cooked chickpeas can be tucked into a pita with Greek yogurt, chopped tomatoes, and fresh Italian (flat-leaf) parsley. Sprinkle with ground cumin or smoked paprika.

- Toss chickpeas into Brown Rice with Sesame Oil (page 216), adding salt and more sesame oil and sesame seeds to taste.

ROASTED ROSEMARY RED POTATOES

TOTAL TIME: 20 minutes   **ACTIVE TIME:** 10 minutes   **YIELD:** Serves 4

Sautéing these potatoes first in butter gives them a little bit of browning on the exterior that you can't get from pressure-cooking alone. Does it take a little extra time? Yes. But it's worth it. And the Instant Pot lets you do it all in one fell swoop.

---

3 tablespoons unsalted butter

1/2 teaspoon finely chopped fresh rosemary leaves, plus 1 sprig fresh rosemary

3 medium red potatoes (about 1 pound total), each cut into 8 wedges (see Note)

1/4 teaspoon salt

1/4 teaspoon freshly ground black pepper

3/4 cup water

Salted butter, for serving

---

1 Press Sauté and use the Sauté or Adjust button to select the middle temperature ("Normal"). Place the unsalted butter in the inner pot, wait about 1 minute for the butter to melt, then add the chopped rosemary leaves, potatoes, salt, and pepper. Cook with the lid off, stirring occasionally, until the potatoes are browned on most sides, about 10 minutes.

2 Add the water and the rosemary sprig. Close and lock the lid. Set the valve to Sealing. Press Cancel, then press Manual or Pressure Cook and use the Pressure or Pressure Level button to select High Pressure. Use the − or + button to set the time to 3 minutes.

3 When the cooking cycle ends, carefully use a wooden spoon to release the pressure by turning the pressure-release valve to Venting. (The pressure is released when the small metal float valve next to the pressure-release valve sinks back into the lid and the lid is no longer locked.)

4 Press Cancel and remove the lid. Discard the rosemary sprig and place the potatoes on a serving plate. Serve hot with salted butter dabbed on top.

Roasted Rosemary Red Potatoes will keep, in an airtight container in the refrigerator, for up to 3 days (store the cooking liquid separately). To reheat, preheat the oven to 350°F and place the potatoes in a shallow baking dish with about ¼ inch of the cooking liquid on the bottom. Cover the baking dish tightly with aluminum foil and bake until hot, about 15 minutes.

Note: The potato wedges should be roughly equal in size to ensure even cooking. If one potato is much smaller than others, cut it into quarters instead of eighths.

PRESSURE-COOKER "BAKED" POTATOES

TOTAL TIME: 30 minutes   **ACTIVE TIME:** 5 minutes   **YIELD:** Serves 4   V VN DF X2 30

Baked potatoes are great as a base for leftovers, whether it's stew, soup, or bits of meat and vegetables from the fridge or freezer. But oven-baked potatoes can take an hour or more. Good news: The Instant Pot can tackle them in about 30 minutes. While these may not have crisp, oven-baked skins, I'll take 30 minutes over an hour any day. (And, time permitting, you can always slather them in oil, throw them on a baking sheet, and bake in a 450°F oven for about 10 minutes to crisp the skin a bit.)

4 medium russet potatoes
(about 12 ounces each)

1 cup water

1 Pierce each potato all over several times with a fork. Place the steaming rack in the inner pot, pour in the water, and then place the potatoes on the steaming rack.

2 Close and lock the lid. Set the valve to Sealing. Press Manual or Pressure Cook and use the Pressure or Pressure Level button to select High Pressure. Use the – or + button to set the time to 15 minutes.

3 When the cooking cycle ends, carefully use a wooden spoon to release the pressure by turning the pressure-release valve to Venting. (The pressure is released when the small metal float valve next to the pressure-release valve sinks back into the lid and the lid is no longer locked.) Press Cancel, remove the lid, and serve the potatoes hot.

Pressure-Cooker "Baked" Potatoes will keep, in an airtight container in the refrigerator, for up to 3 days. To reheat, preheat the oven to 350°F. Wrap each potato tightly in aluminum foil, place it on the oven rack, and bake until hot, about 15 minutes.

CREAMY BUTTERNUT SQUASH

TOTAL TIME: 25 minutes   **ACTIVE TIME:** 5 minutes   **YIELD:** Serves 6

Putting the squash in a steaming basket serves an important purpose here: Squash that is cooked directly in the water will become too soft and risk clogging the valve when the pressure is released. The creaminess in this dish comes not just from the crème fraîche—although that certainly does help—but from the texture of the mashed squash itself. Serve this naturally sweet side dish with a beef roast or a roasted chicken.

1 cup water

1 medium butternut squash (about 2 pounds), peeled, seeded, and cut into 1-inch cubes

2 tablespoons Crème Fraîche (page 233) or heavy (whipping) cream

½ teaspoon salt

¼ teaspoon freshly ground black pepper

Salted butter, for serving

1 Place the steaming rack on the bottom of the inner pot and add the water. Place a silicone or collapsible metal steaming basket on top of the rack and then place the squash inside the basket.

2 Close and lock the lid. Set the valve to Sealing. Press Manual or Pressure Cook and use the Pressure or Pressure Level button to select High Pressure. Use the – or + button to set the time to 10 minutes.

3 When the cooking cycle ends, carefully use a wooden spoon to release the pressure by turning the pressure-release valve to Venting. (The pressure is released when the small metal float valve next to the pressure-release valve sinks back into the lid and the lid is no longer locked.)

4 Press Cancel and remove the lid. Wearing oven mitts, remove the steaming basket from the inner pot (be careful—it's hot!) and transfer the squash, crème fraîche, salt, and pepper to a large serving bowl. Use a potato masher to smash the squash and combine thoroughly.

5 Serve hot, topped with butter.

Creamy Butternut Squash will keep, in an airtight container in the refrigerator, for up to 5 days. To reheat, place the squash in a pot, add a splash of water, cover, and warm on the stovetop over medium heat, stirring occasionally, for about 5 minutes.

QUICK-PICKLED VEGETABLES

TOTAL TIME: 3 hours (including cooling time)   **ACTIVE TIME:** 5 minutes   **YIELD:** Serves 8   V VN DF X2

Pressure-cooking happens fast, which is why at first I was afraid that quick-pickling vegetables would make them mushy. But fear not. The key is using next to no pressure-cooking time: just 1 minute. This softens the vegetables a bit while allowing them to maintain a respectable texture. Just as important, the heat gives the vinegar a head start on penetrating the vegetables. Quick-Pickled Vegetables are delicious served with a cheese plate or alongside a sandwich. Note that because these pickles are not processed for room-temperature storage, they must be kept in the refrigerator.

1 cup apple cider vinegar

1 cup water

1 tablespoon sugar

1 tablespoon kosher or pickling salt

1 teaspoon black peppercorns

1 teaspoon mustard seeds

1 pound carrots, peeled, trimmed, and cut into 2-inch segments, or 1 pound English cucumbers, cut into 2-inch segments (or a combination)

1 Place the vinegar, water, sugar, salt, peppercorns, and mustard seeds in the inner pot and stir to dissolve the salt and sugar. Add the carrots and/or cucumbers and stir to coat.

2 Close and lock the lid. Set the valve to Sealing. Press Manual or Pressure Cook and use the Pressure or Pressure Level button to select High Pressure. Use the – or + button to set the time to 1 minute.

3 When the cooking cycle ends, carefully use a wooden spoon to release the pressure by turning the pressure-release valve to Venting. (The pressure is released when the small metal float valve next to the pressure-release valve sinks back into the lid and the lid is no longer locked.)

4 Press Cancel and remove the lid. Use a large spoon to place the vegetables in a heatproof container with a lid.

5 Wearing oven mitts, remove the inner pot (be careful—it's hot!) and carefully pour the liquid into the container with the vegetables.

6 Allow the vegetables to cool, uncovered, to room temperature, about 45 minutes, then cover the container before refrigerating for at least 2 hours to chill. Serve chilled.

Quick-Pickled Vegetables will keep—and continue to develop flavor!—in a covered container in the refrigerator, for up to 2 weeks.

BACON-Y REFRIED BEANS

TOTAL TIME: 1 hour 15 minutes   **ACTIVE TIME:** 5 minutes   **YIELD:** Serves 8

These beans might be reason enough to get in the habit of saving your bacon fat whenever you fry some bacon. Simply pour the hot fat from the pan—carefully!—into a Mason jar with a lid or an airtight glass container, and store it in the refrigerator or freezer. Then, whenever you want a smoky, salty fat to infuse flavor into a dish (or to fry an egg—doesn't get much better than that), just scoop some grease from the jar. It will keep in the fridge for a few months, and indefinitely in the freezer. If you don't have bacon fat, vegetable oil can be used instead.

---

2 tablespoons bacon fat or vegetable oil

1 medium white or yellow onion, chopped

2 cloves garlic, chopped

1 small jalapeño, stemmed, seeded, and finely chopped (see Tip)

2 cups dried pinto beans, rinsed, drained, and picked over to remove debris

1 teaspoon salt

1 teaspoon chili powder

1 teaspoon ground cumin

1/2 teaspoon freshly ground black pepper

3 cups reduced-salt chicken broth or All-Purpose Chicken Stock (page 88)

Shredded Cheddar cheese, for serving

---

1 Press Sauté and use the Sauté or Adjust button to select the middle temperature ("Normal"). Place the bacon fat in the inner pot, wait about 1 minute for the fat to melt and warm, then add the onion, garlic, and jalapeño. Cook with the lid off, stirring occasionally, until the onion softens slightly, about 5 minutes.

2 Add the beans, salt, chili powder, cumin, pepper, and chicken broth to the inner pot and stir to combine. Close and lock the lid. Set the valve to Sealing. Press Cancel, then press Manual or Pressure Cook and use the Pressure or Pressure Level button to select High Pressure. Use the – or + button to set the time to 40 minutes.

3 When the cooking cycle ends, turn off the machine. Allow the appliance to cool and release pressure naturally, about 25 minutes. (The pressure is released when the small metal float valve next to the pressure-release valve sinks back into the lid and the lid is no longer locked.)

4 Remove the lid. Use a potato masher to smash the beans until they are slightly chunky.

5 Serve hot, sprinkled with Cheddar cheese.

Bacon-y Refried Beans will keep, in an airtight container in the refrigerator, for up to 5 days. To reheat, place the beans in a pot, add a splash of water, and warm on the stovetop over medium heat, stirring frequently, for about 5 minutes.

Tip: To easily remove the seeds from a jalapeño, split it in half lengthwise and then run a serrated grapefruit spoon down the inside of each half. The seeds will fall out.

STEEL-CUT OATS WITH CHOCOLATE AND SLIVERED ALMONDS

TOTAL TIME: 35 minutes   **ACTIVE TIME:** 5 minutes   **YIELD:** Serves 4

Steel-cut oats represent the best of what oatmeal can offer: a warm bowl of comfort food that maintains a pleasant bit of chewiness. I have heard that you can even add more chocolate to your bowl if you know it's going to be that kind of day.

2¾ cups water

1 cup steel-cut oats (not instant)

¼ teaspoon salt

¼ cup chocolate chips

¼ cup slivered almonds

---

1 Place the water, oats, and salt in the inner pot and stir to combine.

2 Close and lock the lid. Set the valve to Sealing. Press Manual or Pressure Cook and use the Pressure or Pressure Level button to select High Pressure. Use the – or + button to set the time to 10 minutes.

3 When the cooking cycle ends, press Cancel. Allow the appliance to cool and release pressure naturally, about 15 minutes. (The pressure is released when the small metal float valve next to the pressure-release valve sinks back into the lid and the lid is no longer locked.)

4 Remove the lid and stir to distribute any remaining liquid. Divide the oatmeal among 4 bowls and scatter the chocolate chips and almonds on top. Serve warm.

Steel-Cut Oats with Chocolate and Slivered Almonds will keep, in an airtight container in the refrigerator, for up to 5 days. To reheat, scoop a single serving into a small pot, add a splash of water or milk, and warm on the stovetop over medium-low heat, stirring occasionally, for about 3 minutes.

MAPLE-CINNAMON BREAKFAST QUINOA

TOTAL TIME: 15 minutes   **ACTIVE TIME:** 5 minutes   **YIELD:** Serves 4   `V` `VN` `DF` `X2` `30`

It's amazing that one cinnamon stick can take a somewhat plain and slightly nutty-tasting grain like quinoa and nudge it into perfectly sweet breakfast territory. Of course, the berries and maple syrup don't hurt. They never do.

---

1 cup white quinoa, rinsed and drained (see Note)

1 cup water

1 cinnamon stick, about 3 inches

Pinch of salt

¼ cup pure maple syrup

Fresh blueberries, for garnish

---

1 Place the quinoa in the inner pot, followed by the water, cinnamon stick, and salt. Stir to combine.

2 Close and lock the lid. Set the valve to Sealing. Press Cancel, then press Manual or Pressure Cook and use the Pressure or Pressure Level button to select High Pressure. Use the – or + button to set the time to 1 minute.

3 When the cooking cycle ends, press Cancel. Allow the appliance to cool and release pressure naturally, about 10 minutes. (The pressure is released when the small metal float valve next to the pressure-release valve sinks back into the lid and the lid is no longer locked.)

4 Remove the lid. Discard the cinnamon stick and use a fork to fluff the quinoa. Divide the quinoa among 4 bowls. Top each with 1 tablespoon of maple syrup and then garnish generously with blueberries. Serve warm.

Maple-Cinnamon Breakfast Quinoa will keep, in an airtight container in the refrigerator, for up to 5 days. To reheat, scoop a single serving into a small pot, add a splash of water, and warm on the stovetop over medium-low heat, stirring occasionally, for about 3 minutes.

Note: Rinse the quinoa in a fine-mesh strainer; the grains are so small that they can fall out the bottom of many strainers and colanders.

TAPIOCA CHAI PUDDING

TOTAL TIME: 3 hours (including cooling time)   **ACTIVE TIME:** 15 minutes   **YIELD:** Serves 6   [V]

The Indian spices and tapioca pearls in this pudding make it like the dessert cousin of bubble tea, that sweet drink with a jumbo straw and lots of chewy tapioca. Typically tapioca can require presoaking or long cooking times, but pressure-cooking it in the Instant Pot eliminates any of that hassle.

2/3 cup medium pearl tapioca (see Note)

3 cups water

1 piece (3 inches) peeled fresh ginger, cut crosswise into 1/2-inch-thick pieces

1 tablespoon whole cloves

1 cinnamon stick, about 3 inches

2/3 cup sugar

1/2 teaspoon salt

2 large egg yolks

1 cup whole milk

1 teaspoon pure vanilla extract

1/8 teaspoon ground cardamom, for garnish

---

1 Place the tapioca in a colander and rinse it under running water.

2 Pour the tapioca into the inner pot, add the water, and stir to combine. Close and lock the lid. Set the valve to Sealing. Press Manual or Pressure Cook and use the Pressure Level or Adjust button to select High Pressure. Use the - or + button to set the time to 6 minutes.

3 While the tapioca cooks, wrap the ginger, cloves, and cinnamon stick in cheesecloth and tie the ends together to make a bundle. Set aside until step 7.

4 When the cooking cycle ends, press Cancel. Allow the appliance to cool and release pressure naturally, about 20 minutes. (The pressure is released when the small metal float valve next to the pressure-release valve sinks back into the lid and the lid is no longer locked.)

5 Remove the lid and use a whisk to incorporate the sugar and salt into the tapioca. (The tapioca will be quite thick.)

6 In a liquid measuring cup or small bowl, use a fork to beat together the egg yolks and milk until combined.

7 With the lid off, press Cancel and then press Sauté and use the Sauté or Adjust button to select the lowest temperature ("Less"). Stir in the egg yolk mixture and then add the bundle of spices. Cook the pudding with the lid off, stirring occasionally, until it very gently gurgles and a few bubbles break the surface, about 10 minutes. Remove and discard the spice bag, add the vanilla to the pudding, and stir until it is well distributed.

8 Turn off the machine, use oven mitts to remove the inner pot (be careful—it's hot!), and divide the pudding among 6 ramekins or heatproof bowls. Cover and refrigerate for 2 hours to chill. (To avoid developing a "skin" on the pudding, press plastic wrap tightly against the surface. Or just cover loosely and stir any skin back into the pudding before serving.) Serve chilled, dusted very lightly with ground cardamom.

Tapioca Chai Pudding will keep, covered in the refrigerator, for up to 5 days.

Note: Tapioca comes in many sizes and types. You don't want instant tapioca. Instead, you want spheres about 1/4 inch in diameter in a package that calls for pre-soaking. (You won't presoak it; you'll use the Instant Pot.)

CHOCOLATE LAVA CAKES WITH DULCE DE LECHE

TOTAL TIME: 30 minutes   **ACTIVE TIME:** 10 minutes   **YIELD:** Serves 4   V 30

When I lived in Argentina, I used to joke that there were three taps in the kitchen—hot water, cold water, and dulce de leche. And, really, it seems like only a slight exaggeration to say that the sweet, sticky caramel sauce flowed from the faucet, since it was just about everywhere and in just about everything. Not that I was complaining. Not at all. In these cakes, the dulce de leche remains hidden at first, enveloped in the moist chocolate cake, before bursting on the scene as a warm river of caramel. It makes for an impressive dessert that happens quickly in your Instant Pot.

Nonstick cooking spray

¼ cup semisweet chocolate chips

2 ounces unsweetened chocolate, finely chopped

½ cup (1 stick) unsalted butter

1 cup confectioners' sugar, plus extra for garnish

2 large eggs plus 2 large egg yolks

¼ cup all-purpose flour

Pinch of salt

4 teaspoons dulce de leche (see Note)

1 cup water

1 Coat four 5- to 6-ounce ramekins with nonstick cooking spray. Place the chocolate chips and chopped chocolate in a medium bowl.

2 Melt the butter in a small bowl in the microwave on high for 2 minutes. Or place the butter in the inner pot, then press Sauté and use the Sauté or Adjust button to select the lowest temperature ("Less"). Wait for the butter to melt, about 3 minutes.

3 Add the melted butter to the chocolate and stir until well combined. (If you used the inner pot to melt the butter, wash it.)

4 Add the confectioners' sugar to the chocolate mixture and use a fork to mix until no streaks remain. Add the eggs and egg yolks and mix until well combined.

5 Add the flour and salt and mix gently with a rubber spatula until no streaks remain.

6 Coat a spoon with nonstick cooking spray and use it to fill each ramekin with batter halfway. Coat a 1-teaspoon measuring spoon with nonstick cooking spray and use it to place 1 teaspoon of dulce de leche in the center of the batter in each ramekin, then cover with the remaining batter. (The batter should cover the dulce de leche but will not fill the ramekins.)

7 Place the steaming rack on the bottom of the inner pot and pour the water into the inner pot. Place the ramekins on the steaming rack, tilting them slightly if necessary to fit them. Place a sheet of aluminum foil over the ramekins. (It's not necessary to cover the ramekins tightly; the foil is there to prevent water from dripping onto the cakes.)

8 Close and lock the lid. Set the valve to Sealing. Press Manual or Pressure Cook and use the Pressure or Pressure Level button to select High Pressure. Use the – or + button to set the time to 10 minutes.

9 When the cooking cycle ends, carefully use a wooden spoon to release the pressure by turning the pressure-release valve to Venting. (The pressure is released when the small metal float valve next to the pressure-release valve sinks back into the lid and the lid is no longer locked.)

10 Press Cancel and remove the lid. Carefully remove the foil with tongs, trying to avoid spilling water on the cakes. Allow the cakes to cool in the appliance for 10 minutes.

11 Remove the ramekins and dust the top of each cake with confectioners' sugar before serving warm.

Chocolate Lava Cakes with Dulce de Leche are best served when freshly made. (That said, no one needs to know what you cover with plastic wrap and stash in the refrigerator. Just eat it chilled the next day—I mean, hypothetically, that's how it would be best enjoyed the next day.)

Note: Dulce de leche—literally "milk jam"—is a caramel spread popular in many parts of Latin America and is sometimes available in a variation known as *cajeta*. Look for it in the supermarket near the jams and jellies or at a grocer with a selection of Latin American products.

Chapter 3
SLOW COOKER

have always had a special place in my heart for a good slow-cooker recipe; I just haven't always had a place on my countertop for a slow cooker. The Instant Pot solved that quandary.

Slow-cooking is probably the Instant Pot function with which the most home cooks are already familiar. If you're not familiar with slow-cooking, or if you just want an overview and a look at some special considerations for slow-cooking, read on.

WHY USE A SLOW COOKER?

- Rarely in life do we wish things would take longer, but that's the strength of the slow cooker: While the pressure cooker might make a meal in an hour, the slow cooker might take 10 hours. This allows you to start a recipe in the morning, let it cook all day, and have it ready for dinner.

- Cooking low and slow can make tough, inexpensive cuts of meat more tender by breaking down the connective tissue that makes meat chewy.

TEMPERATURE AND TIMING

The Instant Pot has three slow-cooker temperature settings that—depending on the model—are accessed by pushing the Adjust button after the Slow Cook button, or by pressing the Slow Cook button a second time. The temperatures can vary slightly as the heating element cycles on and off, but for most models they are generally:

- "Less" (low): 190°F

- "Normal" (medium): 200°F

- "More" (high): 210°F

CONVERTING TRADITIONAL RECIPES FOR THE SLOW COOKER

If you'd like to try making a conventional, oven-based recipe in the slow cooker, these cooking-time conversions can serve as starting points. As always, experiment and take notes on what works for you.

- 15 to 30 minutes in the oven: Slow-cook for 1 to 2 hours on High or 4 to 6 hours on Low

- 30 minutes to 1 hour in the oven: Slow-cook for 2 to 3 hours on High or 5 to 7 hours on Low

- 1 to 2 hours in the oven: Slow-cook for 3 to 4 hours on High or 6 to 8 hours on Low

SLOW-COOKER TIPS AND PITFALLS

The recipes in this section were all developed for the Instant Pot slow cooker. If you're developing your own recipes, here are some things to keep in mind:

- Do not use frozen meat or poultry in the slow cooker; the meat may hover at unsafe temperatures for too long.

- Removing the lid frequently to check on the food or cooking with the lid off will result in longer cooking times.

- Milk, cheese, and cream do not benefit from slow-cooking (milk and cheese in particular tend to curdle or separate if cooked too long) and should be added during the last hour of cooking unless otherwise directed.

- Soft vegetables such as raw tomatoes, mushrooms, and zucchini should be added in the last 30 minutes to avoid overcooking.

- Generally speaking, to avoid mushiness, pasta should be added toward the end of the cooking or cooked separately and added just before serving. (With that said, you'll see I violate my own rule in the Ziti with Italian Sausage recipe on page 151 It may seem counterintuitive but trust me—it works.)

- Go easy on the booze. As with a pressure cooker, any alcohol in a recipe will not have a chance to evaporate in the relatively low-temperature, sealed cooking process.

KOREAN-STYLE SHORT RIBS WITH GARLIC AND GINGER

TOTAL TIME: 9 hours 30 minutes   **ACTIVE TIME:** 20 minutes   **YIELD:** Serves 4

The beef here becomes fall-off-the-bone tender from the long cooking time and takes on a beautiful salty-sweet balance from the soy sauce and fall fruit. (Pear is more traditional in the grilled beef *bulgogi* that inspired this recipe, but apple works very well.) White rice (see page 211) makes the perfect accompaniment for soaking up the juices.

Korean-style ribs are cut through the bone, meaning each length of meat is thin (about ½ inch) and contains several bones in cross-section. They are often available in Asian markets or by request from a butcher. If they are unavailable, try using 2-inch cubes of chuck roast.

---

4 pounds bone-in Korean-style beef short ribs (see above)

Salt and freshly ground black pepper

1 medium pear or apple, peeled, cored, and coarsely chopped

½ cup soy sauce

3 cloves garlic, minced

3 scallions, white and green parts, thinly sliced, plus extra for garnish

2 tablespoons peeled and finely grated fresh ginger

2 tablespoons toasted sesame oil

1 tablespoon rice vinegar

1 cup water

Sesame seeds, for garnish

Cooked white rice, for serving

---

1 Season the ribs lightly on both sides with salt and pepper and set them aside. Place the pear, soy sauce, garlic, scallions, ginger, sesame oil, vinegar, and water in the inner pot and stir to combine. Add the ribs to the inner pot and turn them in the sauce to coat them.

2 Close and lock the lid. Set the valve to Venting. Attach the condensation collector. Press Slow Cook and use the Slow Cook or Adjust button to select the lowest temperature ("Less"). Use the − or + button to set the time to 9 hours.

3 When the cooking time is finished, press Cancel and remove the lid. The beef will be very tender. Carefully remove the ribs from the inner pot and place them on a serving platter. Drizzle them with some of the cooking liquid, garnish them with scallions and sesame seeds, and serve hot with the rice, passing the remaining cooking liquid in a small bowl. If you're among friends or family, this may be a good time to wash your hands thoroughly and eat the ribs with your hands.

Korean-Style Short Ribs with Garlic and Ginger will keep, in an airtight container in the refrigerator, for up to 4 days. To reheat, place the ribs along with a few spoonfuls of the cooking liquid in a frying pan on the stovetop over medium heat, flipping the ribs occasionally, for about 5 minutes.

SLOW-COOKER POT ROAST AND CARROTS

TOTAL TIME: 9 hours 30 minutes   **ACTIVE TIME:** 30 minutes   **YIELD:** Serves 8

I love the idea of taking a classic dish like pot roast and pairing it with newfangled technology like the Instant Pot. Another thing to love: This recipe creates both the main course and side dish at the same time. It's the perfect dish for a weekend evening, though the Instant Pot means you can also prepare it at the beginning of a weekday and have it waiting for dinner no matter where that weekday takes you.

---

2 tablespoons neutral-flavored vegetable oil, such as canola or peanut

3 pounds boneless beef chuck roast (see Note)

Salt and freshly ground black pepper

2 small white or yellow onions, chopped

1 pound carrots, peeled and cut into 2-inch chunks

2 cloves garlic, chopped

1 teaspoon dried thyme

2 cups reduced-salt beef or chicken broth or All-Purpose Beef or Chicken Stock (pages 90 and 88)

1 tablespoon Worcestershire sauce

¼ cup all-purpose flour

½ cup water

---

1 Press Sauté and use the Sauté or Adjust button to select the highest temperature ("More"). Place the vegetable oil in the inner pot. Sprinkle the beef on all sides with salt and pepper. Wait until the display reads "Hot," about 5 minutes, then add the beef. Cook with the lid off, turning the beef every 2 minutes, until the beef is browned on most sides, about 8 minutes.

2 Add the onions and cook with the lid off, stirring occasionally, until the onions soften slightly, about 5 minutes.

3 Add the carrots, garlic, and thyme and then pour the broth and Worcestershire sauce over the meat and vegetables. Close and lock the lid. Set the valve to Venting. Attach the condensation collector. Press Cancel, then press Slow Cook and use the Slow Cook or Adjust button to select the middle temperature ("Normal"). Use the – or + button to set the time to 9 hours.

4 When the cooking time is finished, press Cancel and remove the lid. Remove the roast and the vegetables to a serving platter and cover with aluminum foil to keep warm.

5 Allow the liquid in the inner pot to settle for about 5 minutes before using a large spoon to skim off any noticeable fat from the surface.

6 Press Sauté and use the Sauté or Adjust button to select the highest temperature ("More"). Cook the liquid with the lid off, stirring occasionally, until it bubbles vigorously, about 2 minutes. Continue cooking, stirring occasionally, until it has thickened and reduced to about half of its original volume, about 10 minutes.

7 Press Cancel, then press Sauté and use the Sauté or Adjust button to select the middle temperature ("Normal"). In a small bowl, use a fork to stir the flour into the water until fully incorporated. Add the flour mixture to the inner pot and stir constantly until the liquid has thickened, about 2 minutes.

8 Press Cancel to turn off the Instant Pot. Taste the sauce and adjust the seasoning, adding salt and pepper as needed before pouring the sauce over the beef and vegetables. Serve warm.

Slow-Cooker Pot Roast and Carrots will keep, in an airtight container in the refrigerator, for up to 4 days. To reheat, preheat the oven to 350°F and place the beef and carrots in a shallow baking dish. Add some sauce and a splash of water to reach a depth of about ¼ inch on the bottom. Cover the baking dish tightly with aluminum foil and bake until hot, about 15 minutes.

Note: Three pounds of meat is going to be a tight fit in a 6-quart Instant Pot, but it works. Don't worry about browning every side of the roast, just try to get some color on large parts of it. If you're using an 8-quart Instant Pot, it's best not to scale up this recipe. Just take advantage of the extra room in the pot to brown more of the meat's surface.

MARVELOUS SLOW-COOKER MEATBALLS

Maybe we tend to think of meatballs as a classic accompaniment to pasta, and served with a marinara sauce, they certainly are that (see below). But don't stop there. Serve sweet-and-sour meatballs (see page 126) with rice and a side of vegetables, or make meatballs with feta and mint (see page 128) for a Greek-inspired twist. Heads up: These recipes densely pack the inner pot to maximize the number of meatballs. Handle the meatballs gently to keep them intact.

Master Method

① BASIL-PARMESAN MEATBALLS

TOTAL TIME: 5 hours 20 minutes

ACTIVE TIME: 20 minutes

YIELD: Serves 6

---

1 pound 85% lean ground beef, ground veal, ground pork, or a combination

¾ cup plain bread crumbs

¾ cup pesto sauce (see Note)

¼ cup freshly grated Parmesan cheese, plus extra for garnish

1 large egg yolk, lightly beaten

1 tablespoon neutral-flavored vegetable oil, such as canola or peanut

1 jar (24 ounces) favorite marinara sauce

½ cup water

Fresh basil leaves, for garnish

---

1 Line a large plate with waxed paper or parchment paper. Place the ground meat, bread crumbs, pesto, Parmesan, and egg yolk in a medium bowl and mix with your hands until well combined. Use your hands to pat and gently roll the meat into 12 equal-size balls, setting them on the prepared plate.

2 Press Sauté and use the Sauté or Adjust button to select the highest temperature ("More"). Place the vegetable oil in the inner pot. Wait until the display reads "Hot," about 5 minutes, then add the meatballs. Cook with the lid off until the meatballs are browned on one side, about 2 minutes.

3 Add the marinara sauce and water and stir very gently to distribute the meatballs evenly.

4 Close and lock the lid. Set the valve to Venting. Attach the condensation collector. Press Cancel, then press Slow Cook and use the Slow Cook or Adjust button to select the lowest temperature ("Less"). Use the – or + button to set the time to 5 hours.

5 When the cooking time is finished, press Cancel and remove the lid. Place the meatballs and sauce on a serving platter and garnish with basil leaves and Parmesan. Serve hot.

Basil-Parmesan Meatballs will keep, in an airtight container in the refrigerator, for up to 4 days. To reheat, place the meatballs and sauce in a pot and warm on the stovetop over medium heat, stirring occasionally, for about 5 minutes.

Note: Pesto sauce is often sold in shelf-stable jars, in the refrigerated case in tubs, and in the freezer section as cubes. The refrigerated or frozen versions are usually superior in flavor.

2 SWEET-AND-SOUR MEATBALLS DF

TOTAL TIME: 5 hours 20 minutes
ACTIVE TIME: 20 minutes
YIELD: Serves 6

---

1 pound 85% lean ground beef, ground veal, ground pork, or a combination

¾ cup plain bread crumbs

4 small cloves garlic, finely chopped

1 small white or yellow onion, finely chopped

½ teaspoon salt

½ teaspoon freshly ground black pepper

1 large egg yolk, lightly beaten

1 tablespoon neutral-flavored vegetable oil, such as canola or peanut

½ cup apple cider vinegar

½ cup ketchup

1 cup water

1 cup brown sugar

2 tablespoons soy sauce

Finely chopped green, red, and yellow bell peppers, for garnish

Cooked white rice (see page 211; optional), for serving

---

1 Line a large plate with waxed paper or parchment paper. Place the ground meat, bread crumbs, garlic, onion, salt, pepper,

Clockwise from top: Greek-Inspired
Meatballs with Mint and Feta,
Basil-Parmesan Meatballs,
Sweet-and-Sour Meatballs

and egg yolk in a medium bowl and mix with your hands until well combined. Use your hands to pat and gently roll the meat into 12 equal-size balls, setting them on the prepared plate.

2 Press Sauté and select the highest temperature. Place the vegetable oil in the inner pot. Wait until the display reads "Hot," about 5 minutes, then add the meatballs. Cook with the lid off until meatballs are browned on one side, about 2 minutes.

3 Add the vinegar, ketchup, water, brown sugar, and soy sauce and stir very gently to distribute the meatballs evenly.

4 Close and lock the lid. Set the valve to Venting. Attach the condensation collector. Press Cancel, then press Slow Cook and select the lowest temperature. Set the time to 5 hours.

5 When the cooking time is finished, press Cancel and remove the lid. Place the meatballs and sauce on a serving platter and garnish with the finely chopped peppers. Serve hot, with or without rice.

Sweet-and-Sour Meatballs will keep, in an airtight container in the refrigerator, for up to 4 days.

3 GREEK-INSPIRED MEATBALLS WITH MINT AND FETA

TOTAL TIME: 5 hours 20 minutes
ACTIVE TIME: 20 minutes
YIELD: Serves 6

---

1 pound ground lamb

3/4 cup plain bread crumbs

2 cloves garlic, finely chopped

1/2 small white or yellow onion, finely chopped

1/2 cup (about 2 ounces) crumbled feta cheese, plus extra for garnish

1/4 cup finely chopped fresh Italian (flat-leaf) parsley leaves

2 tablespoons finely chopped fresh mint leaves

2 teaspoons dried oregano

1/2 teaspoon freshly ground black pepper

1 large egg yolk, lightly beaten

1 tablespoon neutral-flavored vegetable oil, such as canola or peanut

1 jar (24 ounces) favorite marinara sauce

1/2 cup water

Freshly grated zest of 1 lemon

Chopped, pitted black olives, for garnish

---

1 Line a large plate with waxed paper or parchment paper. Place the ground lamb, bread crumbs, garlic, onion, feta, parsley, mint, 1 teaspoon of the oregano, pepper, and egg yolk in a medium bowl and mix with your hands until well combined. Use your hands to pat and gently roll the meat into 12 equal-size balls, setting them on the prepared plate.

2 Press Sauté and select the highest temperature. Place the vegetable oil in the inner pot. Wait until the display reads "Hot," about 5 minutes, then add the meatballs. Cook with the lid off until the meatballs are browned on one side, about 2 minutes.

3 Add the marinara sauce, water, lemon zest, and remaining teaspoon of oregano and stir very gently to distribute the meatballs evenly.

4 Close and lock the lid. Set the valve to Venting. Attach the condensation collector. Press Cancel, then press Slow Cook and select the lowest temperature. Set the time to 5 hours.

5 When the cooking time is finished, press Cancel and remove the lid. Place the meatballs and sauce on a serving platter and garnish with chopped olives and feta. Serve hot.

Greek-Inspired Meatballs with Mint and Feta will keep, in an airtight container in the refrigerator, for up to 4 days.

MORE FLAVORING AND SERVING IDEAS FOR MARVELOUS SLOW-COOKER MEATBALLS

- Add some heat: Spike the meat mixture with a little of your favorite hot sauce.

- No matter which kind of meatball you choose, it will be at home in a sandwich (with or without mozzarella or provolone cheese for the tomato-based meatballs, or roasted red peppers for the sweet-and-sour version). Split a bun in half and pile the meatballs in between. Or go the slider route, serving each meatball between a small bun for single-meatball sliders.

- Serve atop a bed of lightly steamed spinach.

- Serve atop couscous or polenta (see page 52).

- Add the leftovers to soups just before serving. Try them with Creamy Chipotle Tomato Soup (page 166) or Tomato and White Bean Soup (page 177).

- Place halved leftover meatballs atop pizza, adding them just a few minutes before the pizza is finished baking.

MEATLOAF, MEET THE INSTANT POT

TOTAL TIME: 4 hours 15 minutes   **ACTIVE TIME:** 15 minutes   **YIELD:** Serves 8

The tall, round geometry of the Instant Pot means this will not be a typical meatloaf in appearance. It's more scoopable than sliceable, but all the customary flavor is there. And it's perfect for spooning out over a "baked" potato (see page 100) or serving with a baguette. I won't even mention meatloaf sandwiches for the leftovers. Oops. I guess I just did.

¼ cup ketchup

2 tablespoons packed brown sugar

2 teaspoons apple cider vinegar

1 tablespoon neutral-flavored vegetable oil, such as canola or peanut

1 small white or yellow onion, minced

2 cloves garlic, minced

2 slices white sandwich bread, torn into small pieces

½ cup whole milk

2 large eggs

1 tablespoon Dijon mustard

1 tablespoon Worcestershire sauce

1½ teaspoons salt

1 teaspoon freshly ground black pepper

2 pounds 85% lean ground beef

Nonstick cooking spray

1 Stir together the ketchup, brown sugar, and vinegar in a small bowl. Set aside.

2 Press Sauté and use the Sauté or Adjust button to select the lowest temperature ("Less"). Place the vegetable oil in the inner pot, wait about 1 minute for it to warm, then add the onion and garlic. Cook with the lid off, stirring occasionally, until the onion softens slightly, about 5 minutes.

3 Meanwhile, combine the bread and milk in a large mixing bowl and use a fork to mash them into a paste. In a small bowl, use a fork to beat together the eggs, mustard, Worcestershire sauce, salt, and pepper.

4 When the onion is soft, remove the inner pot and place it on a trivet or other heat-resistant surface. Add the egg mixture to the bread paste in the large bowl, followed by the onion and garlic. Add the ground beef and then use your hands to mix the ingredients until evenly distributed.

5 Spray the inner pot with cooking spray. (There's no need to clean out any residue from the onion.) Add the meatloaf mixture, using the back of a spoon to press it gently into an even layer. Brush the top of the meatloaf with the reserved ketchup mixture.

6 Return the inner pot to the appliance. Close and lock the lid. Set the valve to Venting. Attach the condensation collector. Press Cancel, then press Slow Cook and use the Slow Cook or Adjust button to select the middle temperature ("Normal"). Use the – or + button to set the time to 4 hours.

7 When the cooking time is finished, press Cancel and remove the lid. Serve the meatloaf hot, spooning it out into serving bowls.

Meatloaf, Meet the Instant Pot will keep, in an airtight container in the refrigerator, for up to 4 days. To reheat, preheat the oven to 350°F and place the meatloaf in a shallow baking dish with water to a depth of about ¼ inch. Cover the baking dish tightly with aluminum foil and bake until hot, about 15 minutes.

SLOW-AND-LOW PORK ROAST

These pork dishes rank as favorites because they squeeze a lot of flavor out of a few ingredients. Pork shoulder in general—here, the boneless blade roast—is a great match for the slow cooker, becoming meltingly tender as it cooks nearly all day. Make this pork roast with maple and mustard (see below), or switch things up a bit with a beer-braised pork roast (see page 134) and a version flavored with a quick homemade barbecue sauce (see page 133).

① MAPLE-MUSTARD PORK ROAST **DF**

TOTAL TIME: 8 hours 15 minutes
ACTIVE TIME: 15 minutes
YIELD: Serves 8

½ cup whole-grain Dijon mustard

½ cup pure maple syrup

2 tablespoons apple cider vinegar

1 boneless pork blade roast (about 3 pounds), any butcher's twine removed

1 teaspoon salt

1 teaspoon freshly ground black pepper

2 tablespoons neutral-flavored vegetable oil, such as canola or peanut

4 medium white or yellow onions, chopped

3 cloves garlic, finely chopped

1 Stir together the mustard, maple syrup, and vinegar in a small bowl until combined. Set aside.

2 Rub the pork all over with the salt and pepper.

3 Press Sauté and use the Sauté or Adjust button to select the highest temperature ("More"). Place the vegetable oil in the inner pot. Wait until the display reads "Hot," about 5 minutes, then add the pork. Cook with the lid off, turning the pork every 2 minutes, until the pork is browned on most sides, about 8 minutes.

4 Move the pork to one side of the inner pot and nestle the onions and garlic in the center, stirring to distribute them evenly. Nudge the pork back into the center of the pot, placing it atop the onions and garlic.

5 Pour the maple-mustard mixture over the pork. Close and lock the lid. Set the valve to Venting. Attach the condensation collector. Press Cancel, then press Slow Cook and use the Slow Cook or Adjust button to select the middle temperature ("Normal"). Use the − or + button to set the time to 8 hours.

6 When the cooking time is finished, press Cancel and remove the lid. Use tongs to remove the pork and set it on a cutting board. Use a chef's knife to carve it into 1-inch slices or large chunks. Transfer them to a serving platter and drizzle the sauce from the inner pot on top. Serve hot.

Maple-Mustard Pork Roast will keep, in an airtight container in the refrigerator, for up to 4 days. To reheat, preheat the oven to 350°F and place the pork in a shallow baking dish with sauce to a depth of about ¼ inch. Cover the baking dish tightly with aluminum foil and bake until hot, about 15 minutes.

2 BARBECUE PORK ROAST DF

TOTAL TIME: 8 hours 15 minutes
ACTIVE TIME: 15 minutes
YIELD: Serves 8

¾ cup ketchup

2 tablespoons brown sugar

1 tablespoon Worcestershire sauce

1 tablespoon apple cider vinegar

1 teaspoon chili powder

1 boneless pork blade roast (about 3 pounds), any butcher's twine removed

1 teaspoon salt

1 teaspoon freshly ground black pepper

2 tablespoons neutral-flavored vegetable oil, such as canola or peanut

4 medium white or yellow onions, chopped

3 cloves garlic, finely chopped

1 Stir together the ketchup, brown sugar, Worcestershire sauce, vinegar, and chili powder in a small bowl until combined. Set aside.

2 Rub the pork all over with the salt and pepper.

3 Press Sauté and select the highest temperature. Place the vegetable oil in the inner pot. Wait until the display reads "Hot," then add the pork. Cook with the lid off, turning the pork occasionally, until the pork is browned on most sides.

4 Move the pork to one side of the inner pot and nestle the onions and garlic in the center, stirring to distribute them evenly. Nudge the pork back into the center of the pot, placing it atop the onions and garlic.

5 Pour the ketchup mixture over the pork. Close and lock the lid. Set the valve to Venting. Attach the condensation collector. Press Cancel, then press Slow Cook and select the middle temperature. Set the time to 8 hours.

6 When the cooking time is finished, press Cancel and remove the lid. Remove the pork to a cutting board and carve it into 1-inch slices or large chunks. Serve hot, drizzled with sauce from the inner pot.

Barbecue Pork Roast will keep, in an airtight container in the refrigerator, for up to 4 days.

3 BEER-BRAISED PORK ROAST DF

TOTAL TIME: 8 hours 25 minutes
ACTIVE TIME: 25 minutes
YIELD: Serves 8

1 boneless pork blade roast (about 3 pounds), any butcher's twine removed

2 teaspoons salt

1 teaspoon freshly ground black pepper

1 teaspoon ground mustard seed

1 teaspoon chili powder

1 teaspoon ground coriander

2 tablespoons neutral-flavored vegetable oil, such as canola or peanut

2 medium white or yellow onions, chopped

3 cloves garlic, finely chopped

1 bottle (12 ounces) beer (domestic lager is the way to go here)

1 Rub the pork all over with the salt, pepper, ground mustard seed, chili powder, and ground coriander.

2 Press Sauté and select the highest temperature. Place the vegetable oil in the inner pot. Wait until the display reads "Hot," then add the pork. Cook with the lid off, turning the pork occasionally, until the pork is browned on most sides.

3 Move the pork to one side of the inner pot and nestle the onions and garlic in the center, stirring to distribute them evenly. Nudge the pork back into the center of the pot, placing it atop the onions and garlic.

4 Pour the beer over the pork. Close and lock the lid. Set the valve to Venting. Attach the condensation collector. Press Cancel, then press Slow Cook and select the middle temperature. Set the time to 8 hours.

5 When the cooking time is finished, press Cancel and remove the lid. Remove the pork to a cutting board and tent it with aluminum foil to keep it warm. Press Sauté and select the middle temperature ("Normal"). Cook the liquid with the lid off until it has reduced by half, about 10 minutes. Drizzle the liquid over the pork, slice, and serve hot.

Beer-Braised Pork Roast will keep, in an airtight container in the refrigerator, for up to 4 days.

PORK SHOULDER RAGÙ

TOTAL TIME: 10 hours   **ACTIVE TIME:** 20 minutes   **YIELD:** Serves 8

Pork shoulder turns fork-tender from low and slow cooking in the Instant Pot. A few minutes of effort at the beginning of your day can mean looking forward to a warm, hearty bowl of pasta and sauce toward the end of it. Rich with the flavor of slow-cooked onions and suffused with the complexity of red wine, this sauce knows few limits. As delicious as it is on pasta, it's terrific over polenta, too (see page 52). Make the polenta the day before and reheat it or reheat this sauce from a previous day's cooking and serve it with freshly made polenta. Like a lot of slow-cooked meats and sauces, it's not only great the next day, it's quite possibly at its best. Note that this sauce serves 8 people, while the polenta recipe serves 4. This means that serving this with polenta gives you leftover sauce. Lucky you.

---

1 medium white or yellow onion, finely chopped

3 cloves garlic, minced

1/2 cup dry red wine, such as Syrah or Zinfandel

1 can (28 ounces) whole, peeled tomatoes, drained

2 bay leaves

4 sprigs fresh thyme

1 teaspoon crushed red pepper flakes

1 teaspoon salt

1/2 teaspoon freshly ground black pepper

3 pounds bone-in pork shoulder, trimmed of most fat

1 box (16 ounces) dried short pasta, such as wagon wheels, orecchiette, or rigatoni, cooked, or 4 cups polenta, for serving

Freshly grated Parmesan cheese, for serving

Finely chopped fresh flat-leaf (Italian) parsley, for garnish

---

1 Place the onion, garlic, wine, tomatoes, bay leaves, thyme, red pepper flakes, salt, and pepper in the inner pot and stir to combine before adding the pork shoulder. Close and lock the lid. Set the valve to Venting. Attach the condensation collector. Press Slow Cook and use the Slow Cook or Adjust button to select the

middle temperature ("Normal"). Use the
– or + button to set the time to 9 hours
30 minutes.

2 When the cooking time is finished,
remove the lid. The pork will be very
tender. Remove it from the inner pot and
transfer it to a cutting board. Discard the
thyme sprigs and bay leaves. Use a potato
masher in the inner pot to break up the
chunks of tomato and help discover any
pieces of bone remaining in the sauce.
Allow the pork to rest until cool enough
to handle, about 10 minutes.

3 While the pork rests, press Cancel and
then press the Sauté or Adjust button to
select the highest temperature ("More").
Allow the sauce to cook with the lid off
until it thickens and loses about one third
of its volume, about 10 minutes, and then
press Cancel.

4 Use one fork to pull off a chunk of the
pork and then use two forks to shred that
piece, holding down the meat with one fork
and pulling at it with the other. Repeat with
the remaining pork, discarding the fat and
bones. Return the meat to the sauce and
stir to distribute the meat.

5 Serve hot, spooned over pasta and
sprinkled with freshly grated Parmesan.
Garnish with fresh parsley.

Pork Shoulder Ragù will keep, in an airtight
container in the refrigerator, for up to
4 days. (A layer of fat will form atop the
sauce. Stir it back into the sauce to enjoy
the richness it adds, or scoop it off and
discard it before reheating.) To reheat,
place the sauce in a pot and warm on the
stovetop over medium-low heat, stirring
occasionally, for about 5 minutes.

TOMATILLO PORK STEW

TOTAL TIME: 8 hours 15 minutes **ACTIVE TIME:** 15 minutes **YIELD:** Serves 8

Tomatillos look like little green tomatoes with paper wrappings, but their flavor is quite different from a tomato's—it's brighter and more piquant. The tomatillo's papery coating hides an unpleasantly sticky skin when fresh, but here we avoid dealing with that by using the canned version.

¼ cup extra-virgin olive oil

2½ pounds bone-in pork shoulder, trimmed of most outside fat, meat cut into 1½-inch cubes (reserve the bone and any meat attached to it)

1 bulb garlic, cloves peeled and chopped

½ teaspoon salt, plus extra as needed

½ teaspoon freshly ground black pepper, plus extra as needed

2 medium white or yellow onions, coarsely chopped

1 can (28 ounces) tomatillos, drained and halved

1 medium jalapeño, stemmed, seeded (or seeds left in for more heat), and chopped

1 cup water

1 cup reduced-salt chicken broth or All-Purpose Chicken Stock (page 88)

Crema Mexicana or Crème Fraîche (page 233), for serving

½ bunch of fresh cilantro leaves, chopped, for garnish

Corn tortillas, for serving

1 Press Sauté and use the Sauté or Adjust button to select the highest temperature ("More"). Place the olive oil in the inner pot. Wait until the display reads "Hot," about 5 minutes, then add the cubed pork (and the bone and meat attached to it), garlic, salt, and pepper to the inner pot. Cook with the lid off, turning the pork with a silicone spatula or wooden spoon, until it is lightly browned on most sides, about 7 minutes.

2 Add the onions to the inner pot (it will be quite full). Cook, undisturbed, with the lid off until the onions are fragrant, about 2 minutes.

3 Add the tomatillos, jalapeño, water, and broth and stir to combine. Close and lock the lid. Set the valve to Venting. Attach the condensation collector. Press Cancel, then press Slow Cook and use the Slow Cook or Adjust button to select the middle temperature ("Normal"). Use the − or + button to set the time to 8 hours.

4 When the cooking time is finished, remove the lid. Remove the bone. Press Cancel, then press Sauté and use the Sauté or Adjust button to select the middle temperature ("Normal"). The liquid will bubble vigorously. Cook with the lid off until the stew thickens, about 30 minutes. Check the seasoning and add more salt and pepper to taste.

5 Serve hot in bowls, garnishing each with a dollop of crema Mexicana and some chopped cilantro, and accompanied by corn tortillas.

Tomatillo Pork Stew will keep, in an airtight container in the refrigerator, for up to 4 days. To reheat, place the stew in a pot and warm on the stovetop over medium heat, stirring occasionally, for about 5 minutes.

KIMCHEE CHICKEN

TOTAL TIME: 8 hours   **ACTIVE TIME:** 5 minutes   **YIELD:** Serves 6

Kimchee can be any number of Korean fermented vegetables, but it is most readily available in its cabbage variety. You can typically find it at a Korean market or a well-stocked Asian market in the refrigerated section. Here it provides a powerful punch of vinegary, salty heat suffused through the chicken in the low, slow cooking time. Rice is the natural accompaniment to this dish.

1½ cups chopped cabbage kimchee, drained

1 cup reduced-salt chicken broth or
   All-Purpose Chicken Stock (page 88)

2 tablespoons packed brown sugar

2 tablespoons toasted sesame oil

1 tablespoon soy sauce

1 tablespoon peeled, grated fresh ginger

2 pounds boneless, skinless chicken thighs

Sesame seeds, for garnish

Cooked white rice (see page 211)
   or Garlic-Ginger White Rice (page 212),
   for serving (optional)

1 Place the kimchee, chicken broth, brown sugar, sesame oil, soy sauce, and ginger in the inner pot and stir to combine. Add the chicken thighs and stir to coat them.

2 Close and lock the lid. Set the valve to Venting. Attach the condensation collector. Press Slow Cook and use the Slow Cook or Adjust button to select the lowest temperature ("Less"). Use the − or + button to set the time to 8 hours.

3 When the cooking time is finished, press Cancel and remove the lid. The chicken will be very tender. Using tongs, carefully transfer the chicken to a serving platter. Spoon some of the cooking liquid and kimchee over the chicken, garnish it with sesame seeds, and serve hot with rice, if you like.

Kimchee Chicken will keep, in an airtight container in the refrigerator, for up to 4 days. To reheat, place the chicken along with a few spoonfuls of the cooking liquid in a frying pan over medium-low heat, flipping the chicken occasionally, for about 5 minutes.

MISO SESAME CHICKEN

TOTAL TIME: 8 hours **ACTIVE TIME:** 5 minutes **YIELD:** Serves 6

Miso, a fermented soybean concoction perhaps best known outside of Japan as a base for soup, is a simple way to add a punch of umami, that flavor often described simply as "savory." This recipe does not use much of it, but don't despair about having leftovers. Kept sealed in the refrigerator, miso will last at least a year and it's fantastic in everything from plain yogurt to soup.

---

1 cup reduced-salt chicken broth or
   All-Purpose Chicken Stock (page 88)

3 tablespoons honey

2 tablespoons toasted sesame oil

1 tablespoon rice vinegar

2 tablespoons yellow miso

¼ teaspoon crushed red pepper flakes

2 pounds boneless, skinless chicken thighs

Sesame seeds, for garnish

---

1 Place the chicken broth, honey, sesame oil, vinegar, miso, and red pepper flakes in the inner pot and stir to combine. Add the chicken thighs and turn them in the sauce to coat them.

2 Close and lock the lid. Set the valve to Venting. Attach the condensation collector. Press Slow Cook and use the Slow Cook or Adjust button to select the lowest temperature ("Less"). Use the − or + button to set the time to 8 hours.

3 When the cooking time is finished, press Cancel and remove the lid. The chicken will be very tender. Using tongs, carefully remove the chicken from the inner pot and place it on a serving platter. Spoon some of the cooking liquid over the chicken, garnish it with sesame seeds, and serve hot.

Miso Sesame Chicken will keep, in an airtight container in the refrigerator, for up to 4 days. To reheat, place the chicken along with a few spoonfuls of the cooking liquid in a frying pan on the stovetop over medium-low heat, flipping the chicken occasionally, for about 5 minutes.

SHREDDED CHICKEN TACOS WITH TOMATO AND LIME

TOTAL TIME: 4 hours 15 minutes **ACTIVE TIME:** 15 minutes **YIELD:** Serves 6

The brightness of the lime shines through in these tacos because it's added to the cooked shredded chicken at the last minute, along with a healthy dose of cooking liquid to keep everything moist and flavorful. A blend of white meat and dark meat keeps partisans of both satisfied, while cooking low and slow in the Instant Pot yields tender chicken that falls apart easily.

2 tablespoons neutral-flavored vegetable oil, such as canola or peanut

1 small white or yellow onion, finely chopped

2 cloves garlic, finely chopped

3 tablespoons chili powder

2 teaspoons ground coriander

2 teaspoons ground cumin

1 can (8 ounces) tomato sauce

2 teaspoons sugar

½ teaspoon salt, plus extra as needed

½ teaspoon freshly ground black pepper, plus extra as needed

1 pound boneless, skinless chicken thighs

1 pound boneless, skinless chicken breasts

1 tablespoon freshly squeezed lime juice

Soft corn tortillas, shredded lettuce, diced tomatoes, crema Mexicana or sour cream, and hot sauce, for serving

1 Press Sauté and use the Sauté or Adjust button to select the middle temperature ("Normal"). Place the vegetable oil in the inner pot, wait about 1 minute for it to warm, then add the onion, garlic, chili powder, coriander, and cumin. Cook with the lid off, stirring occasionally, until the onion softens slightly, about 5 minutes.

2 Add the tomato sauce, sugar, salt, and pepper and stir to combine. Add the chicken thighs and breasts and turn to coat the pieces evenly in the sauce. Close and lock the lid. Set the valve to Venting. Attach the condensation collector. Press Cancel, then press Slow Cook and use the Slow Cook or Adjust button to select the middle temperature ("Normal"). Use the – or + button to set the time to 4 hours.

3 When the cooking time is finished, press Cancel and remove the lid. Remove one piece of chicken from the inner pot and place it in a large bowl. Shred the chicken using two forks: Hold down the meat with one fork and pull at it with the other. Repeat with the remaining pieces until all the chicken is shredded.

4 Transfer 1 cup of the cooking liquid to a small bowl (discard the rest), add the lime juice, and stir to incorporate. Pour this sauce evenly over the shredded chicken and toss to combine. Taste and adjust the seasoning, adding more salt and pepper as needed. Serve the shredded chicken warm, nestled in tortillas and topped with lettuce, tomato, crema Mexicana, and hot sauce.

The shredded chicken will keep, in an airtight container in the refrigerator, for up to 4 days. To reheat, preheat the oven to 350°F and place the chicken in a shallow baking dish with enough of its juices to reach a depth of about 1/4 inch. Cover tightly with aluminum foil and bake until hot, about 15 minutes.

STUFFED BELL PEPPERS WITH SAUSAGE AND CORN

TOTAL TIME: 4 hours 45 minutes   **ACTIVE TIME:** 15 minutes   **YIELD:** Serves 4

So now that you own a rice maker and are a few simple steps away from rice at all times, how about a great way to use up a little extra? This recipe takes cooked rice and turns it into a whole new meal with the help of sausage, corn, and cheese—and the Instant Pot, of course. Any color of bell pepper will work, but for maximum visual impact try a mix of green, red, yellow, and orange.

---

4 medium green, red, yellow, and/or orange bell peppers

1 tablespoon extra-virgin olive oil

1 small white or yellow onion, finely chopped

2 cloves garlic, finely chopped

1 tablespoon tomato paste

1/4 teaspoon crushed red pepper flakes

8 ounces sweet Italian sausage, removed from its casings

3/4 cup frozen corn kernels

3/4 cup shredded mozzarella cheese

3/4 cup cooked long-grain white rice (see page 211)

1/2 teaspoon salt

1/2 teaspoon freshly ground black pepper

3/4 cup water

Small bunch of fresh basil, finely chopped, for garnish

---

1 Using a chef's knife, cut off the upper 1/2 inch of each pepper and set the tops aside. Core and seed the peppers. Remove the stems from the pepper tops and finely chop the remaining flesh.

2 Press Sauté and use the Sauté or Adjust button to select the lowest temperature ("Less"). Place the olive oil in the inner pot, wait about 1 minute for it to warm, then add the onion, garlic, tomato paste, and red pepper flakes. Cook with the lid off, stirring occasionally, until the onion softens, about 5 minutes. Press Cancel.

3 Transfer the onion mixture to a medium mixing bowl and add the chopped pepper, sausage, corn, cheese, rice, salt, and black pepper. Use your hands to combine everything thoroughly.

4 Divide the sausage stuffing among the peppers, packing each one full and creating a mound that rises slightly above the edge of each pepper.

5 Pour the water in the inner pot and then add the stuffed peppers, keeping them upright. (There's no need to clean out any residue from the onion.) Close and lock the lid. Set the valve to Venting. Attach the condensation collector. Press Slow Cook and use the Slow Cook or Adjust button to select the lowest temperature ("Less"). Use the – or + button to set the time to 4 hours 30 minutes.

6 When the cooking time is finished, press Cancel and remove the lid. Use a slotted spoon or tongs to remove the peppers and place them on a serving platter. Garnish with basil and serve hot.

Stuffed Bell Peppers with Sausage and Corn will keep, in an airtight container in the refrigerator, for up to 3 days. To reheat, place the stuffed peppers upright in a pot, add water to a depth of about 1/4 inch, and cover. Warm on the stovetop over medium-low heat for about 10 minutes.

> *Tip:* Leftover sausage stuffing? Refrigerate it in an airtight container for up to 1 day. To cook, sauté it in a skillet and serve with scrambled eggs.

ZITI WITH ITALIAN SAUSAGE

TOTAL TIME: 3 hours 30 minutes   **ACTIVE TIME:** 30 minutes   **YIELD:** Serves 6

This is on the shorter side of slow-cooking times, which means you can plan to make it in the afternoon rather than the morning. Maybe the weather turns lousy and you decide to take on a tiny, delicious cooking project. This dish turns out almost like a casserole with the tomato infused into the soft pasta. It's made for a chilly evening and a glass of red wine (chilly evening optional). Round out the meal with a tossed salad or grilled vegetables.

1 tablespoon extra-virgin olive oil

1 pound sweet Italian sausage, removed from its casings

2 small white or yellow onions, finely chopped

1 green bell pepper, stemmed, seeded, and chopped

1 red bell pepper, stemmed, seeded, and chopped

2 cloves garlic, finely chopped

1 teaspoon dried oregano

1 can (28 ounces) crushed tomatoes

1 can (15 ounces) tomato sauce

1/2 cup heavy (whipping) cream

1/4 teaspoon freshly ground black pepper

8 ounces dried ziti or rigatoni

1 cup shredded mozzarella cheese

1 Press Sauté and use the Sauté or Adjust button to select the middle temperature ("Normal"). Place the olive oil in the inner pot, wait about 2 minutes for the oil to heat, then add the sausage. Cook with the lid off, stirring occasionally to break up any large pieces, until the sausage is browned, about 5 minutes.

2 Add the onions, bell peppers, garlic, and oregano and cook until the vegetables are soft, about 10 minutes.

3 Add the crushed tomatoes, tomato sauce, cream, and black pepper and use a silicone spatula or wooden spoon to scrape up any brown bits on the bottom. Allow the sauce to come to a simmer, about 3 minutes, and then simmer until thickened slightly, about 5 minutes more.

4 Add the ziti. Stir the pasta into the sauce, spreading the sauce evenly over the pasta and mixing with a large spoon to ensure the pasta doesn't clump together. Avoid pushing the pasta to the bottom, where it might burn. Close and lock the lid. Set the valve to Venting. Attach the condensation collector. Press Cancel, then press Slow Cook and use the Slow Cook or Adjust button to select the highest temperature ("More"). Use the − or + button to set the time to 3 hours.

5 When the cooking time is finished, press Cancel and remove the lid. Stir the pasta gently, then divide the pasta, sausage, and sauce among 6 bowls. Top with mozzarella before serving hot.

Ziti with Italian Sausage will keep, in an airtight container in the refrigerator, for up to 4 days. To reheat, place the pasta and sauce in a pot with a splash of water and warm on the stovetop over medium heat, stirring occasionally, for about 5 minutes.

FAUX CASSOULET

TOTAL TIME: 4 hours 45 minutes **ACTIVE TIME:** 15 minutes **YIELD:** Serves 8 **DF**

Cassoulet is a rich French dish often made with duck, but here we use chicken legs as a stand-in. Meanwhile, kielbasa makes a readily available substitute for the garlic sausage traditionally used. Is this dish heavy on the meat? Yes. Tradition dictates that it is. This makes it the perfect dish for a cold evening when you don't have to be anywhere the next morning.

¾ cup dried navy beans, rinsed, drained, and picked over to remove debris

6 cloves garlic, peeled and crushed

1 medium white or yellow onion, chopped

2 medium carrots, peeled and chopped

1 can (28 ounces) diced tomatoes

½ teaspoon dried thyme

2 bay leaves

4 ounces bacon, coarsely chopped

2 large sweet Italian sausages (about 8 ounces total)

8 ounces kielbasa, cut into ¾-inch chunks

1 pound boneless pork stew meat, such as shoulder, cut into 2-inch cubes

2 skin-on chicken drumsticks (about 8 ounces total)

1½ cups water

¼ teaspoon salt, plus extra as needed

½ teaspoon freshly ground black pepper, plus extra as needed

Crusty baguette, for serving

1 Place the beans, garlic, onion, carrots, tomatoes, thyme, bay leaves, bacon, whole Italian sausages, kielbasa, pork, and chicken in the inner pot. Add the water, salt, and pepper and stir to combine.

2 Close and lock the lid. Set the valve to Venting. Attach the condensation collector. Slow Cook and use the Slow Cook or Adjust button to select the highest temperature ("More"). Use the − or + button to set the time to 4 hours 30 minutes.

3 When the cooking time is finished, press Cancel and remove the lid. Discard the bay leaves. The drumstick meat will have fallen off the bones; remove the bones and discard. Remove the Italian sausages, place them on a cutting board, and cut them into bite-size pieces before returning them to the inner pot.

4 Taste and adjust the seasoning, adding salt and pepper as needed. Serve hot with slices of baguette for soaking up juices.

Faux Cassoulet will keep, in an airtight container in the refrigerator, for up to 4 days. To reheat, place the cassoulet in a pot, add a splash of water, and cover. Warm on the stovetop over medium heat, stirring occasionally, for about 5 minutes.

CRAZY-GOOD SLOW-COOKER CHILI

Slow-cooking and chili-making are a match made in heaven. The tightened lid of the Instant Pot means that the aroma of the chili stays mostly inside the appliance, although sometimes you'll catch some of the chili scent wafting out, maybe when you come home from errands or work. It's bound to whet your appetite. Whether it's a vegetarian version with corn and black beans (see below), a turkey version spiked with citrus (see page 158), or a ground beef version with pleasantly deep, bitter notes from the addition of ground cocoa (see page 159), those aromas are a tempting reminder of what's for dinner—and one of the reasons you have the Instant Pot. For more flavoring and serving ideas, see Quick Chili 1, 2, 3, page 65.

1 VEGETARIAN SLOW-COOKER CHILI V VN DF

TOTAL TIME: 8 hours 10 minutes

ACTIVE TIME: 10 minutes

YIELD: Serves 6

1 tablespoon extra-virgin olive oil

2 medium white or yellow onions, finely chopped

1 medium green or red bell pepper, stemmed, seeded, and chopped

2 cloves garlic, finely chopped

1 small jalapeño, stemmed, seeded, and finely chopped

1 chipotle chile in adobo, finely chopped

2 cups dried black beans, rinsed, drained, and picked over to remove debris

3 tablespoons chili powder

¼ teaspoon salt, plus extra as needed

¼ teaspoon freshly ground black pepper, plus extra as needed

1 can (14½ ounces) diced tomatoes with their juices

4 cups store-bought reduced-salt vegetable broth

1 cup frozen corn

Cornbread, for serving (optional)

---

1 Press Sauté and use the Sauté or Adjust button to select the lowest temperature ("Less"). Place the olive oil in the inner pot, wait about 1 minute for it to warm, then add the onions, bell pepper, garlic, jalapeño, and chipotle. Cook with the lid off, stirring occasionally, until the onions soften slightly, about 5 minutes.

2 Add the beans, followed by the chili powder, salt, and pepper. Add the tomatoes (with their juices) and broth and use a silicone spatula or wooden spoon to scrape up any brown bits off the bottom. Stir to combine.

3 Close and lock the lid. Set the valve to Venting. Attach the condensation collector. Press Cancel, then press Slow Cook and use the Slow Cook or Adjust button to select the middle temperature ("Normal"). Use the − or + button to set the time to 8 hours.

4 When the cooking time is finished, press Cancel and remove the lid. Add the corn, stir to distribute evenly, and then close and lock the lid to allow the residual heat to warm the corn, about 5 minutes.

5 Taste and adjust the seasoning, adding more salt and pepper as needed. Serve hot with cornbread, if you like.

Vegetarian Slow-Cooker Chili will keep, in an airtight container in the refrigerator, for up to 5 days. To reheat, place the chili in a pot and warm on the stovetop over medium heat, stirring occasionally, for about 5 minutes.

② TURKEY AND LIME SLOW-COOKER CHILI

TOTAL TIME: 5 hours 10 minutes

ACTIVE TIME: 10 minutes

YIELD: Serves 6

---

1 tablespoon extra-virgin olive oil

2 medium white or yellow onions, finely chopped

1 medium green or red bell pepper, stemmed, seeded, and chopped

2 cloves garlic, finely chopped

1 small jalapeño, stemmed, seeded, and finely chopped

1 chipotle chile in adobo, finely chopped

1 pound ground turkey

3 tablespoons chili powder

¼ teaspoon salt, plus extra as needed

¼ teaspoon freshly ground black pepper, plus extra as needed

1 can (14½ ounces) diced tomatoes, drained

1 cup store-bought reduced-salt chicken broth or All-Purpose Chicken Stock (page 88)

Finely grated zest and freshly squeezed juice of 2 medium limes

1 can (15 ounces) pinto beans, drained and rinsed

Crema Mexicana or sour cream and tortilla chips, for serving

Lime wedges, for garnish

---

1 Press Sauté and select the lowest temperature. Place the olive oil in the inner pot, wait about 1 minute for it to warm, then add the onions, bell pepper, garlic, jalapeño, and chipotle. Cook with the lid off, stirring occasionally, until the onions soften slightly, about 5 minutes. Add the turkey and sauté until no longer pink, about 5 minutes.

2 Add the chili powder, salt, pepper, tomatoes, broth, and lime zest and juice and stir to combine, scraping up any brown bits off the bottom.

3 Close and lock the lid. Set the valve to Venting. Attach the condensation collector. Press Cancel, then press Slow Cook and select the lowest temperature. Set the time to 5 hours.

4 When the cooking time is finished, press Cancel and remove the lid. Add the beans, stir to distribute evenly, and then close and lock the lid to allow the residual heat to warm the beans, about 5 minutes.

5 Taste and adjust the seasoning, adding more salt and pepper as needed. Serve hot with crema Mexicana and tortilla chips, garnished with lime wedges.

Turkey and Lime Slow-Cooker Chili will keep, in an airtight container in the refrigerator, for up to 4 days.

③ GROUND BEEF AND COCOA SLOW-COOKER CHILI DF

TOTAL TIME: 5 hours 10 minutes

ACTIVE TIME: 10 minutes

YIELD: Serves 6

---

1 tablespoon extra-virgin olive oil

2 medium white or yellow onions, finely chopped

1 medium green or red bell pepper, stemmed, seeded, and chopped

2 cloves garlic, finely chopped

1 small jalapeño, stemmed, seeded, and finely chopped

1 pound ground beef

3 tablespoons chili powder

2 tablespoons unsweetened cocoa powder

1/4 teaspoon salt, plus extra as needed

1/4 teaspoon freshly ground black pepper, plus extra as needed

1 can (14 1/2 ounces) diced tomatoes, drained

1 cup store-bought reduced-salt beef broth or All-Purpose Beef Stock (page 90)

Finely grated zest and freshly squeezed juice of 2 medium limes

1 can (15 ounces) black beans, drained and rinsed

Crushed roasted peanuts, for garnish

---

1 Press Sauté and select the lowest temperature. Place the olive oil in the inner pot, wait about 1 minute for it to warm, then add the onions, bell pepper, garlic, and jalapeño. Cook with the lid off, stirring occasionally, until the onions soften slightly, about 5 minutes. Add the beef and sauté until no longer pink, about 5 minutes.

2 Add the chili powder, cocoa powder, salt, pepper, tomatoes, broth, and lime zest and juice and stir to combine, scraping up any brown bits off the bottom.

3 Close and lock the lid. Set the valve to Venting. Attach the condensation collector. Press Cancel, then press Slow Cook and select the lowest temperature. Set the time to 5 hours.

4 When the cooking time is finished, press Cancel and remove the lid. Add the beans, stir to distribute evenly, and then close and lock the lid to allow the residual heat to warm the beans, about 5 minutes.

5 Taste and adjust the seasoning, adding more salt and pepper as needed. Serve hot, garnished with crushed peanuts.

Ground Beef and Cocoa Slow-Cooker Chili will keep, in an airtight container in the refrigerator, for up to 4 days.

SPICY TOMATO PASTA SAUCE

TOTAL TIME: 9 hours 15 minutes   **ACTIVE TIME:** 15 minutes   **YIELD:** Serves 8

Fish sauce? Soy sauce? What are these things doing in a tomato pasta sauce? The answer: They provide a base of savory saltiness that lends a depth of flavor without contributing any identifiable fish or soy taste. The rest of the flavor comes from low, slow cooking in the Instant Pot. Don't be afraid to take this sauce in a milder direction: Leaving out the red pepper flakes produces a sauce with none of the heat and all of the flavor. Stash leftovers in a zip-top bag in the freezer, where they'll be ready to use just about any time tomato sauce is called for.

2 tablespoons extra-virgin olive oil

2 small white or yellow onions, finely chopped

3 cloves garlic, finely chopped

2 tablespoons tomato paste

2 teaspoons dried oregano

2 teaspoons dried basil

1/2 teaspoon fish sauce (see Notes) or anchovy paste

1/2 teaspoon crushed red pepper flakes

3/4 cup dry red wine, such as Syrah or Zinfandel

1 can (28 ounces) no-salt-added crushed tomatoes

1 can (28 ounces) diced tomatoes, drained

2 cans (15 ounces each) tomato sauce (see Notes)

1 tablespoon soy sauce

2 teaspoons sugar

Salt and freshly ground black pepper

1 box (16 ounces) small dried pasta, such as wagon wheels, orecchiette, or rigatoni, cooked, for serving

Freshly grated Parmesan cheese, for serving

1 Press Sauté and use the Sauté or Adjust button to select the middle temperature ("Normal"). Place the olive oil in the inner pot, wait about 1 minute for it to heat, then add the onions, garlic, tomato paste, oregano, basil, fish sauce, and red pepper flakes. Cook with the lid off, stirring occasionally, until the onions soften and start to brown, about 10 minutes.

2 Add the wine and use a silicone spatula or wooden spoon to scrape up any brown bits off the bottom. Continue cooking until most of the liquid has cooked off, about 5 minutes.

3 Add the crushed tomatoes, diced tomatoes, tomato sauce, soy sauce, and sugar and stir to combine. Close and lock the lid. Set the valve to Venting. Attach the condensation collector. Press Cancel, then press Slow Cook and use the Slow Cook or Adjust button to select the lowest temperature ("Less"). Use the – or + button to set the time to 9 hours.

4 When the cooking time is finished, press Cancel and remove the lid. Taste and adjust the seasoning, adding salt and pepper as needed. Serve hot atop the cooked pasta with freshly grated Parmesan.

Spicy Tomato Pasta Sauce will keep, in an airtight container in the refrigerator, for up to 5 days. To reheat, place the sauce in a pot and warm on the stovetop over medium-low heat, stirring occasionally, for about 5 minutes.

Notes: Fish sauce can be found in the Asian aisle of the supermarket. It is sometimes marketed as Thai fish sauce or *nam pla*.

Canned tomato sauce works best here, since it is typically minimally spiced and made without the sweeteners found in jarred tomato sauce.

KOREAN-STYLE SOFT TOFU STEW

TOTAL TIME: 2 hours   **ACTIVE TIME:** 15 minutes   **YIELD:** Serves 4

While I typically prefer the chewiness of firm tofu, very soft tofu has a place in a dish like this, where its pillowy texture adds to the comfort factor. The spiciness of the kimchee and elemental familiarity of the egg contribute their own dose of comfort, helping create a dish that clears your sinuses and warms your stomach. Slow-cooking it gives the salty, spicy flavors a chance to meld, but because everything except the bacon and the eggs are ready to eat from the start, it's a quick slow-cooker recipe.

---

3 slices bacon, cut crosswise into thin strips

½ cup chopped cabbage kimchee

1 teaspoon toasted sesame oil

1 scallion, trimmed and thinly sliced, plus extra for garnish

1 clove garlic, minced

Pinch of freshly ground black pepper

3 cups reduced-salt chicken broth or All-Purpose Chicken Stock (page 88)

1 package (11 ounces) extra-soft Korean tofu (see Note)

4 large eggs

---

1 Place the bacon in the inner pot. Press Sauté and use the Sauté or Adjust button to select the middle temperature ("Normal"). Cook with the lid off and use a silicone spatula to move the bacon around occasionally so that it cooks evenly. Cook until the bacon is pale pink and the fat is no longer bright white, about 5 minutes.

2 Add the kimchee, sesame oil, scallion, garlic, and pepper. Cook with the lid off, stirring occasionally, until the scallion softens, about 2 minutes.

3 Add the broth and stir to combine. Close and lock the lid. Set the valve to Venting. Attach the condensation collector.

Press Cancel, then press Slow Cook and use the Slow Cook or Adjust button to select the lowest temperature ("Less"). Use the − or + button to set the time to 1 hour.

4 When the cooking time is finished, remove the lid. Add the tofu and gently use a spoon to break up any large lumps. Close and lock the lid. Press Cancel, then press Slow Cook and use the Slow Cook or Adjust button to select the lowest temperature ("Less"). Use the − or + button to set the time to 30 minutes.

5 When the cooking time is finished, remove the lid. Press Cancel, then press Sauté and use the Sauté or Adjust button to select the middle temperature ("Normal"). Cook with the lid off until the stew bubbles vigorously, about 5 minutes.

6 Press Cancel, then press Sauté and use the Sauté or Adjust button to select the lowest temperature ("Less"). Carefully crack the eggs into the inner pot, trying to avoid breaking the yolks up. Cook with the lid off

until the whites are set and the yolks are soft but thick, about 4 minutes.

7 Press Cancel and serve hot, garnished with scallion.

Korean-Style Soft Tofu Stew will keep, in an airtight container in the refrigerator, for up to 3 days. To reheat, place the stew in a pot and warm on the stovetop over medium heat, stirring occasionally, for about 5 minutes.

Note: Extra-soft Korean tofu is typically labeled "soon tofu" and is often sold in tubes at Asian markets. If that is unavailable, look for "silken tofu" or use the softest tofu available.

Tip: Frozen bacon is easier to slice. Place the bacon on a cutting board and place the cutting board in the freezer for 15 minutes until it firms up.

CREAMY CHIPOTLE TOMATO SOUP

TOTAL TIME: 8 hours 15 minutes   **ACTIVE TIME:** 15 minutes   **YIELD:** Serves 6

Chipotles are smoked jalapeños and so they contribute not only heat but also smoky notes to this soup. When it comes to spiciness in food, one person's three-alarm fire can be another person's "What, *this* is hot?" Taking that into consideration, I would place this soup in the "spicy but not ridiculously spicy" category, and note that you can reduce or increase the amount of chipotle to adjust the heat.

---

1 tablespoon neutral-flavored vegetable oil, such as canola or peanut

1 small white or yellow onion, finely chopped

1 tablespoon tomato paste

1 chipotle chile in adobo, finely chopped

2 cans (28 ounces each) diced tomatoes with their juices

2 cups reduced-salt chicken broth or All-Purpose Chicken Stock (page 88)

¼ teaspoon salt, plus extra as needed

½ teaspoon freshly ground black pepper, plus extra as needed

½ teaspoon Worcestershire sauce

1 cup heavy (whipping) cream

Tortilla chips, for garnish

---

1 Press Sauté and use the Sauté or Adjust button to select the middle temperature ("Normal"). Place the vegetable oil in the inner pot, wait about 1 minute for it to warm, then add the onion, tomato paste, and chipotle. Cook with the lid off, stirring occasionally, until the onion softens slightly, about 5 minutes.

2 Add the tomatoes and their juices, broth, salt, pepper, and Worcestershire sauce and stir to combine. Close and lock the lid. Set the valve to Venting. Attach the condensation collector. Press Cancel, then press Slow Cook and use the Slow Cook or Adjust button to select the lowest temperature ("Less"). Use the − or + button to set the time to 8 hours.

3 When the cooking time is finished, press Cancel and remove the lid. Use an immersion blender to puree the soup, or carefully transfer the soup to a blender and puree it. (Take care when pureeing the hot soup and do not overfill your blender; you may need to puree the soup in batches.) Return the pureed soup to the inner pot.

4 Add the cream to the pureed soup and stir to incorporate it. Taste and adjust the seasoning, adding more salt and pepper as needed. Serve hot, garnished with crumbled tortilla chips.

Creamy Chipotle Tomato Soup will keep, in an airtight container in the refrigerator, for up to 5 days. To reheat, place the soup in a pot and warm on the stovetop over medium heat, stirring occasionally, for about 5 minutes.

CORN *OFF* THE COB SOUP

TOTAL TIME: 4 hours 20 minutes   **ACTIVE TIME:** 20 minutes   **YIELD:** Serves 6

Good, fresh corn is only available for about one month a year where I live, so when it's in season we eat it just about every day. With something this precious, I don't want any to go to waste, which is why cooking this soup with the corn cobs is key; it ensures that no corn flavor is lost. Pro tip: Remember to take the cobs out before serving. A bay leaf you might be able to shrug off; a corn cob is harder.

---

5 ears sweet corn, husks and silk removed (see Note)

2 tablespoons unsalted butter

1 shallot, finely chopped

1 clove garlic, finely chopped

1 teaspoon chili powder, plus more for garnish

¼ teaspoon ground cumin

½ teaspoon salt, plus extra as needed

½ teaspoon freshly ground black pepper, plus extra as needed

4 cups reduced-salt chicken broth or All-Purpose Chicken Stock (page 88)

1 teaspoon sugar

1 cup half-and-half

Chopped fresh chives, for garnish

---

1 Cut the kernels from the corn: Place one ear of corn in a large bowl, stand it on the wide end, and use a sharp knife to scrape off the kernels, allowing the kernels to fall in the bowl and rotating the cob until no kernels remain. Repeat with each cob.

2 Cut the stripped cobs in half crosswise and set them aside.

3 Press Sauté and use the Sauté or Adjust button to select the middle temperature ("Normal"). Place the butter in the inner pot, wait about 1 minute for the butter to melt, then add the shallot, garlic, chili powder, cumin, salt, and pepper. Cook with the lid off, stirring occasionally, until the shallot softens slightly, about 3 minutes.

4 Add the broth and sugar and stir to combine, then add the corn cobs and kernels. Close and lock the lid. Set the valve to Venting. Attach the condensation collector. Press Cancel, then press Slow Cook and use the Slow Cook or Adjust button to select the lowest temperature ("Less"). Use the − or + button to set the time to 4 hours.

5 When the cooking time is finished, press Cancel and remove the lid. Use a slotted spoon to remove the cobs from the inner pot, allowing any liquid clinging to them to drip back into the soup. Add the half-and-half and stir thoroughly to combine. Taste and adjust seasoning, adding more salt and pepper as needed.

6 Serve hot, garnished with chopped chives and a dusting of chili powder or freshly ground black pepper.

Corn *Off* the Cob Soup will keep, in an airtight container in the refrigerator, for up to 5 days. To reheat, place the soup in a pot and warm on the stovetop over medium heat, stirring occasionally, for about 5 minutes.

Note: Let your microwave help you shuck corn: Cut about 2 inches off each cob from the stalk end (that's where nature provides the cob's "handle"), leaving the husk intact. Place the corn on a plate and microwave on high for 2 minutes. Remove the plate from the microwave and use a kitchen towel to grasp a cob by the uncut end. (Be careful! The corn is hot.) Shake the corn until the shucked corn falls out from the husk, leaving that bothersome silk behind.

CHICKEN SOUP

1·2·3

Chicken soup is practically the definition of comfort food. When you want to do better than what comes out of a can, your Instant Pot is there for you. In fact, it's there for you at least three ways in chicken soup alone. Make a traditional chicken noodle soup (see below), incorporate southwestern flavors with chipotle and tortillas (see page 172), or try a Thai-inspired version with lemongrass and rice noodles (see page 175).

① CLASSIC CHICKEN NOODLE SOUP DF

TOTAL TIME: 8 hours 30 minutes

ACTIVE TIME: 30 minutes

YIELD: Serves 8

---

1 tablespoon neutral-flavored vegetable oil, such as canola or peanut

1 medium white or yellow onion, chopped

2 cloves garlic, finely chopped

2 large stalks celery, leaves discarded, chopped

2 medium carrots, peeled and coarsely chopped

1½ pounds boneless, skinless chicken breasts

2 bay leaves

½ teaspoon salt, plus extra as needed

½ teaspoon freshly ground black pepper, plus extra as needed

½ teaspoon dried thyme

8 cups reduced-salt chicken broth or All-Purpose Chicken Stock (page 88)

2½ cups dried wide egg noodles

Chopped fresh Italian (flat-leaf) parsley, for garnish

---

1 Press Sauté and use the Sauté or Adjust button to select the lowest temperature ("Less"). Place the vegetable oil in the inner pot, wait about 1 minute for it to warm, then add the onion, garlic, celery, and carrots. Cook with the lid off, stirring occasionally, until the onion softens slightly, about 5 minutes.

2 Add the chicken breasts, followed by the bay leaves, salt, pepper, thyme, and broth. Stir to combine.

3 Close and lock the lid. Set the valve to Venting. Attach the condensation collector.

Press Cancel, then press Slow Cook and use the Slow Cook or Adjust button to select the lowest temperature ("Less"). Use the − or + button to set the time to 8 hours.

4 When the cooking time is finished, press Cancel and remove the lid. Remove the chicken breasts from the inner pot and place them on a cutting board. Discard the bay leaves.

5 Press Sauté and use the Sauté or Adjust button to select the middle temperature ("Normal"). Cook with the lid off until bubbling, about 5 minutes. Add the noodles and allow them to cook, uncovered, until al dente, about 5 minutes.

6 While the noodles cook, slice the chicken breasts into bite-size pieces.

7 When the noodles have finished cooking, press Cancel and return the chicken to the soup, stirring to distribute. Taste and adjust the seasoning, adding more salt and pepper as needed. Serve hot, garnished with parsley.

Classic Chicken Noodle Soup will keep, in an airtight container in the refrigerator, for up to 4 days. To reheat, place the soup in a pot and warm on the stovetop over medium heat, stirring occasionally, for about 5 minutes.

② CHIPOTLE-TORTILLA CHICKEN SOUP

TOTAL TIME: 8 hours 45 minutes
ACTIVE TIME: 45 minutes
YIELD: Serves 8

---

1 tablespoon neutral-flavored vegetable oil, such as canola or peanut

1 medium white or yellow onion, chopped

2 cloves garlic, finely chopped

2 large stalks celery, leaves discarded, chopped

2 medium carrots, peeled and coarsely chopped

1 chipotle chile in adobo, finely chopped

1½ pounds boneless, skinless chicken breasts

2 bay leaves

½ teaspoon salt, plus extra as needed

½ teaspoon freshly ground black pepper, plus extra as needed

1 can (14½ ounces) diced tomatoes, drained

1 tablespoon tomato paste

8 cups reduced-salt chicken broth or All-Purpose Chicken Stock (page 88)

5 small (6-inch) corn tortillas, cut into 1-inch pieces

Crushed tortilla chips, crema Mexicana or sour cream, sliced avocado, and shredded Monterey Jack cheese, for serving

Chopped fresh cilantro, for garnish

Clockwise from top: Lemongrass and Rice Noodle Chicken Soup, Chipotle-Tortilla Chicken Soup, Classic Chicken Noodle Soup

1 Press Sauté and select the lowest temperature. Place the vegetable oil in the inner pot, wait about 1 minute for it to warm, then add the onion, garlic, celery, carrots, and chipotle. Cook with the lid off, stirring occasionally, until the onion softens slightly, about 5 minutes.

2 Add the chicken breasts, followed by the bay leaves, salt, pepper, tomatoes, tomato paste, and broth. Stir to combine.

3 Close and lock the lid. Set the valve to Venting. Attach the condensation collector. Press Cancel, then press Slow Cook and select the lowest temperature. Set the time to 8 hours.

4 When the cooking time is finished, press Cancel and remove the lid. Remove the chicken breasts from the inner pot and place them on a cutting board. Discard the bay leaves.

5 Press Sauté and select the highest temperature. Add the tortillas to the soup and cook with the lid off until the soup comes to a boil, then change to the lowest temperature and cook, uncovered, until the tortillas have started to disintegrate, about 30 minutes.

6 Meanwhile, slice the chicken breasts into bite-size pieces.

7 Return the chicken to the soup and allow it to heat through. Taste and adjust the seasoning, adding more salt and pepper as needed. Serve with crushed tortilla chips, crema Mexicana, avocado, and cheese. Garnish with cilantro.

Chipotle-Tortilla Chicken Soup will keep, in an airtight container in the refrigerator, for up to 4 days.

③ LEMONGRASS AND RICE NOODLE CHICKEN SOUP DF

TOTAL TIME: 8 hours 30 minutes

ACTIVE TIME: 30 minutes

YIELD: Serves 8

---

1 tablespoon neutral-flavored vegetable oil, such as canola or peanut

1 medium white or yellow onion, chopped

2 cloves garlic, finely chopped

2 large stalks celery, leaves discarded, chopped

2 medium carrots, peeled and coarsely chopped

1/4 cup Thai red curry paste

1 1/2 pounds boneless, skinless chicken breasts

1/2 teaspoon salt, plus extra as needed

1/2 teaspoon freshly ground black pepper, plus extra as needed

2 small stalks (about 8 inches each) lemongrass, slightly smashed with the back of a knife

8 cups reduced-salt chicken broth or All-Purpose Chicken Stock (page 88)

8 ounces flat rice noodles (not vermicelli-style noodles)

Lime wedges and chopped fresh cilantro, for garnish

---

1 Press Sauté and select the lowest temperature. Place the vegetable oil in the inner pot, wait about 1 minute for it to warm, then add the onion, garlic, celery, carrots, and curry paste. Cook with the lid off, stirring occasionally, until the onion softens slightly, about 5 minutes.

2 Add the chicken breasts, followed by the salt, pepper, lemongrass, and broth. Stir to combine.

3 Close and lock the lid. Set the valve to Venting. Attach the condensation collector. Press Cancel, then press Slow Cook and select the lowest temperature. Set the time to 8 hours.

4 Ten minutes before the end of the cooking time, remove the chicken breasts, discard the lemongrass, and chop the chicken into bite-size pieces (keep the pot set to Slow Cook).

5 Return the chicken to the soup and add the noodles. Cover and cook, stirring occasionally and testing a noodle for doneness, until the noodles are tender and the chicken is heated through, about 10 minutes.

6 Serve hot, garnished with lime wedges and cilantro.

Lemongrass and Rice Noodle Chicken Soup will keep, in an airtight container in the refrigerator, for up to 4 days.

MORE FLAVORING AND SERVING IDEAS FOR CHICKEN SOUP

- Replace the noodles with leftover cooked white rice, Cilantro-Lime White Rice, Coconut White Rice, or Garlic-Ginger White Rice (page 212).

- Add a handful of chopped fresh dill, large stems removed, to Classic Chicken Noodle Soup when you add the noodles.

- Sprinkle a handful of croutons into the bowl before serving Classic Chicken Noodle Soup.

- A dash of curry powder adds a twist to Classic Chicken Noodle Soup.

- Add large slices of peeled ginger to Classic Chicken Noodle Soup or Lemongrass and Rice Noodle Chicken Soup. Remove before serving.

- Stir in frozen peas with the noodles in Classic Chicken Noodle Soup or Lemongrass and Rice Noodle Chicken Soup.

- Stir in coconut milk at the end of cooking Classic Chicken Noodle Soup or Lemongrass and Rice Noodle Chicken Soup.

- Add a few drops of your favorite hot sauce.

- You know what goes well in chicken soup? Just about every leftover cooked vegetable on Earth. Think spinach, carrots, cabbage, potatoes, sweet potatoes, or mushrooms.

- Cooked beans make a hearty addition.

- One word: bacon. (Okay, four more words: Crumble it on top.)

TOMATO AND WHITE BEAN SOUP

TOTAL TIME: 4 hours 15 minutes   **ACTIVE TIME:** 15 minutes   **YIELD:** Serves 6

This simple dish has no meat and can be made vegetarian by substituting vegetable broth for the chicken broth and replacing the Parmesan with a cheese made without animal rennet. The short list of shelf-stable ingredients means it's a good recipe to have in your back pocket when dinner inspiration just isn't happening. The Instant Pot is there for you. And so is this soup.

2 tablespoons unsalted butter

3 cans (14½ ounces each) diced tomatoes, drained with juice reserved

1 medium white or yellow onion, finely chopped

1 tablespoon brown sugar

1 tablespoon tomato paste

¼ teaspoon salt, plus more as needed

¼ teaspoon freshly ground black pepper, plus more as needed

2 tablespoons all-purpose flour

3 cups reduced-salt chicken broth or All-Purpose Chicken Stock (page 88)

2 bay leaves

1 can (15 ounces) white beans, such as cannellini, drained and rinsed

Freshly grated Parmesan cheese, for garnish

Chopped fresh basil, for garnish

1 Press Sauté and use the Sauté or Adjust button to select the middle temperature ("Normal"). Place the butter in the inner pot, wait about 1 minute for the butter to melt, then add the tomatoes, onion, brown sugar, tomato paste, salt, and pepper. Cook with the lid off, stirring occasionally, until the tomatoes are lightly browned and most of the liquid has evaporated, about 10 minutes.

2 Add the flour to the inner pot and cook for 1 minute before slowly whisking in 1 cup of the broth, dragging the whisk along the bottom of the inner pot to scrape up any brown bits.

3 Stir in the remaining 2 cups of broth, the reserved juice from the tomatoes, and the bay leaves. Close and lock the lid. Set the valve to Venting. Attach the condensation collector. Press Cancel, then press Slow Cook and use the Slow Cook or Adjust button to select the lowest temperature ("Less"). Use the − or + button to set the time to 4 hours.

4 Five minutes before the cooking time is finished, remove the lid. Discard the bay leaves. Add the beans and continue cooking with the lid off until the beans are warm, about 5 minutes.

5 When the cooking time is finished, press Cancel. Taste and adjust the seasoning, adding more salt and pepper as needed. Serve hot, garnished with Parmesan, basil, and pepper.

Tomato and White Bean Soup will keep, in an airtight container in the refrigerator, for up to 5 days. To reheat, place the soup in a pot and warm on the stovetop over medium heat, stirring occasionally, for about 5 minutes.

FRENCH ONION SOUP

TOTAL TIME: 10 hours 15 minutes   **ACTIVE TIME:** 15 minutes   **YIELD:** Serves 6

This classic soup gets a chance to develop deep flavor with a long, slow cook in the Instant Pot. While soy sauce is not a traditional French ingredient, it contributes not only salinity but depth of flavor here, just as the little bit of brown sugar does. If you're trying to impress someone—or just feeling generous—it might pay to stray just briefly from your Instant Pot and run this under the broiler for an unbeatable cheesy finish. Simply put each serving of soup in an oven-safe bowl, place the bowls on a rimmed baking sheet, top each with a slice of baguette and a handful of cheese, and broil in the oven until the cheese is melted and bubbly, about 5 minutes. (Because broiler intensities vary, check after about 2 minutes and frequently thereafter to avoid burnt cheese—and tears.)

---

4 medium white or yellow onions, thinly sliced

¼ cup (½ stick) unsalted butter

½ teaspoon salt, plus extra as needed

½ teaspoon freshly ground black pepper, plus extra as needed

1 tablespoon soy sauce

1 tablespoon brown sugar

½ teaspoon dried thyme

6 cups reduced-salt beef broth or All-Purpose Beef Stock (page 90)

Gruyère cheese, shredded, for garnish

Crusty baguette, for serving

---

1 Place the onions, butter, salt, pepper, soy sauce, brown sugar, and thyme in the inner pot. Close and lock the lid. Set the valve to Venting. Attach the condensation collector and place a towel under the appliance to catch any overflow. (Onions contain a lot of water; some of that water may escape the appliance.) Press Slow Cook and use the Slow Cook or Adjust button to select the highest temperature ("More"). Use the – or + button to set the time to 10 hours.

2 When the cooking time is finished, remove the lid. Add the beef broth and use a silicone spatula or wooden spoon to scrape up any brown bits off the bottom and stir them into the broth.

3 Press Cancel, then press Sauté and use the Sauté or Adjust button to select the middle temperature ("Normal"). Cook with the lid off, stirring occasionally, until the soup is heated through, about 5 minutes. Press Cancel.

4 Ladle into individual bowls. Serve hot with a generous handful of cheese atop each bowl and slices of baguette on the side.

French Onion Soup will keep, in an airtight container in the refrigerator, for up to 5 days. To reheat, place the soup in a pot and warm on the stovetop over medium heat, stirring occasionally, for about 5 minutes.

BARLEY-MUSHROOM STEW

TOTAL TIME: 3 hours 15 minutes   **ACTIVE TIME:** 15 minutes   **YIELD:** Serves 8

Using both fresh and dried mushrooms in this soup creates layers of mushroom flavor and yields a tasty vegetarian stew. The barley cooks and softens relatively quickly and the flavors get a chance to meld nicely, even in what might qualify as a "quick" slow-cooker recipe. A little dairy at the end in the form of crème fraîche or shredded Gruyère adds a rich finish to this earthy, satisfying dish. (If you're preparing this for strict vegetarians, look for a mild cheese made without animal rennet that melts well.)

---

1 tablespoon extra-virgin olive oil

2 cloves garlic, finely chopped

1 medium white or yellow onion, chopped

2 large stalks celery, leaves discarded, coarsely chopped

3 large carrots, peeled and coarsely chopped

¾ cup pearl barley

1 pound white mushrooms, trimmed and quartered

¼ ounce dried chanterelle mushrooms, soaked, drained, rinsed, and finely chopped (see Note)

2 bay leaves

1 teaspoon dried thyme

1 teaspoon salt, plus extra as needed

½ teaspoon freshly ground black pepper, plus extra as needed

4 cups store-bought reduced-salt vegetable broth

2 cups water

Crème Fraîche (page 233) or shredded Gruyère cheese, for garnish

---

1 Press Sauté and use the Sauté or Adjust button to select the lowest temperature ("Less"). Place the olive oil in the inner pot, wait about 1 minute for it to warm, then add the garlic, onion, celery, and carrots. Cook with the lid off, stirring occasionally, until the onion softens slightly, about 5 minutes.

2 Add the barley, followed by the white mushrooms, chanterelle mushrooms, bay leaves, thyme, salt, and pepper. Stir to combine and then add the broth and water.

3 Close and lock the lid. Set the valve to Venting. Attach the condensation collector. Press Cancel, then press Slow Cook and use the Slow Cook or Adjust button to select the middle temperature ("Normal"). Use the − or + button to set the time to 3 hours.

4 When the cooking time is finished, press Cancel and remove the lid. Discard the bay leaves. Taste and adjust the seasoning, adding more salt and pepper as needed. Spoon into serving bowls and garnish with a dollop of crème fraîche or a sprinkling of Gruyère and serve hot.

Barley-Mushroom Stew will keep, in an airtight container in the refrigerator, for up to 5 days. To reheat, place the soup in a pot and warm on the stovetop over medium heat, stirring occasionally, for about 5 minutes.

Note: Dried mushrooms can be gritty, but soaking and rinsing them takes care of this: Place the dried chanterelles in a bowl, add 1 cup of water, and soak for 20 minutes (weigh them down with a plate if necessary to prevent them from floating). Remove the mushrooms, place them in a colander, and rinse them under running water, using your fingers to toss them occasionally to make sure they are thoroughly rinsed before using.

SPLIT PEA SOUP

TOTAL TIME: 8 hours 30 minutes   **ACTIVE TIME:** 15 minutes   **YIELD:** Serves 8 DF

Pea soup will always make me think of childhood road trips that inevitably involved a stop at a restaurant dedicated to pea soup. Why pea soup? I have no idea. It does seem like an odd thing to build a restaurant around. But when you're a kid, you don't question these things. In any case, as an adult I've come to realize: Pea soup is better without the long car ride. And even better with the Instant Pot.

---

1 tablespoon extra-virgin olive oil

2 medium white or yellow onions, coarsely chopped

2 large stalks celery, leaves discarded, coarsely chopped

2 medium carrots, peeled and coarsely chopped

2 cloves garlic, finely chopped

2 cups split green peas, rinsed, drained, and picked over to remove debris

2 bay leaves

1/4 teaspoon salt, plus extra as needed

1/2 teaspoon freshly ground black pepper, plus extra as needed

1 smoked ham hock (about 2 pounds)

6 cups water

---

1 Press Sauté and use the Sauté or Adjust button to select the lowest temperature ("Less"). Place the olive oil in the inner pot, wait about 1 minute for it to warm, then add the onions, celery, carrots, and garlic. Cook with the lid off, stirring occasionally, until the onions soften slightly, about 5 minutes.

2 Add the split peas, followed by the bay leaves, salt, and pepper. Stir to combine, then add the ham hock and water.

3 Close and lock the lid. Set the valve to Venting. Attach the condensation collector. Press Cancel, then press Slow Cook and use the Slow Cook or Adjust button to select the middle temperature ("Normal"). Use the – or + button to set the time to 8 hours.

4 When the cooking time is finished, press Cancel and remove the lid. Remove the ham hock and place it on a cutting board. Discard the bay leaves. Replace the lid to keep the soup warm. When the ham is cool enough to handle, after about 10 minutes, use one fork to pull off a chunk and then use two forks to shred that piece, holding down the ham with one fork and pulling at it with the other. Repeat with the remaining ham, discarding the skin, fat, and bone.

5 Use a large spoon to skim any accumulated fat from the surface of the soup, then return the ham to the soup and stir to distribute it. Taste and adjust the seasoning, adding more salt and pepper as needed. Serve hot.

Split Pea Soup will keep, in an airtight container in the refrigerator, for up to 5 days. To reheat, place the soup in a pot and warm on the stovetop over medium heat, stirring occasionally, for about 5 minutes.

GARLICKY WHITE BEAN SOUP WITH CRISPY PANCETTA

TOTAL TIME: 7 hours 20 minutes **ACTIVE TIME:** 20 minutes **YIELD:** Serves 6

Sautéing the pancetta in the Instant Pot before making this soup accomplishes two things: It allows the rendered fat to flavor the soup *and* it provides a crispy, salty counterpart to the beans when serving. While sautéing and slow-cooking conventionally might require two pans or pots, with the Instant Pot there's no need for more than one.

2 tablespoons extra-virgin olive oil, plus extra for serving

6 ounces pancetta, finely chopped (see Note)

3 small white or yellow onions, finely chopped

4 cloves garlic, finely chopped

1/4 teaspoon salt, plus extra as needed

1/4 teaspoon freshly ground black pepper, plus extra as needed

1/4 teaspoon crushed red pepper flakes

4 cups reduced-salt chicken broth or All-Purpose Chicken Stock (page 88)

4 cups water

2 cups dried navy beans, rinsed, drained, and picked over to remove debris

1/4 cup freshly grated Parmesan cheese

2 bay leaves

Crusty baguette, for serving

1 Press Sauté and use the Sauté or Adjust button to select the middle temperature ("Normal"). Place the olive oil in the inner pot, wait about 1 minute for it to warm, then add the pancetta. Cook with the lid off, stirring occasionally, until the pancetta is crisp, about 10 minutes.

2 Use a slotted spoon to remove the pancetta from the inner pot, leaving behind the fat. Place the pancetta in a container with a lid and allow it to cool uncovered at room temperature until no longer hot, about 20 minutes. Cover the container and refrigerate until step 6.

3 Add the onions, garlic, salt, pepper, and red pepper flakes to the fat in the inner pot. Cook with the lid off, stirring occasionally, until the onions soften and start to brown, about 10 minutes. (Press Cancel and stop cooking if the garlic starts to burn.)

4 Add the broth and water and use a silicone spatula or wooden spoon to scrape up any brown bits off the bottom and stir them into the soup.

5 Add the beans, Parmesan, and bay leaves and stir to combine. Close and lock the lid. Set the valve to Venting. Attach the condensation collector. Press Cancel, then press Slow Cook and use the Slow Cook or Adjust button to select the highest temperature ("More"). Use the − or + button to set the time to 7 hours.

6 When the cooking time is finished, press Cancel and remove the lid. Discard the bay leaves. Taste and adjust the seasoning, adding more salt and pepper as needed. Serve hot, garnished with the reserved pancetta and olive oil, accompanied by a sliced baguette.

Garlicky White Bean Soup will keep, in an airtight container in the refrigerator, for up to 5 days. To reheat, place the soup in a pot and warm on the stovetop over medium heat, stirring occasionally, for about 5 minutes.

Note: Pancetta can be a slippery beast. If you're having trouble slicing it, place it in the freezer for 15 minutes until very cold and then slice. Or, look for pancetta sold prechopped in your supermarket's refrigerated case. Can't find pancetta? Don't worry. Use bacon. I promise it'll taste good.

ORANGE-GLAZED CARROTS

TOTAL TIME: 4 hours   **ACTIVE TIME:** 5 minutes   **YIELD:** Serves 6

Orange is a natural match not only for the color of carrots but for the flavor, too. The easiest way to incorporate that flavor here is a little marmalade, but if you have an orange on hand, you can use finely grated orange zest (see Note). Either way, with just a handful of ingredients and a few minutes of prep work, you have a reliable step up from plain carrots that no one will accuse of being boring or bland.

---

2 pounds carrots, peeled and sliced crosswise into ¼-inch-thick rounds

1 cup water

1 teaspoon sugar

½ teaspoon salt, plus extra as needed

1 tablespoon unsalted butter

¼ cup orange marmalade (see Note)

¼ teaspoon freshly ground black pepper, plus extra as needed

---

1 Place the carrots, water, sugar, and salt in the inner pot and stir to combine.

2 Close and lock the lid. Set the valve to Venting. Attach the condensation collector. Press Slow Cook and use the Slow Cook or Adjust button to select the lowest temperature ("Less"). Use the − or + button to set the time to 4 hours.

3 When the cooking cycle ends, press Cancel and remove the lid. Wearing oven mitts, remove the inner pot (be careful—it's hot!), drain the carrots through a colander, and then return them to the inner pot. Return the inner pot to the appliance. Add

the butter, marmalade, and pepper and stir gently to combine. Check the seasoning and add more salt and pepper to taste. Serve hot.

Orange-Glazed Carrots will keep, in an airtight container in the refrigerator, for up to 5 days. To reheat, place them in a small pot, add water to a depth of ½ inch, and warm on the stovetop over medium-low heat, stirring occasionally, for about 5 minutes.

Note: No orange marmalade? No problem. Use 3 tablespoons of honey and the finely grated zest of 1 orange in its place.

PARMESAN BREAD PUDDING WITH BACON AND BROCCOLI

TOTAL TIME: 4 hours 15 minutes   **ACTIVE TIME:** 15 minutes   **YIELD:** Serves 8

If you think of bread pudding solely as a dessert, this dish will be a pleasant revelation. Serve this savory pudding at a brunch or gathering of friends or family and be prepared to answer requests for the recipe.

---

4 slices bacon, halved crosswise to make 8 short strips

6 large eggs

1½ cups whole milk

1 clove garlic, minced

½ cup finely grated Parmesan cheese

½ teaspoon crushed red pepper flakes

1½ teaspoons salt

½ teaspoon freshly ground black pepper

1 small head of broccoli (about 1 pound), stalks and florets cut into ½-inch pieces

10 ounces (5 slices) thick-cut white sandwich bread, cut into 1-inch cubes (about 8 cups)

Nonstick cooking spray

---

1 Line the bottom of the inner pot with bacon. (Place the slices as close together as possible so that little if any creeps up the side of the inner pot.) Press Sauté and use the Sauté or Adjust button to select the lowest temperature ("Less"). Cook with the lid off until the bacon is pale pink and the fat is no longer bright white, about 5 minutes.

2 While the bacon cooks, whisk together the eggs in a large mixing bowl, then whisk in the milk, garlic, Parmesan, red pepper flakes, salt, and pepper. Add the broccoli and bread to the bowl and use a rubber spatula to toss the mixture until the bread is thoroughly coated.

3 Leaving the bacon on the bottom of the inner pot, coat the sides with nonstick cooking spray. Carefully pour the egg mixture on top of the bacon, using a rubber spatula to make sure the bread and broccoli are evenly distributed. Close and lock the lid. Set the valve to Venting. Attach the condensation collector. Press Cancel, then press Slow Cook and use the Slow Cook or Adjust button to select the lowest temperature ("Less"). Use the – or + button to set the time to 4 hours.

4 When the cooking time is finished, press Cancel and remove the lid. Use a large spoon to scoop out portions and serve hot.

Parmesan Bread Pudding with Bacon and Broccoli will keep, in an airtight container in the refrigerator, for up to 3 days. Serve leftovers chilled.

MAPLE-SWEETENED FRENCH TOAST CASSEROLE

TOTAL TIME: 2 hours   **ACTIVE TIME:** 5 minutes   **YIELD:** Serves 8

Yes, this version of French toast does take longer than the traditional stovetop version, but there's a big advantage: This recipe lets you just walk away and come back when it's done. Best of all, the complex sweetness of maple syrup—such a great match for French toast of all types—is baked right into this dish.

6 large eggs

¾ cup whole milk

½ cup heavy (whipping) cream

¾ cup pure maple syrup

1 tablespoon pure vanilla extract

½ teaspoon ground cinnamon, plus extra for garnish

Pinch of ground nutmeg

Pinch of salt

1 pound thin-crusted seedless Italian bread, torn into large bite-size chunks

Nonstick cooking spray

Whipped cream, for serving (optional)

1 Whisk together the eggs in a large mixing bowl to combine. Whisk in the milk, cream, maple syrup, vanilla extract, cinnamon, nutmeg, and salt. Add the bread to the bowl and use a rubber spatula to toss the mixture until the bread has absorbed the liquid.

2 Coat the bottom and side of the inner pot with nonstick cooking spray. Transfer the bread mixture to the inner pot, pouring any remaining liquid on top.

3 Close and lock the lid. Set the valve to Venting. Attach the condensation collector. Press Slow Cook and use the Slow Cook or Adjust button to select the highest temperature ("More"). Use the – or + button to set the time to 2 hours.

4 When the cooking time is finished, press Cancel and remove the lid. Serve hot, scooped into bowls and topped with a dollop of whipped cream and a sprinkling of cinnamon, if desired.

Maple-Sweetened French Toast Casserole is best served the day it is made, though leftover casserole can be kept, in an airtight container in the refrigerator, for up to 3 days and served chilled. (Like cold pizza, it has its devotees.)

MULLED CIDER

TOTAL TIME: 1 hour 45 minutes   **ACTIVE TIME:** 15 minute   **YIELD:** Serves 12

What is the difference between apple cider and apple juice? It depends in part on who does the labeling, but in general apple juice has been filtered to remove any trace of apple solids, while apple cider—especially fresh apple cider sold in season—contains apple solids and may be slightly cloudy. Other differences:

• Fresh cider must be refrigerated to avoid fermenting, whereas apple juice is usually pasteurized and vacuum sealed to be shelf-stable.

• Apple juice may be made from concentrate and sometimes contains added sugar.

If you can't find anything labeled apple cider, try using unfiltered, unsweetened apple juice instead.

1 gallon apple cider

2-inch piece peeled fresh ginger, cut into thick rounds

3 cinnamon sticks (about 3 inches each)

1 tablespoon whole cloves

Pinch of freshly grated nutmeg

1 medium orange, sliced crosswise into thin rounds

Calvados (apple brandy), for serving (optional)

1 Place the cider, ginger, cinnamon sticks, cloves, and nutmeg in the inner pot.

2 Close and lock the lid. Set the valve to Venting. Attach the condensation collector. Press Slow Cook and use the Slow Cook or Adjust button to select the lowest temperature ("Less"). Use the – or + button to set the time to 1 hour 30 minutes.

3 When the cooking cycle ends, allow the Instant Pot to switch to Keep Warm mode. (A timer on the display will begin counting up.) Remove the lid and use a slotted spoon or fine-mesh strainer to remove the ginger, cinnamon sticks, and cloves.

4 Add the orange slices to the cider and stir gently to distribute. Serve hot, adding Calvados to taste to individual mugs.

Mulled Cider is best served when freshly made.

LEMON-CHOCOLATE BREAD PUDDING

TOTAL TIME: 4 hours 15 minutes   **ACTIVE TIME:** 15 minutes   **YIELD:** Serves 8

Lemon and chocolate may sound like an odd combination at first, but it works. While the flavor pairing of chocolate-orange is relatively well established, this is just one surprising and delicious step sideways. Using only the zest here and balancing it with vanilla extract ensures that the lemon flavor comes through without overpowering sourness. It's the aroma and almost floral essence of the lemon that shines. No small thing: Sprinkling the chocolate chips on top allows them to melt into a perfectly gooey sauce.

6 large eggs

1½ cups whole milk

1 tablespoon pure vanilla extract

Finely grated zest of 2 small lemons

1 cup sugar

Pinch of salt

10 ounces (5 slices) thick-cut white sandwich bread, cut into 1-inch cubes (about 8 cups)

Nonstick cooking spray

½ cup bittersweet or semisweet chocolate chips

Whipped cream, for serving (optional)

1 Whisk together the eggs in a large mixing bowl, then whisk in the milk, vanilla extract, lemon zest, sugar, and salt. Add the bread to the bowl and use a rubber spatula to toss the mixture until the bread is thoroughly coated.

2 Coat the bottom and side of the inner pot with nonstick cooking spray. Transfer the bread mixture to the inner pot, pouring any remaining liquid on top. Sprinkle the chocolate chips over the egg mixture. Close and lock the lid. Set the valve to Venting. Attach the condensation collector. Press Slow Cook and use the Slow Cook or Adjust button to select the lowest temperature ("Less"). Use the − or + button to set the time to 4 hours.

3 When the cooking time is finished, press Cancel and remove the lid. Serve hot, scooped into bowls and topped with a dollop of whipped cream, if desired.

Lemon-Chocolate Bread Pudding will keep, in an airtight container in the refrigerator, for up to 3 days. Serve chilled.

MORE FLAVORING AND SERVING IDEAS FOR LEMON-CHOCOLATE BREAD PUDDING

- In step 1, add a drop of almond extract. (Go easy on it. No matter how much you like almond flavor, a little extract goes a long way.)

- Serve with a dab of Blueberry Jam (page 201) or Apricot-Vanilla Compote (page 206).

- Add a small pinch of ground cardamom or grated ginger to the egg mixture.

- Add a splash of rum to the egg mixture.

- Substitute finely grated orange zest for the lemon zest.

- Serve with slivered almonds atop the chocolate.

- Serve with a sprig of fresh basil.

- Toss some fresh blackberries or blueberries onto the finished pudding before serving.

- Serve with a dollop of mascarpone instead of whipped cream.

SAFFRON RICE PUDDING

TOTAL TIME: 2 hours   **ACTIVE TIME:** 5 minutes   **YIELD:** Serves 8

Rice pudding is one of the desserts with the best effort-to-taste ratio, especially when you make it in the Instant Pot and don't have to stand over it stirring. This version is very lightly sweet, but can be tweaked to increase the sugar. Saffron adds not just a shade of gold but a subtle, pleasing floral flavor to the pudding.

Nonstick cooking spray

1 cup white long-grain rice

¼ teaspoon salt

3 cups water

3 cups whole milk

½ cup sugar, plus extra as needed

Pinch of saffron threads, plus extra for garnish

1 Coat the inner pot with cooking spray. Add the rice, salt, water, milk, and sugar.

2 Crush the saffron between two fingers and add it to the rice mixture. Stir to combine. Close and lock the lid. Set the valve to Venting. Attach the condensation collector. Press Slow Cook and use the Slow Cook or Adjust button to select the highest temperature ("More"). Use the – or + button to set the time to 2 hours.

3 When the cooking time is finished, press Cancel and remove the lid. The pudding should be thick, not watery. If the pudding is too watery, press Sauté and use the Sauté or Adjust button to select the lowest temperature ("Less"). Cook with the lid off and stir occasionally until more liquid is absorbed, about 10 minutes.

4 Taste to check the sweetness of the pudding. If it is not sweet enough, add 1 tablespoon of sugar and stir well; taste and repeat if necessary. Serve warm, each serving garnished with a saffron thread or two.

Saffron Rice Pudding will keep, in an airtight container in the refrigerator, for up to 5 days. Serve warm or chilled. To reheat, place the pudding in a small pot and warm on the stovetop over medium-low heat, stirring occasionally, for about 5 minutes.

BLUEBERRY JAM

TOTAL TIME: 4 hours 15 minutes **ACTIVE TIME:** 15 minutes **YIELD:** Makes about 7 cups `V` `VN` `DF`

Making jam in the Instant Pot eliminates most of the stirring and monitoring necessary on the stovetop. It also wipes out the need to wrangle hot jars and fuss with canning lids. (I like doing that sometimes, but I like not doing it sometimes, too.) While this recipe uses frozen blueberries, fresh will work, too. But frozen blueberries know no season, and much of the time they are a better value, too.

---

4 cups frozen (or fresh) blueberries	2 tablespoons freshly squeezed lemon juice
4 cups sugar	1 package (1¾ ounces) dry pectin (see Note)

---

1 Place the blueberries, sugar, and lemon juice in the inner pot and stir to combine. Close and lock the lid. Set the valve to Venting. Attach the condensation collector. Press Slow Cook and use the Slow Cook or Adjust button to select the lowest temperature ("Less"). Use the – or + button to set the time to 4 hours.

2 After 20 minutes, remove the lid and lightly mash the berries with a potato masher, crushing most berries but allowing a few whole berries to remain. Replace the lid.

3 When the cooking time is finished, remove the lid. Press Cancel, then press Sauté and use the Sauté or Adjust button to select the highest temperature ("More"). Cook with the lid off until boiling, about 5 minutes. Add the pectin and continue to boil for 1 minute, stirring frequently.

4 Press Cancel. Wearing oven mitts, remove the inner pot (be careful—it's hot!) and place it on a trivet or other heat-resistant surface. Allow the jam to cool for about 5 minutes, then scoop it into Mason jars.

Blueberry Jam will keep, in a covered Mason jar in the refrigerator, for up to 1 month.

Note: Pectin is what helps jams set. It's a powder often available near the jams and jellies in the supermarket.

AUTUMN SPICE APPLE BUTTER

TOTAL TIME: 7 hours 30 minutes **ACTIVE TIME:** 30 minutes **YIELD:** Makes about 4 cups

Whenever I go apple-picking and come home with too many apples (those two things always go hand in hand), my mind turns to apple butter. Perfect for spreading on French toast or stirring into yogurt, apple butter tastes and smells like autumn. Don't worry too much about the variety of apple you use—sweet or tart apples are all fair game, though a blend of varieties will capture a nicely rounded apple flavor. A bonus: The aroma suggests you've been laboring over a hot stove all day, even if the Instant Pot makes it considerably less work than that.

---

4 pounds apples, peeled, cored, and cut into ½-inch cubes

2 tablespoons freshly squeezed lemon juice

¾ cup sugar

1½ teaspoons ground cinnamon

½ teaspoon ground cardamom

¼ teaspoon ground allspice

Pinch of ground nutmeg

¼ teaspoon salt

1 vanilla bean, split lengthwise

---

1 Place the apples and lemon juice in the inner pot and stir to combine.

2 Combine the sugar, cinnamon, cardamom, allspice, nutmeg, and salt in a small bowl and stir to incorporate.

3 Add the sugar mixture to the apples and stir until the apples are evenly coated. Use a dull knife to scrape in the vanilla seeds,

and then add the scraped vanilla bean as well. Stir until the vanilla seeds are evenly distributed.

4 Close and lock the lid. Set the valve to Venting. Attach the condensation collector. Press Slow Cook and use the Slow Cook or Adjust button to select the highest temperature ("More"). Use the − or + button to set the time to 5 hours.

5 After 1 hour, remove the lid, stir the apples, and replace the lid. Repeat about every hour. When the cooking time is finished, remove the lid. Wearing oven mitts, remove the inner pot (be careful—it's hot!) and set it on a trivet or other heat-resistant surface. The apples should be very soft. Remove and discard the vanilla bean.

6 Transfer the apples to a blender and puree them. (Take care when pureeing the hot apples.) Place the pureed apples in the inner pot.

7 Return the inner pot to the appliance. Press Cancel, then press Slow Cook and use the Slow Cook or Adjust button to select the highest temperature ("More"). Use the − or + button to set the time to 2 hours. Cook with the lid off, stirring occasionally, until the apple butter is thick and a spoon dragged through it leaves a trail that does not quickly fill back in. The apple butter will thicken further as it cools.

8 Press Cancel. Spoon the apple butter into containers with lids and refrigerate. Serve chilled or at room temperature.

Autumn Spice Apple Butter will keep, in an airtight container in the refrigerator, for up to 4 weeks.

SIMPLY POACHED PEARS

TOTAL TIME: 2 hours 30 minutes   **ACTIVE TIME:** 5 minutes   **YIELD:** Serves 4

The fact that the Instant Pot allows these pears to happen while I do other things has moved them up on my dessert menu. The fruit comes out sweet and perfumed with the vanilla and cinnamon, perfect for serving with Saffron Rice Pudding (page 199), ice cream, or a dollop of homemade Crème Fraîche (page 233). Bonus: Not only can these be made ahead, they're better the next day. Soaking in syrup does that to you.

---

4 cups water

1 cup sugar

1 cinnamon stick (about 3 inches)

1 vanilla bean, split lengthwise

4 Bosc pears, peeled, halved, and cored

---

1 Place the water and sugar in the inner pot and stir until the sugar is mostly dissolved. Add the cinnamon stick, vanilla bean, and pears.

2 Close and lock the lid. Set the valve to Venting. Attach the condensation collector. Press Slow Cook and use the Slow Cook or Adjust button to select the lowest temperature ("Less"). Use the − or + button to set the time to 2 hours.

3 When the cooking time is finished, remove the lid. The pears will be tender but still intact. Use a slotted spoon to remove them from the inner pot and divide them among 4 plates. Set the pears aside.

4 Press Cancel, then press Sauté and use the Sauté or Adjust button to select the middle temperature ("Normal"). Cook the liquid with the lid off, stirring occasionally, until it has thickened and reduced to one third of its original volume, about 30 minutes. Remove the cinnamon stick and vanilla bean and discard. Press Cancel and spoon some liquid over each pear. Serve warm or at room temperature.

Simply Poached Pears will keep, stored in their cooking liquid in an airtight container in the refrigerator, for up to 5 days. Serve chilled or warm. To reheat, place the liquid and the pears in a small pot and warm on the stovetop over medium-low heat for about 10 minutes.

APRICOT-VANILLA COMPOTE

TOTAL TIME: 3 hours 10 minutes   **ACTIVE TIME:** 10 minutes   **YIELD:** Makes about 3 cups

Don't be shy about using soft or bruised fruit here. This recipe can take advantage of apricots that are, shall we say, past their prime. A little slow-cooking turns even such imperfect apricots into an ideal accompaniment to plain yogurt (see page 226) or buttered toast. You can even serve a dab or two of this alongside roast pork or lamb.

²/₃ cup sugar

½ cup water

2 tablespoons freshly squeezed lemon juice

Pinch of salt

2 pounds apricots, halved and pitted

1 vanilla bean, split lengthwise

1 Place the sugar, water, lemon juice, and salt in the inner pot and stir to combine. Add the apricots and stir until they are well coated.

2 Use a dull knife to scrape the vanilla seeds into the inner pot and then add the scraped vanilla bean. Stir until the vanilla seeds are evenly distributed.

3 Close and lock the lid. Set the valve to Venting. Attach the condensation collector. Press Slow Cook and use the Slow Cook or Adjust button to select the lowest temperature ("Less"). Use the − or + button to set the time to 3 hours.

4 When the cooking time is finished, press Cancel and remove the lid. Discard the vanilla bean and stir the compote. Serve warm or at room temperature.

Apricot-Vanilla Compote will keep, in an airtight container in the refrigerator, for up to 2 weeks.

Chapter 4

RICE MAKER

Rice cookers can be divisive appliances, with some who swear by them and some who scratch their heads and wonder what's wrong with making rice on the stovetop. I'm not here to take sides. I don't have to, and neither do you. You own an Instant Pot, so by default you own a rice cooker.

The push-button convenience of making rice in a separate appliance can spoil you; no more futzing with the heat on the stovetop or moving pots on and off the heat. Making rice in the Instant Pot is easy, but knowing a little bit about the rice-making function can make it even easier.

WHAT'S DIFFERENT ABOUT THE RICE CYCLE?

The Instant Pot bills itself as a rice maker and indeed turns out rice quickly and easily. There's even a button on the front of the machine that says Rice. Must be the best way to make rice in the Instant Pot, right?

Not exactly.

That button is designed for white rice and cooks at low pressure, which takes longer. The Instant Pot does not have any of the "fuzzy logic" circuitry that more sophisticated, dedicated rice cookers use to determine when the rice is cooked.

The bottom line: While the Instant Pot makes great rice quickly, I prefer to skip the Rice button and stick with the Manual or Pressure Cook button, as explained in the recipes that follow.

TEMPERATURE AND TIMING

Following the recipes in this book is great (of course, I would say that; I wrote them), but sometimes you may want to strike out on your own. When you do, there are a few things to keep in mind when making rice:

- **Brown rice takes longer:** Just as on the stovetop, whole-grain rice will take longer in the Instant Pot than white rice varieties. As a rule, brown rice will take 25 minutes.

- **You won't use as much water:** Remember that there is much less evaporation in the Instant Pot than in a covered pot on the stove. Also, the rice will be cooking under pressure. Both factors mean that less water will be needed than on the stovetop.

- **Cooking time does not increase with the volume of rice:** One cup of rice cooks in the same amount of time as 3 cups.

- **Write it down:** Save yourself frustration and take notes on your preferred rice-to-water ratio (see below) and cooking times.

IS THERE A MAGIC RICE-TO-WATER RATIO?

I'll answer that question upfront: Maybe. The real answer is, of course, longer.

America's Test Kitchen has done experiments suggesting that all rice absorbs the same amount of water, whether long grain, short grain, or brown. This might seem ridiculous at first, if you've cooked different kinds of rice on the stovetop. The difference in the recommended amounts of water for each type of rice, they suggest, is because each type of rice takes a different amount of time to cook and therefore either more or less water evaporates. (Thus, brown rice needs more water on the stovetop because it takes longer to cook and more of that water evaporates.)

With that in mind, the Instant Pot's manufacturer recommends a ratio of 1:1 between rice and water, and I pass that along with three caveats:

- The 1:1 ratio assumes that you're starting with rinsed (or "wet") rice. This is rice that has been rinsed in a colander. While most of the water drains through the colander, some does stick to the rice. The recipes in this book use wet rice.

- The 1:1 ratio is best viewed as a starting point. Because people like their rice done differently, you are ultimately the judge of the best ratio in your cooking.

- If you're using liquid that isn't pure water—say, coconut milk, broth, or tomato juice—the 1:1 ratio may not apply, since some of that liquid consists of dissolved solids that will not hydrate the rice.

MEASUREMENT

If your inner pot has cup lines marked inside, they are not standard 8-ounce cups and are best ignored. When it comes to using the 1:1 ratio, there is no magic cup size, though for note-taking purposes and consistency I recommend standard measuring cups. Keep in mind, too, that you can achieve the best results by cooking no less than 1 cup of rice at a time.

Clockwise from top: Garlic-Ginger White Rice, Cilantro-Lime White Rice, Coconut White Rice

LICKETY-SPLIT WHITE RICE

1·2·3

The Instant Pot takes the guesswork out of making rice, which means you can focus on the rest of dinner while it takes care of the side dish. Unadorned, basic white rice pairs well with a flavorful main course such as Pineapple Skirt Steak (page 33). Cilantro-Lime White Rice (page 212) is an easy way to add a little zip and makes a great accompaniment to Mexican food or Thai-Spiced Beef Stew (page 36). Adding coconut milk is another simple variation (page 212) that turns white rice into the perfect side dish for a spicy curry. Garlic-Ginger White Rice (page 212) makes a standout side dish to a stovetop stir-fry. If you wish to double the recipe, double the ingredients and keep the cooking time the same.

Master Method

V | VN | DF | X2 | 30

TOTAL TIME: 20 minutes

ACTIVE TIME: 5 minutes

YIELD: Serves 6

1½ cups long-grain white rice

1½ cups water

¾ teaspoon salt

---

1 Rinse the rice: Place the rice in a fine-mesh strainer or colander with small holes and run cold water over it, swirling the strainer gently for about 15 seconds to make sure all the rice is rinsed. It's not necessary for every last drop of water to drain away; in fact, a little water clinging to the rice is what we're looking for.

2 Place the slightly damp rice, water, and salt in the inner pot and stir to combine. Close and lock the lid. Set the valve to Sealing. Press Manual or Pressure Cook and use the Pressure or Pressure Level button to select High Pressure. Use the – or + button to set the time to 6 minutes.

3 When the cooking cycle ends, wait 10 minutes, and then carefully use a wooden spoon to release the pressure by turning the pressure-release valve to Venting. (The pressure is released when the small metal float valve next to the pressure-release valve sinks back into the lid and the lid is no longer locked.)

4 Press Cancel and remove the lid. Use a fork to fluff the rice and serve hot.

Lickety-Split White Rice will keep, in an airtight container in the refrigerator, for up to 3 days. To reheat, place the rice in a pot, add a splash of water, and cover. Warm on the stovetop over medium-low heat, stirring occasionally until hot, about 5 minutes.

❶ CILANTRO-LIME WHITE RICE V VN DF X2 30

TOTAL TIME: 20 minutes
ACTIVE TIME: 5 minutes
YIELD: Serves 6

Add 1 teaspoon sugar with the rice, water, and salt. When the rice is finished cooking, add the finely grated zest of 1 small lime, 3 tablespoons of freshly squeezed lime juice, and ¾ cup chopped fresh cilantro leaves. Toss with the rice until well distributed.

❷ COCONUT WHITE RICE V VN DF X2 30

TOTAL TIME: 20 minutes
ACTIVE TIME: 5 minutes
YIELD: Serves 6

Use 1 can (13½ ounces) coconut milk plus ¼ cup water for the liquid and add 1 teaspoon sugar. Some crunchy, browned bits of rice will await you at the bottom of the inner pot; this is normal and delicious.

❸ GARLIC-GINGER WHITE RICE V VN DF X2 30

TOTAL TIME: 20 minutes
ACTIVE TIME: 5 minutes
YIELD: Serves 6

Press Sauté and use the Adjust button to select the lowest temperature ("Less"). Place 1 tablespoon neutral-flavored vegetable oil, such as canola or peanut, in the inner pot. Wait about 1 minute for it to warm, then add 1 tablespoon peeled and finely grated fresh ginger and 2 cloves garlic, finely chopped. Cook with the lid off, stirring occasionally with a silicone spatula or wooden spoon, until fragrant, about 1 minute. Press Cancel and then continue with step 1 of the Master Method (page 211).

MORE FLAVORING AND SERVING IDEAS FOR WHITE RICE

- Use All-Purpose Chicken Stock (page 88) or store-bought vegetable broth in place of the water. (Omit the salt.)

- Add a knob of unsalted butter with the rice and water in the Master Method.

- Use fresh herbs to flavor the Master Method rice: Add finely chopped fresh dill or Italian (flat-leaf) parsley to the finished rice just before fluffing it with a fork.

- Combine the Garlic-Ginger and Coconut Rice methods to make Garlic-Ginger Coconut White Rice.

- Place whole spices in the inner pot with the Master Method rice: Cinnamon sticks or star anise work particularly well. Remove before serving.

- Add saffron to the Master Method rice: Warm the water. Place a pinch of saffron threads between two fingers and rub them together to allow the saffron to break apart and fall into the water. Allow the saffron to soak for a few minutes before proceeding.

THAI-STYLE STICKY RICE

TOTAL TIME: 1 hour   **ACTIVE TIME:** 5 minutes   **YIELD:** Serves 4

One of my favorite parts of going to a Thai restaurant is the sticky rice, fragrant and faintly sweet. There is no magic in cooking it at home, though it does require starting with the right rice. The one you want is called "glutinous rice" and has opaque, white grains. It's often available at Asian supermarkets and can be ordered online. Sticky rice requires a little soaking in warm water to start softening the grain. When it comes to the actual cooking, the water you use will quickly be heated by the Instant Pot, so lukewarm (or even cold) water is fine.

---

2 cups Thai glutinous ("sticky") rice

2 cups warm water (about 110°F)

2 cups lukewarm or cold water

---

1 Place the rice and 2 cups of warm water in a medium bowl and stir well to make sure the rice is submerged. Allow the rice to soak for 20 minutes.

2 Pour the soaked rice into a silicone or collapsible metal steaming basket over the sink. Much of the soaking water will drain away, but some of it will cling to the rice. Allow the rice to remain damp.

3 Place the steaming rack on the bottom of the inner pot and pour the 2 cups of lukewarm or cold water into the inner pot. Place the steaming basket on top of the rack.

4 Close and lock the lid. Set the valve to Sealing. Press Steam and use the − or + button to set the time to 13 minutes.

5 When the cooking cycle ends, press Cancel. Allow the appliance to cool and release pressure naturally, about 15 minutes. (The pressure is released when the small metal float valve next to the pressure-release valve sinks back into the lid and the lid is no longer locked.)

6 Remove the lid. Wearing oven mitts, remove the steaming basket from the inner pot (be careful—it's hot!). Serve hot.

Thai-Style Sticky Rice will keep, in an airtight container in the refrigerator, for up to 3 days. To reheat, follow the instructions in steps 2 through 4, but reduce steaming time to 1 minute and release the pressure immediately after the cooking cycle ends by using a wooden spoon to carefully turn the pressure-release valve to Venting. Remember, this will release hot steam!

BROWN RICE WITH SESAME OIL

TOTAL TIME: 45 minutes   **ACTIVE TIME:** 5 minutes   **YIELD:** Serves 8   V VN DF X2 60

Brown rice has the fiber and nutrition that has been stripped away from white rice and thus is often my preference for side dishes and stir-fries. The downside can be that it takes more time to cook. Fortunately, the Instant Pot is about as simple as it gets. To highlight the sesame flavor when serving as a side dish, sprinkle toasted sesame seeds on the rice. Serve alongside a rich, fatty fish such as salmon, whether grilled, steamed, or oven-roasted.

---

2 cups long-grain brown rice

2 cups water

2 tablespoons toasted sesame oil

½ teaspoon salt

Toasted sesame seeds, for garnish (optional)

---

1 Rinse the rice: Place the rice in a fine-mesh strainer or colander with small holes and run cold water over it, swirling the strainer gently for about 15 seconds to make sure all the rice is rinsed. It's not necessary for every last drop of water to drain away; in fact, a little water clinging to the rice is what we're looking for.

2 Place the water, sesame oil, and salt in the inner pot. Spoon or scrape the rice from the strainer into the inner pot. Stir to combine. Close and lock the lid. Set the valve to Sealing. Press Manual or Pressure Cook and use the Pressure or Pressure Level button to select High Pressure. Use the − or + button to set the time to 25 minutes.

3 When the cooking cycle ends, wait 10 minutes, and then carefully use a wooden spoon to release the pressure by turning the pressure-release valve to Venting. (The pressure is released when the small metal float valve next to the pressure-release valve sinks back into the lid and the lid is no longer locked.) Press Cancel, remove the lid, and serve the rice hot, sprinkled with sesame seeds if desired.

Brown Rice with Sesame Oil will keep, in an airtight container in the refrigerator, for up to 3 days. To reheat, place the rice in a pot, add a splash of water, and cover. Warm on the stovetop over medium-low heat, stirring occasionally, for about 5 minutes.

WHOLESOME WILD RICE WITH GOLDEN RAISINS

TOTAL TIME: 50 minutes   **ACTIVE TIME:** 5 minutes   **YIELD:** Serves 4   `V` `VN` `DF` `X2` `60`

Set against the dark wild rice, golden raisins look like little jewels. Not only do they appeal to the eye, they're a quick way to add sweetness and contrasting texture. Wild rice on the stovetop can be a bit of a chore, but the Instant Pot makes it simple enough to focus on the rest of dinner while the rice cooks away on its own.

¼ cup golden raisins

1 cup warm water (about 110°F)

1 cup wild rice

1 cup lukewarm or cold water

½ teaspoon salt

---

1 Soak the raisins: Place the raisins in a small bowl and cover with the warm water. Set aside until step 5.

2 Rinse the rice: Place the rice in a fine-mesh strainer or colander with small holes and run cold water over, swirling the strainer gently for about 15 seconds to make sure all the rice is rinsed. It's not necessary for every last drop of water to drain away; in fact, a little water clinging to the rice is what we're looking for.

3 Place the rice, 1 cup lukewarm or cold water, and salt in the inner pot and stir to combine. Close and lock the lid. Set the valve to Sealing. Press Manual or Pressure Cook and use the Pressure or Pressure Level button to select High Pressure. Use the − or + button to set the time to 27 minutes.

4 When the cooking cycle ends, wait 10 minutes, and then carefully use a wooden spoon to release the pressure by turning the pressure-release valve to Venting. (The pressure is released when the small metal float valve next to the pressure-

release valve sinks back into the lid and the lid is no longer locked.)

5 Press Cancel and remove the lid. Drain the raisins, place them in the inner pot, and use a fork to fluff the rice and mix in the raisins. Close and lock the lid to allow the residual heat to plump the raisins slightly and warm them, about 5 minutes. Remove the lid and serve the rice hot.

Wholesome Wild Rice with Golden Raisins will keep, in an airtight container in the refrigerator, for up to 3 days. To reheat, place the rice in a pot, add a splash of water, and cover. Warm on the stovetop over medium-low heat, stirring occasionally until hot, about 5 minutes.

Chapter 5
YOGURT MAKER

··

Before the Instant Pot entered my life, I had tried making yogurt with some success. But no method I tried was simple enough for me to do regularly. (Swaddling a jar with a towel and heating pad, for example, was not going to become part of my routine. It sounds kind of like a spa day for a dairy product, and I can't get behind treating my yogurt better than I treat myself.)

Buying a stand-alone yogurt maker was tempting, but I could never justify the price or the counter space. Fortunately, the Instant Pot more than justifies its counter space and raises the prospect of homemade yogurt from "possible" to "probable."

WHAT DOES THE YOGURT FUNCTION DO?

The yogurt function has three temperatures. Two of them are used for making yogurt, while a third is used for making Crème Fraîche (page 233)—and a popular Chinese dish of fermented glutinous rice. You can also make ricotta (page 229).

- "Normal" mode for making yogurt after pasteurizing the milk: 97°F to 109°F.

- "Less" mode for making Crème Fraîche and Jiu Niang (fermented glutinous rice): 86°F to 93°F.

- "More" for pasteurizing milk: 160°F to 180°F. (Yes, even store-bought pasteurized milk is re-pasteurized in the Instant Pot before making yogurt. This ensures that no bad bacteria compete with the good, yogurt-making bacteria to colonize the yogurt.)

YOGURT-MAKING BASICS

Making yogurt is a three-step process:

1. Scald the milk to kill any harmful bacteria and denature the proteins. The heat unfolds the proteins, which allows them to later form a mesh and yield yogurt.

2. Allow the milk to cool and add yogurt bacteria ("starter") to the milk. The starter is often simply yogurt with live bacteria— including the stuff you buy at the market. The milk must first be cooled because high temperatures can kill the yogurt bacteria.

3. Incubate the yogurt to allow the bacteria to do their job.

That's it.
There are a few other things to know:

- Whole milk is typically easiest for beginners, yielding the creamiest results.

- No need for fancy milk. Pasteurized, homogenized milk—the milk most readily available at the supermarket—works just fine. UHT milk (ultra-pasteurized, shelf-stable milk—the kind sold in boxes) can work, though it may produce a thinner yogurt.

- A previous batch of homemade yogurt can be used as starter in a new yogurt, but this will only work for so long. After a half dozen times or so, the yogurt may not set as well; it's time for a new starter in the form of yogurt from the supermarket.

- Different brands of starter yogurt may use different bacteria and therefore yield different results in your finished yogurt. If you make a particularly good batch of yogurt with a certain brand of starter, take note; you may have just found your favorite bacteria! (It's not everyone who can say that.)

- The style of yogurt starter—whether Greek, Australian, or Canadian (I think I made that last one up)—does not entirely determine the style of yogurt produced, since those products can be a result of straining the yogurt at the end to thicken it.

- Use only plain, unflavored yogurt as a starter, ideally one without additives or thickeners (such as gelatin, cornstarch, or guar gum).

MAKING YOGURT IN CONTAINERS

The recipes in this book use just the inner pot to make a single large batch of yogurt, but it is also possible to make the yogurt in containers within the inner pot using Mason jars or heat-safe glass bottles:

- Instead of using the Boil function described in the recipes, pasteurize the milk by steaming it: Place 1 cup of water in the inner pot, set the steaming rack inside it, and rest your uncovered, filled containers on top of the rack. Note that this step is necessary even for milk sold as pasteurized.

- Close and lock the lid. Set the valve to Sealing, press the Steam button, and set the time for 1 minute. When the cycle ends, turn off the machine. Allow the appliance to cool and release pressure naturally, about 20 minutes. Proceed with the recipe as directed, placing the uncovered containers directly in the inner pot. (No water is necessary for this second step.)

YOGURT EXPERIMENTATION

More than some other cooking projects, making yogurt is a bit of a journey. Many bread bakers know that part of the fun of bread-making can be tweaking a recipe and observing the difference in the finished product. The same is true here. Possibilities for variation abound:

• Try different fat levels of milk (whole, 2%, nonfat). As I mentioned, whole milk is generally easier to work with for first-timers and will give you creamier yogurt, but try various fat contents to find what suits you best.

• Try different milks: Any milk from a mammal (such as sheep, goat, or water buffalo if you happen to have one around) should behave much the same way (though the flavors of the resulting yogurt will vary).

• Nondairy milks such as coconut and soy milk *can* yield yogurt, but they require a starter specially designed for them (often available at natural foods stores) and may also require a starch or agar-agar to thicken. The recipes in this book use dairy milk, but consult the package of nondairy starter for recipe suggestions and use your Instant Pot to experiment.

• Add a little more or a little less of the yogurt starter: While 1 tablespoon per quart of milk is a good guideline, adding twice as much can produce a thicker, more sour yogurt; adding half as much can yield a thinner yogurt with less bite.

• Try a different starter and take note of what works for you: If you're using commercial yogurt as a starter, pay attention to the strain of bacteria mentioned on the back of the package.

• Scald the milk twice in the initial step, allowing more proteins to denature and creating a thicker yogurt.

• Experiment with different times in the final step of the process. Try 10 hours instead of the prescribed 8 to get a tangier, thicker yogurt.

YOGURT TROUBLESHOOTING

Making yogurt involves many variables—the bacterial starter, the milk, and the length of incubation time, to name a few. Things can go wrong, even if you do everything right.

Here are some possible glitches and how to address them:

There are lumps: Incubating the yogurt for too long or using an old starter can cause small lumps to form in the yogurt. Also, homemade yogurt is often simply not as smooth and homogenous as its commercial counterpart. In either case, there is hope: Pour off some of the liquid (the whey), and then beat the yogurt with a whisk until smooth.

The yogurt's too sour: In general, yogurt becomes more sour the longer it incubates. Try reducing the incubation time for the next batch. Until the next batch, it's a good candidate to eat with jam (see page 240), dried fruit (see page 240), or vanilla syrup (see page 239).

It does not set: The bacteria in the starter may have died, sometimes from old age if the starter is not fresh. The bacteria may also have died because the starter was added to the milk before it cooled sufficiently. The milk must cool to 110°F before the starter is added. When taking the temperature of the milk, stir it first to mix it well, since the milk on the top may be cooler than the milk at the bottom.

There's a layer of liquid: This is normal. The liquid, whey, can be poured off, drained through cheesecloth to create a thicker yogurt, or stirred back into the yogurt.

It's too thin: Homemade yogurt is often thinner than its store-bought counterparts, which usually contain thickeners. If the yogurt is not as thick as you'd like, try draining some of the whey as directed in the 2% Greek Yogurt instructions (page 227).

HOMEMADE PLAIN YOGURT

1·2·3

If you've never made yogurt at home, you're in for a treat. It's a rewarding process that gives you an appreciation for the role that bacteria play in our lives—and it yields delicious, versatile yogurt you can enjoy without any additives or artificial ingredients. There are so many ways to make yogurt—varying levels of fat, various degrees of straining to thicken it, various types of milks as raw ingredients. Here, I give you three kinds and encourage you to experiment. Make a luscious full-fat yogurt that gets its body from the dairy fat naturally included (see below). Try a part-skim yogurt that is strained to produce a thicker, Greek-style yogurt (see page 227). Finally, a skim-milk yogurt has powdered milk added to bulk up its body (see page 228). Don't be put off by the long preparation time; for most of that time, the yogurt is unattended while the Instant Pot does its thing.

Note that the small amount of yogurt in the ingredients is used for its live bacteria, which will convert the milk into yogurt. Look for a yogurt with as few ingredients as possible, ideally just milk and bacteria. Additives and thickeners may interfere with the results.

① WHOLE MILK YOGURT Ⓥ

TOTAL TIME: 12 hours 30 minutes (including cooling time)

ACTIVE TIME: 10 minutes

YIELD: Makes about 8 cups

2 quarts whole milk

2 tablespoons whole-milk, 2%, or skim yogurt with active (live) cultures

---

1 Place the milk in the inner pot. Close and lock the lid. Set the valve to Sealing. Press the Yogurt button and then press the Yogurt or Adjust button until the display reads "Boil."

2 Allow about 30 minutes for the program to finish. When it has finished, press Cancel until the display reads "Off." Use oven mitts to remove the inner pot (be careful—it's hot!) and place it on a trivet or other heat-resistant surface. Allow the milk to cool, stirring occasionally, until the temperature drops to 110°F as measured on an instant-read thermometer, about 1 hour. (If you do not have a thermometer, use a small spoon to drip a few drops of the milk on the inside of your wrist. It should feel just above body temperature—very slightly warm but not hot. Err on the side of too cool, since too much heat will kill the necessary bacteria in the yogurt in the next step.)

3 Add the yogurt to the inner pot and stir thoroughly.

4 Return the inner pot to the Instant Pot. Press the Yogurt button and use the Yogurt or Adjust button to select the middle temperature ("Normal"). Use the − or + button to set the time to 8 hours. Close and lock the lid. Set the valve to Sealing.

5 When the cycle ends, press Cancel and remove the lid. Stir the yogurt and then use a large spoon to scoop it into a container with a lid or single-serving containers with lids. Place the covered container(s) in the refrigerator to cool, about 3 hours, before serving.

Whole Milk Yogurt will keep, in an airtight container in the refrigerator, for up to 2 weeks.

2 2% GREEK YOGURT V

TOTAL TIME: 13 hours 30 minutes (including cooling time)
ACTIVE TIME: 15 minutes
YIELD: Makes about 6 cups

2 quarts 2% milk

2 tablespoons whole-milk, 2%, or skim yogurt with active (live) cultures

Follow the recipe for Whole Milk Yogurt (page 226) using the 2% milk. In step 3, add the yogurt as directed. In step 5, when the 8-hour cycle ends, remove the lid and set a large strainer lined with a clean tea towel, several layers of cheesecloth, or coffee filters over a large bowl. Spoon the yogurt into the strainer and drain until thickened, at least 1 hour but no more than 2 hours. Refrigerate as directed.

Variation: For an even thicker, Icelandic-style yogurt, strain the yogurt in the refrigerator for at least 12 hours.

> ***Tip:*** The liquid leftover from straining is whey and is rich in protein. Substitute it for water in pizza or bread dough, or incorporate it into smoothies.

3 NONFAT YOGURT v

TOTAL TIME: 12 hours 30 minutes (including cooling time)

ACTIVE TIME: 10 minutes

YIELD: Makes about 8 cups

---

2 quarts skim (nonfat) milk

2 tablespoons whole-milk, 2%, or skim yogurt with active (live) cultures

1 cup powdered skim milk

Follow the recipe for Whole Milk Yogurt (page 226) using the skim milk. In step 3, add the yogurt and powdered skim milk and whisk thoroughly until the powdered milk is dissolved. Continue with the recipe as directed.

DO-IT-YOURSELF RICOTTA

The transformation that occurs in cheesemaking can seem almost magical. You start with the same milk you'd pour on your cereal and end up with something perfect for spreading on crackers or smearing on a baguette. In this case, of course, you get a major assist from the Instant Pot. Enjoy the ricotta unadorned—the results of the Master Method—or transform it into a spread with dill (see page 231), a morning treat with smoked salmon and capers (see page 231), or a savory dip for crackers with sun-dried tomatoes and basil (see page 232).

Master Method

V **X2**

TOTAL TIME: 2 hours 45 minutes (including cooling time)

ACTIVE TIME: 15 minutes

YIELD: Makes about 2 cups

---

1 quart whole milk

1 teaspoon salt

4 tablespoons freshly squeezed lemon juice

---

1 Place the milk in the inner pot. Close and lock the lid. Set the valve to Venting. Press Yogurt and press the Yogurt or Adjust button until the display reads "Boil."

2 Allow about 20 minutes for the program to finish. When it has finished, press Cancel. Use oven mitts to remove the inner pot (be careful—it's hot!) and place it on a trivet or other heat-resistant surface.

3 Stir in the salt. Slowly stir in the lemon juice, 1 tablespoon at a time. The milk will coagulate, gathering together in small lumps as the lemon juice is added. Wait about 5 minutes for the milk to coagulate further.

4 Place a fine-mesh strainer over a medium bowl and pour the milk through it. Let it drain until only the solids remain in the strainer, about 10 minutes.

Clockwise from bottom: Ricotta Spread with Dill,
Ricotta Spread with Sun-Dried Tomatoes and Basil,
Ricotta Spread with Smoked Salmon and Capers

5 Use a spatula to scrape the solids into a container with a lid. Cover the container and refrigerate it until chilled, about 2 hours.

Do-It-Yourself Ricotta will keep, in an airtight container in the refrigerator, for up to 1 week.

> ***Tip:*** The liquid leftover from straining is whey and is rich in protein. Substitute it for water in pizza or bread dough, or incorporate it into smoothies.

1 RICOTTA SPREAD WITH DILL

TOTAL TIME: 5 minutes
ACTIVE TIME: 5 minutes
YIELD: Makes about 2 cups

---

2 cups chilled Do-It-Yourself Ricotta (page 229)

1 small bunch fresh dill (about 1 ounce), large stems removed, finely chopped

¼ teaspoon salt, plus extra as needed

¼ teaspoon freshly ground black pepper, plus extra as needed

Crackers or baguette, for serving (optional)

Place the ricotta in a medium serving bowl. Add the dill, salt, and pepper and stir to distribute evenly. Taste and adjust the seasoning, adding more salt and pepper as needed. Serve chilled or at room temperature with crackers or baguette.

Ricotta Spread with Dill will keep, in an airtight container in the refrigerator, for up to 2 days. Serve leftover spread chilled.

2 RICOTTA SPREAD WITH SMOKED SALMON AND CAPERS

TOTAL TIME: 5 minutes
ACTIVE TIME: 5 minutes
YIELD: Makes about 2½ cups

---

2 cups chilled Do-It-Yourself Ricotta (page 229)

8 ounces smoked salmon, chopped

2 tablespoons drained capers in brine, chopped

1 small bunch fresh chives (about 1 ounce), finely chopped

Finely grated zest of 1 small lemon

Bagels, for serving (optional)

Place the ricotta in a medium serving bowl. Add the salmon, capers, chives, and lemon zest and stir to distribute evenly. Serve chilled or at room temperature with bagels.

Ricotta Spread with Smoked Salmon and Capers will keep, in an airtight container in the refrigerator, for up to 2 days. Serve leftover spread chilled.

3 RICOTTA SPREAD WITH SUN-DRIED TOMATOES AND BASIL

V X2 30

TOTAL TIME: 5 minutes
ACTIVE TIME: 5 minutes
YIELD: Makes about 2¼ cups

2 cups chilled Do-It-Yourself Ricotta (page 229)

¼ cup drained sun-dried tomatoes in oil, finely chopped

¼ cup freshly grated Parmesan cheese

2 tablespoons finely chopped fresh basil leaves

Extra-virgin olive oil, for garnish

Crackers or baguette, for serving (optional)

Place the ricotta in a medium serving bowl. Add the sun-dried tomatoes, Parmesan, and basil and stir to distribute evenly. Serve chilled or at room temperature, garnished with olive oil, with crackers and/or baguette.

Ricotta Spread with Sun-Dried Tomatoes and Basil will keep, in an airtight container in the refrigerator, for up to 2 days. Serve leftover spread chilled.

MORE FLAVORING AND SERVING IDEAS FOR DO-IT-YOURSELF RICOTTA

- Whip with mascarpone and add shavings of dark chocolate, instant espresso, sugar, and a dusting of ground cinnamon.

- Add dried fruits such as blueberries, chopped apricots, or dates.

- Drizzle with honey.

- Add orange zest and dried cranberries.

- Garnish with candied walnuts.

- Stir in flakes of dried vegetables (sometimes available in bulk for use in soups), which will soften once added.

- Stir in thawed, drained, and finely chopped frozen spinach, and season to taste with salt and freshly ground black pepper for use as a topping on pasta.

CRÈME FRAÎCHE

TOTAL TIME: 8 hours   **ACTIVE TIME:** 5 minutes   **YIELD:** 2 cups

Crème fraîche is sort of like French sour cream, but with a richer flavor that's less overtly sour and more nuanced. Spooned on a bowl of soup or dolloped on Simply Poached Pears (page 204) or fresh berries, it adds an almost nutty flavor and creaminess.

2 cups heavy (whipping) cream

2 tablespoons buttermilk (see Note)

1 Place the cream and buttermilk in the inner pot and stir to combine. Close and lock the lid. Set the valve to Venting. Attach the condensation collector. Press Yogurt and use the Yogurt or Adjust button to select the lowest temperature ("Less"). Use the – or + button to set the time to 8 hours.

2 When the cycle ends, press Cancel and remove the lid. Remove the inner pot. Spoon the crème fraîche into a container with a lid, cover it, and place it in the refrigerator to cool before using.

Crème Fraîche will keep, in an airtight container in the refrigerator, for up to 2 weeks.

Note: While it is often possible to make a buttermilk substitute by combining vinegar and milk, this is one time when you want real cultured buttermilk, because it contains the bacteria necessary to turn the cream into crème fraîche.

NO-KNEAD BREAD

TOTAL TIME: 6 hours 30 minutes   **ACTIVE TIME:** 10 minutes   **YIELD:** 1 loaf

Jim Lahey's no-knead bread went viral before going viral as we know it was a thing. People photocopied and passed along newspaper clippings. It was a phenomenon. Whether you remember the origins of the recipe or not, you may remember that it spawned a seemingly endless number of variations. That brings us to the Instant Pot.

Here's a fresh, hot, delicious loaf of bread that you can make in the Instant Pot. While it does not *cook* in the Instant Pot—no chance for it to get a beautiful, crispy crust in there—it does use the inner pot as a cooking vessel in the oven. (It might require a little scrubbing to get clean afterward. If you'd prefer less clean-up, line the inner pot with parchment paper before applying the nonstick cooking spray.) And though it does require several hours from start to finish, the active prep time clocks in at a mere 10 minutes.

While it is possible to use only unbleached all-purpose flour in this recipe, a mix of bread flour and white whole wheat flour (available at some specialty and health food stores) creates an unbeatable texture and flavor.

Nonstick cooking spray

2¼ cups bread flour, plus extra for sprinkling

1 cup white whole wheat flour

1½ teaspoons salt

1 teaspoon instant dry yeast

1 teaspoon sugar

1½ cups room temperature water, plus extra as needed

---

1 Coat the bottom and side of the inner pot generously with nonstick cooking spray.

2 Stir together the flours, salt, yeast, and sugar in a large bowl. Using a large spoon, stir in the 1½ cups of water until the dough no longer sticks to the sides of the bowl. The dough should look dry and shaggy. If there is loose flour, add an additional tablespoon of water and stir again.

3 Use the spoon or your hands to scrape the dough into the inner pot. Press the Yogurt button and use the Yogurt or Adjust button to select the middle temperature ("Normal"). Use the – or + button to set the time to 4½ hours. Close and lock the lid. Set the valve to Sealing.

4 When the countdown timer has 25 minutes remaining, preheat the oven to 450°F with an oven rack in the lower position.

5 Scatter about 1 tablespoon of flour on a work surface. Press Cancel and remove the inner pot from the Instant Pot. Taking care to deflate the dough as little as possible, gently remove the dough from the inner pot and place it on the floured surface. (A wet spatula can be used to gently pry the dough from the side of the pot.) Fold one side of the top edge of the dough to the center. Repeat around the edges, until you form a round loaf.

6 Coat the bottom and side of the inner pot with nonstick cooking spray. Gently place the loaf seam side down in the inner pot. Return the inner pot to the Instant Pot.

7 Press the Yogurt button and use the Yogurt or Adjust button to select the middle temperature ("Normal"). Use the – or + button to set the time to 1 hour. Close and lock the lid. Set the valve to Sealing.

8 Press Cancel. Remove the inner pot from the Instant Pot and tightly cover the top with aluminum foil. Bake in the center of the preheated oven for 35 minutes. Remove the foil and continue baking until the top of the loaf is dark golden brown, about 20 more minutes.

9 Using oven mitts and taking great care because the inner pot is very hot, remove the inner pot from the oven. Allow the inner pot to cool on a rack for 5 minutes before removing the bread from it. (Wear oven mitts when handling the still-hot inner pot. The bread may fall out on its own or it may require gentle prying with a spatula to come loose.) Allow the bread to cool on a rack until very slightly warm, about 30 minutes, before serving.

Note: Because this uses an oven, the usual Instant Pot rules for varying sizes don't apply. If using a 3-quart Instant Pot, halve the ingredients and keep the rising times the same. Bake with the foil on for 30 minutes. Bake with the foil off for 15 minutes. If using an 8-quart Instant Pot, bake first with the foil on for 40 minutes, then with the foil off for 25 minutes.

Tips: Before you start, make sure there is enough clearance in your oven for the inner pot to sit on the rack. It's much easier to move oven racks when cool.

Inner pot a bit dirty after baking? Use a non-abrasive powder cleanser such as Bar Keepers Friend to reclaim its shine.

SAVORY YOGURT

Maybe you tend to think of the sweet side of yogurt, but its tangy, bright flavor lends itself to savory preparations, too. Try it as a spicy dip (see below), serve it with cucumber as a refreshing counterpart to a hearty dish such as Fragrant Lamb and Chickpea Stew (page 49), or take it in an avocado-citrus direction (see page 238) for a smooth, creamy complement to raw vegetables.

1 SPICY YOGURT DIP

TOTAL TIME: 5 minutes
ACTIVE TIME: 5 minutes
YIELD: Makes about 2 cups

2 cups Whole-Milk Yogurt (page 226) or 2% Greek Yogurt (page 227)

1 teaspoon chili powder

1 teaspoon ground cumin

1/2 cup chopped fresh Italian (flat-leaf) parsley leaves

Finely grated zest of 1 small lime

1/2 teaspoon salt, plus extra as needed

1/4 teaspoon freshly ground black pepper, plus extra as needed

Pinch of cayenne pepper, plus extra as needed

Crackers and/or crudités, for serving

Stir together the yogurt, chili powder, cumin, parsley, lime zest, salt, pepper, and cayenne pepper in a medium serving bowl. Taste and adjust the seasoning, adding more salt, pepper, and cayenne pepper as needed. Serve chilled with crackers and/or crudités.

Spicy Yogurt Dip will keep, in an airtight container in the refrigerator, for up to 2 days.

② CUCUMBER YOGURT SAUCE ⓥ ⓧ2 ㉚

TOTAL TIME: 5 minutes

ACTIVE TIME: 5 minutes

YIELD: Makes about 2 cups

1½ cups Whole Milk Yogurt (page 226) or 2% Greek Yogurt (page 227)

½ medium English cucumber, peeled, quartered, and sliced ¼ inch thick

1 tablespoon finely chopped fresh Italian (flat-leaf) parsley leaves

1 small clove garlic, finely chopped

¼ teaspoon ground cumin

¼ teaspoon salt, plus extra as needed

¼ teaspoon freshly ground black pepper, plus extra as needed

Stir together the yogurt, cucumber, parsley, garlic, cumin, salt, and pepper in a medium serving bowl. Taste and adjust the seasoning, adding more salt and pepper as needed. Serve chilled.

Cucumber Yogurt Sauce will keep, in an airtight container in the refrigerator, for up to 2 days.

MORE FLAVORING AND SERVING IDEAS FOR SAVORY YOGURT

Stir in . . .
- Chopped toasted walnuts

- Finely chopped fresh chives

- Finely chopped fresh mint

- Toasted pumpkin seeds (pepitas)

- Finely chopped jalapeño

- White or yellow miso paste and finely chopped scallions

- Finely chopped preserved lemon and fresh dill

- Finely chopped shallots and extra-virgin olive oil

- Chopped sun-dried tomatoes, finely chopped fresh basil, and freshly ground black pepper

③ ZIPPY AVOCADO-YOGURT DIP Ⓥ ⓧ2 ㉚

TOTAL TIME: 10 minutes

ACTIVE TIME: 10 minutes

YIELD: Makes about 1 cup

---

1 large avocado, pitted, peeled, and cut into chunks

¼ cup freshly squeezed lime juice, plus extra as needed

½ cup Whole Milk Yogurt (page 226) or 2% Greek Yogurt (page 227)

Finely grated zest and juice of 1 medium orange

1 medium shallot, finely chopped

¼ teaspoon salt, plus extra as needed

¼ teaspoon freshly ground black pepper, plus extra as needed

Small bunch fresh cilantro, large stems removed, finely chopped

Crudités, for serving

Combine the avocado, lime juice, yogurt, orange zest, orange juice, shallot, salt, pepper, and cilantro in a blender or food processor and pulse until smooth. Taste and adjust the seasoning, adding more salt and pepper as needed. Transfer to a medium bowl and serve with crudités for dipping.

Zippy Avocado-Yogurt Dip is best served when freshly made.

SWEETENED YOGURT

Commercially made yogurt can be overpoweringly sweet, and even the ones that aren't often contain quite a bit of sugar to overcome yogurt's natural tang. So now that you have a yogurt maker—thank you, Instant Pot—it's time to look at making homemade sweetened yogurt. These recipes give store-bought versions a run for their money. Make a simple vanilla syrup that works as a stir-in (see below), swirl in fruit jam (see page 240), or try dried fruit and nuts (see page 240). All help rescue your homemade yogurt—and you—from cloyingly sweet commercial territory.

① YOGURT WITH VANILLA SYRUP

V · X2 · 30

TOTAL TIME: 10 minutes

ACTIVE TIME: 10 minutes

YIELD: Makes about 1½ cups syrup
(enough to flavor about 36 servings of yogurt)

1 cup water

1 cup sugar

2 teaspoons pure vanilla extract

1 whole vanilla bean, split lengthwise

Homemade Plain Yogurt (any percentage of milkfat, see pages 226–228), for serving

1 Place the water, sugar, and vanilla extract in the inner pot and stir to combine.

2 Use a dull knife to scrape the vanilla seeds into the inner pot. Add the scraped vanilla bean as well and stir until the vanilla seeds are evenly distributed.

3 Press Sauté and use the Sauté or Adjust button to select the middle temperature ("Normal"). Cook with the lid off, stirring frequently, until the sugar has dissolved. The liquid will bubble gently at first and then vigorously. Cook until no sugar is visible and the liquid is slightly reduced, about 10 minutes.

4 Press Cancel. Wearing oven mitts, remove the inner pot (be careful—it's hot!) and place it on a trivet or other heat-resistant surface. Use a fork or tongs to remove the vanilla bean, and pour the syrup into a container with a cover.

5 Stir 2 teaspoons of syrup into each ½ cup of yogurt, taste, and then add more syrup if necessary.

Vanilla Syrup will keep, in an airtight container in the refrigerator, for up to 3 weeks (once stirred into the yogurt, the yogurt will keep for up to 2 weeks).

❷ YOGURT WITH FRUIT SWIRL V X2 30

TOTAL TIME: 5 minutes
ACTIVE TIME: 5 minutes
YIELD: Serves 1

½ cup Homemade Plain Yogurt (any percentage of milkfat, see pages 226–228)

1 tablespoon Blueberry Jam (page 201), Apricot-Vanilla Compote (page 206), or store-bought jam, plus extra as needed

Dash of ground cinnamon, for garnish

Place the yogurt in a serving bowl, add the jam, and stir to swirl. Taste and add more jam as needed. Garnish with a dash of cinnamon before serving.

Yogurt with Fruit Swirl will keep, in an airtight container in the refrigerator, for up to 2 weeks.

❸ YOGURT WITH DRIED CHERRIES AND ALMONDS V X2 30

TOTAL TIME: 5 minutes
ACTIVE TIME: 5 minutes
YIELD: Serves 1

½ cup Homemade Plain Yogurt (any percentage of milkfat, see pages 226–228)

2 tablespoons dried cherries, plus extra as needed

2 tablespoons slivered almonds, plus extra as needed

Finely grated orange zest, for garnish

Place the yogurt in a serving bowl and stir in the cherries and almonds. Taste and add more as needed. Garnish with orange zest before serving.

Yogurt with Dried Cherries and Almonds will keep, in an airtight container in the refrigerator, for up to 2 weeks.

Clockwise from bottom: Yogurt with Fruit Swirl, Yogurt with Vanilla Syrup, Yogurt with Dried Cherries and Almonds

MORE FLAVORING AND SERVING IDEAS FOR SWEETENED YOGURT

Stir in . . .

- Honey

- Maple syrup and blueberries (frozen berries when not in season)

- Sliced bananas

- Toasted wheat germ and sliced peaches (fresh or frozen)

- Raisins and walnuts

- Breakfast cereal

- Rainbow sprinkles (Okay, chocolate sprinkles work, too.)

- Vanilla extract and finely grated lemon zest

- Granola

- Crumbled graham crackers

- Chopped pineapple or mango

- Honey and pulp from fresh passion fruit

- Crumbled chocolate sandwich cookies or vanilla wafers

- Cooked steel-cut oats

- Almond butter and a dusting of ground cinnamon

- Chocolate chips

- Lemon curd

- Grape jelly and roasted, salted peanuts

- Chopped dates and finely grated orange zest

MANGO AND POMEGRANATE PARFAITS

TOTAL TIME: 5 minutes   **ACTIVE TIME:** 5 minutes   **YIELD:** Serves 4

Mango and pomegranate are brilliantly colored fruits here beautifully matched with a white backdrop of yogurt and lightly sweetened with honey. To save some labor, look for precut mangoes and seeded pomegranate in the refrigerated case of your supermarket's produce section.

3 cups 2% Greek Yogurt (page 227)

¼ cup honey

3 cups cubed mango (from about 4 medium mangoes; see Note, below, and box on page 245)

1 cup pomegranate seeds (from about 2 medium pomegranates; see box, page 245)

Divide half of the yogurt among four 12-ounce glasses. Drizzle half of the honey over the yogurt in the glasses, then top with half of the mango, dividing it evenly. Top with the remaining yogurt, add the remaining mango, drizzle with the remaining honey, and finish with a sprinkling of pomegranate seeds.

Mango and Pomegranate Parfaits are best served the day they are made. They can be made ahead of time and stored, covered with plastic wrap in the refrigerator, for up to 8 hours.

Note: While Tommy Atkins mangoes with their red-blushed green skin are the most readily available variety, yellow Ataulfo mangoes are sweeter, with less-fibrous flesh, and worth seeking out.

PEELING AND PITTING

To cube a mango: Stand it tall on one end with the narrowest part of the fruit facing you. Use a chef's knife to cut along one flatter side of the fruit, as close to the flat, oval pit as possible. If your knife hits immediate resistance, you likely need to rotate the fruit 90 degrees and try again.

If your knife faces resistance as you cut down into the fruit, lift up the knife, move it farther away from the pit, and try again. Do the same to the other side; you will have two rounded halves. (Some flesh will remain clinging to the pit. This is best enjoyed out-of-hand as a reward for the chef.)

Next, score the flesh: Place a mango half round-side down on a flat surface and use a paring knife to score the flesh in a ½-inch grid, being careful not to cut through the skin. Turn the mango half inside out so the cubes stand out from the skin, then cut the fruit away from the skin with a paring knife. Use the cut mango immediately or store, in an airtight container in the refrigerator, for up to 2 days.

To prepare a pomegranate: Cut off the top and bottom ends. Using a sharp knife, score the fruit from top to bottom, cutting about ½ inch into the flesh and trying to avoid any seeds. Repeat 3 more times around the fruit to score it into quarters. Submerge the fruit in a large bowl of tepid water and, holding the pomegranate underwater, tear the fruit at the score marks to break it into sections and expose the seeds. Use your fingers to comb through the sections and release the seeds. They will sink to the bottom of the bowl; everything else will float. Use the seeds immediately or store, in an airtight container in the refrigerator, for up to 2 days.

HAVE YOGURT, WILL TRAVEL

Looking at a supermarket's massive yogurt assortment, it's hard to believe this dairy product is a relative newcomer to North America. Once mostly a food for immigrants in the know, yogurt didn't win mass acceptance and market share in the United States until the 1950s.

Despite its relatively recent introduction here, yogurt is a very old food. Its origins in the Middle East and Central Asia stretch back thousands of years. Yogurt may have emerged by chance—all it would take would be raw milk sitting in a warm area with the right kind of bacteria. But what a happy accident: Turning milk into yogurt allowed it to resist spoilage. This meant that milk's nutrition could now travel farther and feed more people, laying the foundation for population growth and territorial expansion. (Cheese—that other product of milk and bacteria—offered the same advantages.)

Now, we look to yogurt more for meals or snacks than for food preservation. More than 80 percent of US households buy yogurt, and US yogurt consumption has increased more than 400 percent in the last three decades. Lately, Greek yogurt has driven much of yogurt's sales growth, helping drive national yogurt sales to almost $8 billion per year.

Yogurt has come a long way—from early nomadic shepherds to a multibillion-dollar industry. And now to your Instant Pot.

Chapter 6
STEAMER

n what seems like a former lifetime—before the Great Kitchen Appliance Sell-Off of 2004—I owned a steamer. I liked it and used it, but ultimately not enough to justify the four-piece ensemble that jangled around in my cabinet. The Instant Pot beats the steamer if only because it does not present the same crisis of cabinet space. As with other aspects of the Instant Pot, it helps to understand what's going on with the Steam function to know its limitations and strengths.

WHAT'S DIFFERENT ABOUT THE STEAMING CYCLE?

While steaming on the stovetop also involves placing food over boiling water, the Instant Pot is different in that the steam is sealed under pressure. Combining this cooking method with delicate food such as vegetables and seafood means that the cooking time is set to practically nothing, sometimes as little as 1 minute—or zero minutes, as you will see in some of the recipes.

The Instant Pot's steaming cycle works a little differently from its other cycles. To generate the steam, the Instant Pot heats continuously at full power until it comes to pressure. This nonstop, intense heat is why a steaming rack must be used to raise the food off the bottom of the inner pot (more about that in a minute). The steaming rack avoids the burning that could occur with such intense heat. Once the steam cycle reaches pressure, the Instant Pot regulates pressure and heat by cycling on and off as usual.

Now, about that steaming rack: Two pieces of equipment help steam food effectively in the Instant Pot:

- **Stainless steel steaming rack:** This is typically included with the Instant Pot. It sits on the bottom of the inner pot and supports a steaming basket.

- **Steaming basket:** Some foods can be steamed directly on the included steaming rack, but many smaller foods will fall through the slats. A basket also makes it easier to remove food at the end of the steaming cycle. Although a basket is not included with the pot, one can be purchased readily online. Silicone is my material of choice here because it is flexible and dishwasher safe. (I'm a fan of the one made by OXO.)

VALVE POSITION AND QUICK RELEASE

For all steaming, the valve should be set to Sealing. This ensures that the Instant Pot maintains pressure as it steams.

Because vegetables and seafood cook so quickly with high-pressure steam, a quick release is recommended in all cases, since the extra time taken by a natural release could significantly increase the cooking time (see Natural Release vs. Quick Release, page 26).

OTHER USES FOR THE STEAM FUNCTION

- You can use a little water and the Steam function to clean the Instant Pot before the first use (see Setting Up Your Pot, page 5).

- If you make yogurt in individual containers, use the Steam function to scald the milk (see Making Yogurt in Containers, page 223).

LEMON-THYME STEAMED SHRIMP

TOTAL TIME: 15 minutes   **ACTIVE TIME:** 5 minutes   **YIELD:** Serves 4

A recipe that takes frozen shrimp and turns them into dinner quickly? Yes, please. The risk of making seafood in the Instant Pot can be overcooking it; things happen so quickly in there. But starting with frozen shrimp that have their shells still on offers them a little protection from the heat and yields perfectly cooked shrimp.

---

1 cup water

2 medium lemons, thinly sliced

2 sprigs fresh thyme, plus extra for garnish

1 bag (1 pound) frozen 16- to 20-count shrimp, peels on

Salted butter, melted, for serving

---

1 Pour the water into the inner pot and add the lemons and sprigs of thyme, reserving a few lemon slices for garnish. Place the steaming rack on the bottom of the inner pot, then place a steaming basket on top of the rack and place the shrimp inside the basket.

2 Close and lock the lid. Set the valve to Sealing. Press Steam and use the − or + button to set the time to 1 minute.

3 When the cooking cycle ends, carefully use a wooden spoon to release the pressure by turning the pressure-release valve to Venting. (The pressure is released when the small metal float valve next to the pressure-release valve sinks back into the lid and the lid is no longer locked.)

4 Press Cancel and remove the lid. Wearing oven mitts, remove the bowl from the inner pot (be careful—it's hot!) and pour the shrimp into a serving bowl. Garnish with the reserved lemon slices and thyme and serve warm, with melted butter.

Lemon-Thyme Steamed Shrimp will keep, in an airtight container in the refrigerator, for up to 2 days. Serve leftovers chilled.

SWEET POTATOES WITH PARSLEY AND BALSAMIC VINEGAR

TOTAL TIME: 20 minutes   **ACTIVE TIME:** 5 minutes   **YIELD:** Serves 4   V

The vinegar and fresh parsley in this dish provide a bright contrast to the sweet potatoes. The simple sauce combines the sweet tang of balsamic vinegar and the luxuriously rich finish of butter. Cooking the sweet potatoes in the Instant Pot and then finishing them with the sauce in the same pot brings everything together quickly and saves on dishes.

1 cup water

3 medium sweet potatoes (about 1½ pounds), peeled and cut into 1-inch cubes

¼ cup balsamic vinegar

1 tablespoon packed brown sugar

¼ cup (½ stick) unsalted butter

1 teaspoon salt

¼ teaspoon freshly ground black pepper

1 small bunch fresh Italian (flat-leaf) parsley, large stems removed, chopped

1 Place the steaming rack on the bottom of the inner pot and pour the water into the inner pot. Place a steaming basket on top of the rack and then place the sweet potatoes inside the basket.

2 Close and lock the lid. Set the valve to Sealing. Press Steam and use the – or + button to set the time to 2 minutes.

3 When the cooking cycle ends, carefully use a wooden spoon to release the pressure by turning the pressure-release valve to Venting. (The pressure is released when the small metal float valve next to the pressure-release valve sinks back into the lid and the lid is no longer locked.)

4 Remove the lid. Wearing oven mitts, remove the steaming basket from the inner pot (be careful—it's hot!), and set it aside on a trivet or other heat-resistant surface until step 7.

5 Wearing oven mitts, empty the water from the inner pot, remove the steaming rack, and then return the inner pot to the appliance. Press Cancel, then press Sauté and use the Adjust button to select the middle temperature ("Normal"). Place the balsamic vinegar and brown sugar in the inner pot. Cook with the lid off, stirring until the sugar dissolves and the liquid comes to a boil, about 1 minute.

6 Press Cancel, then press Sauté and use the Adjust button to select the lowest temperature ("Less"). Simmer the liquid with the lid off until it thickens slightly,

about 3 minutes. Add the butter, salt, and pepper to the inner pot and stir until the butter melts, about 1 minute.

7 Press Cancel, then add the potato pieces to the inner pot and toss to coat them. Add the parsley, reserving a handful for garnish, and stir until it just starts to wilt, about 1 minute.

8 Spoon the sweet potatoes into a serving bowl and serve hot, garnished with the reserved parsley.

Sweet Potatoes with Parsley and Balsamic Vinegar will keep, in an airtight container in the refrigerator, for up to 5 days. To reheat, place the sweet potatoes in a pot, add a splash of water, and cover. Warm on the stovetop over medium-low heat, stirring occasionally, for about 5 minutes.

MASHED CAULIFLOWER WITH GARLIC AND CREAM CHEESE

TOTAL TIME: 25 minutes   **ACTIVE TIME:** 5 minutes   **YIELD:** Serves 4   V

I'm not here to trick people into eating their vegetables. I'll merely point out that steaming cauliflower in the Instant Pot and then mashing it turns it into something that could pass for mashed potatoes, in this case a delicious creamy and garlicky version.

---

1 cup water

1 medium head cauliflower (about 1½ pounds), cut into small pieces

4 cloves garlic, unpeeled

2 tablespoons cream cheese, at room temperature

½ teaspoon salt

¼ teaspoon freshly ground black pepper

Salted butter, for serving

Chopped fresh chives, for garnish

---

1 Place the steaming rack on the bottom of the inner pot and pour the water into the inner pot. Place a steaming basket on top of the rack, then place the cauliflower and garlic inside the basket.

2 Close and lock the lid. Set the valve to Sealing. Press Steam and use the – or + button to set the time to 10 minutes.

3 When the cooking cycle ends, carefully use a wooden spoon to release the pressure by turning the pressure-release valve to Venting. (The pressure is released when the small metal float valve next to the pressure-release valve sinks back into the lid and the lid is no longer locked.)

4 Press Cancel and remove the lid. Wearing oven mitts, remove the steaming basket from the inner pot (be careful—it's hot!), and place it on a trivet or other heat-resistant surface.

5 Use a kitchen towel or paper towels to blot the cauliflower dry. Peel the garlic.

6 Place the cauliflower, garlic, cream cheese, salt, and pepper in a large serving bowl. Use a potato masher to smash the cauliflower and combine thoroughly.

7 Serve hot, topped with butter and chives.

Mashed Cauliflower with Garlic and Cream Cheese will keep, in an airtight container in the refrigerator, for up to 3 days. To reheat, place the cauliflower in a pot, add a splash of water, and cover. Warm on the stovetop over medium-low heat, stirring occasionally, for about 5 minutes.

CORN ON THE COB WITH GOCHUJANG BUTTER

TOTAL TIME: 15 minutes   **ACTIVE TIME:** 5 minutes   **YIELD:** Serves 4

Gochujang is a salty, spicy Korean condiment that lasts for eons in the refrigerator and comes in handy for brightening up soups, stir-fries, and just about anything else that needs a little savory punch. Here it livens up butter, already such a natural complement to corn. While fresh corn is often available for months in the supermarket, in many areas its flavor peaks at the height of summer. Try leftover Gochujang Butter on steamed vegetables such as Simply Steamed Baby Carrots (page 260).

½ cup (1 stick) unsalted butter,
   at room temperature

1 tablespoon gochujang chile paste, plus extra
   as needed (see Note)

2 teaspoons toasted sesame oil

1 cup water

4 ears fresh corn, shucked and cobs trimmed
   (see Note on page 170)

Chopped scallions, for garnish (optional)

1 Make the Gochujang Butter: Use an electric mixer to beat together the butter, gochujang, and sesame oil in a medium bowl until well combined. Set aside until step 6.

2 Place the steaming rack on the bottom of the inner pot and pour the water into the inner pot. Place a steaming basket on top of the rack and then place the corn inside the basket. (Large cobs can be cut in half, if necessary, to fit in the inner pot.)

3 Close and lock the lid. Set the valve to Sealing. Press Steam and use the − or + button to set the time to 2 minutes.

4 When the cooking cycle ends, carefully use a wooden spoon to release the pressure by turning the pressure-release valve to Venting. (The pressure is released when the small metal float valve next to the pressure-release valve sinks back into the lid and the lid is no longer locked.)

5 Press Cancel and remove the lid. Use tongs to remove the corn from the steaming basket.

6 Serve the corn hot, slathered in Gochujang Butter and garnished with scallions.

Corn on the Cob is best eaten the day it is prepared.

Gochujang Butter will keep, in an airtight container in the refrigerator, for up to 2 weeks.

Note: Gochujang is available in the Asian foods aisle of many supermarkets. If you can't find it, substitute another garlic-chile sauce, such as sriracha. Because heat levels can vary, use just 1 teaspoon at first and taste before adding more a little at a time.

SIMPLY STEAMED BABY CARROTS

1·2·3

Baby-cut carrots come prewashed and ready to go, no small thing when it comes to putting dinner on the table. Steaming the carrots in the Instant Pot turns them into a quick and appealing side dish, one that can take at least three delicious turns: Serve them with the briny tang of preserved lemon and feta (see page 261), mash them with a generous amount of butter and chives (see page 261), or top them with a sesame-based dressing (see page 261).

Master Method

V VN DF X2 30

TOTAL TIME: 15 minutes
ACTIVE TIME: 5 minutes
YIELD: Serves 4

1 cup water

1 pound baby-cut carrots

1 Place the steaming rack on the bottom of the inner pot and pour the water into the inner pot. Place a steaming basket on top of the rack and then place the carrots inside the basket.

2 Close and lock the lid. Set the valve to Sealing. Press Steam and use the − or + button to set the time to 0 minutes. (Yes, zero minutes. Things happen fast in the Instant Pot.)

3 When the cooking cycle ends, carefully use a wooden spoon to release the pressure by turning the pressure-release valve to Venting. (The pressure is released when the small metal float valve next to the pressure-release valve sinks back into the lid and the lid is no longer locked.)

4 Press Cancel and remove the lid. Wearing oven mitts, remove the steaming basket from the inner pot (be careful—it's hot!) and pour the carrots into a serving bowl. Serve the carrots hot.

Simply Steamed Baby Carrots will keep, in an airtight container in the refrigerator, for up to 3 days. To reheat, place the carrots in a small pot, add a splash of water, and cover. Warm on the stovetop over medium heat, for 5 minutes. Drain the carrots through a colander and serve hot.

❶ CARROT MASH WITH BUTTER AND CHIVES

`V` `X2` `30`

TOTAL TIME: 15 minutes

ACTIVE TIME: 5 minutes

YIELD: Serves 4

Increase the cooking time to 5 minutes. When the carrots are cooked, place them in a medium serving bowl with 1/4 cup (1/2 stick) salted butter, cut into chunks, and 1 small bunch of fresh chives, chopped fine. Use a potato masher to smash the carrots until mostly smooth and combined with the butter and chives.

❷ BABY CARROTS WITH TAHINI DRESSING

`V` `VN` `DF` `X2` `30`

TOTAL TIME: 15 minutes

ACTIVE TIME: 5 minutes

YIELD: Serves 4

While the carrots steam, make the dressing: Combine 1/3 cup tahini (sesame paste), 1/4 cup water, 1/4 cup freshly squeezed lemon juice, 1/2 teaspoon salt, and 1/2 teaspoon sugar in a small bowl. Use a fork or a small whisk to beat until combined and then drizzle over the hot carrots.

❸ BABY CARROTS WITH PRESERVED LEMON AND FETA `V` `X2` `30`

TOTAL TIME: 15 minutes

ACTIVE TIME: 5 minutes

YIELD: Serves 4

Rinse 1 small preserved lemon well (see Note, page 262), chop it finely, and remove the seeds. In a medium serving bowl, toss the cooked carrots with the preserved lemon and 1/2 cup (about 2 ounces) crumbled feta cheese. Garnish with fresh parsley leaves.

Note: Preserved lemons are lemons that have been prepared with salt and water and then sealed in a glass jar. They are not the same as lemon marmalade or lemon curd, both of which are much sweeter than the pleasantly puckery, briny flavor of preserved lemons. Preserved lemons can often be found in specialty food stores, Middle Eastern markets, and in well-stocked supermarkets, typically near the olives and capers.

MORE FLAVORING AND SERVING IDEAS FOR SIMPLY STEAMED BABY CARROTS

- A sprinkle of brown sugar on hot baby carrots goes a long way toward highlighting their natural sweetness. The same goes for a drizzle of maple syrup.

- Nuts such as slivered almonds or chopped walnuts add a bit of visual and textural contrast, as well as flavor.

- Generously coat the cooked baby carrots with a vinaigrette made of 3 parts extra-virgin olive oil and 1 part vinegar along with a little bit of Dijon mustard.

- Sprinkle a flaky, crunchy salt such as Maldon sea salt over the cooked baby carrots just before serving.

- Finely chop Italian (flat-leaf) parsley, dill, or cilantro, large stems removed, and toss the cooked baby carrots with the herbs just before serving.

- Add some zip to the cooked baby carrots by passing around your favorite hot sauce at the table.

- A dollop of Crème Fraîche (page 233) atop the cooked baby carrots adds a tangy touch.

- In step 1 add finely grated orange zest to the water in the inner pot and splash some of the liquid over the baby carrots before serving.

- Place 2 sprigs fresh rosemary in the water below the steaming basket. After opening the lid, remove the rosemary with tongs. Serve carrots hot, garnished with additional fresh rosemary.

MIXED VEGETABLES

1·2·3

With this master recipe in your corner, you can take dinner in quite a few different directions. A zippy, citrusy butter takes ordinary vegetables and elevates them a few notches (see page 265). Try "steam-roasting" garlic with the vegetables and then mashing it and tossing it with them for a garlicky, subtly sweet complement (see page 265). Or add extra virgin olive oil and almonds for a rich flavor with a bit of satisfying crunch (see page 265). Be sure to cut the carrots and broccoli into chunks roughly the same size to ensure even cooking.

Master Method

 V VN DF 30

TOTAL TIME: 15 minutes
ACTIVE TIME: 5 minutes
YIELD: Serves 6

1 cup water

1 pound broccoli, trimmed, stalks and florets cut into large bite-size chunks

1 pound carrots, peeled, cut into large bite-size chunks

1 Place the steaming rack on the bottom of the inner pot and pour the water into the inner pot. Place a steaming basket on top of the rack and then place the vegetables inside the basket.

2 Close and lock the lid. Set the valve to Sealing. Press Steam and use the − or + button to set the time to 0 minutes. (Yes, zero minutes. Things happen fast in the Instant Pot.)

3 When the cooking cycle ends, carefully use a wooden spoon to release the pressure by turning the pressure-release valve to Venting. (The pressure is released when the small metal float valve next to the pressure-release valve sinks back into the lid and the lid is no longer locked.)

4 Press Cancel and remove the lid. Wearing oven mitts, remove the basket from the inner pot (be careful—it's hot!). Spoon the vegetables into a serving bowl. Serve the vegetables hot.

Clockwise from right: Mixed Vegetables with Spicy Lime Butter,
Mixed Vegetables with Garlic, Mixed Vegetables with Olive Oil and Almonds

Mixed Vegetables will keep, in an airtight container in the refrigerator, for up to 2 days. To reheat, place them in a small pot, add water to a depth of 1/2 inch, and warm on the stovetop over medium-low heat, stirring occasionally, for about 5 minutes.

1 MIXED VEGETABLES WITH SPICY LIME BUTTER V 30

TOTAL TIME: 15 minutes
ACTIVE TIME: 10 minutes
YIELD: Serves 6

While the vegetables cook, use an electric mixer to beat together 1/2 cup (1 stick) room-temperature salted butter, 1/4 teaspoon cayenne pepper, and the finely grated zest of 2 medium limes in a medium bowl until well combined. Toss the cooked vegetables with about half of the Spicy Lime Butter and serve hot with more Spicy Lime Butter at the table.

Spicy Lime Butter will keep, in an airtight container in the refrigerator, for up to 2 weeks.

2 MIXED VEGETABLES WITH OLIVE OIL AND ALMONDS V VN DF 30

TOTAL TIME: 15 minutes
ACTIVE TIME: 5 minutes
YIELD: Serves 6

Toss the cooked vegetables with 1/4 cup extra-virgin olive oil, 1/2 cup slivered almonds, and 1/2 teaspoon salt. Serve hot.

3 MIXED VEGETABLES WITH GARLIC V VN DF 30

TOTAL TIME: 15 minutes
ACTIVE TIME: 10 minutes
YIELD: Serves 6

Place 8 cloves unpeeled garlic in the steaming basket with the vegetables. When the vegetables are cooked, wait for the garlic to cool slightly, about 2 minutes, and then squeeze the garlic from its skin into a large serving bowl. Use a fork to mash the garlic with 1/4 cup extra-virgin olive oil and 1/2 teaspoon salt. Toss the vegetables in the serving bowl with the mashed garlic until well coated. Top with shaved Parmesan cheese. Serve hot.

MORE FLAVORING AND SERVING IDEAS FOR MIXED VEGETABLES

- Spritz the cooked vegetables with fresh lemon juice.

- Toss the cooked vegetables with freshly grated ginger.

- Finely chop an anchovy and toss the cooked vegetables with the chopped anchovy, crushed red pepper flakes, and drained pickled capers. To turn it into a main course, toss these vegetables with cooked pasta and olive oil or chopped, cooked chicken breast and olive oil.

- Toss the cooked vegetables with crumbled feta cheese.

- Toss the cooked vegetables with chopped fresh Italian (flat-leaf) parsley and a healthy splash of balsamic vinegar.

- Toss the cooked vegetables with freshly grated Parmesan cheese.

- Toss the cooked vegetables with toasted sesame oil, a pinch of salt, and toasted sesame seeds.

CONVERSION TABLES

APPROXIMATE EQUIVALENTS

1 STICK BUTTER = 8 tbs = 4 oz = ½ cup = 115 g

1 CUP ALL-PURPOSE PRESIFTED FLOUR = 4.7 oz

1 CUP GRANULATED SUGAR = 8 oz = 220 g

1 CUP (FIRMLY PACKED) BROWN SUGAR = 6 oz = 176 g

1 CUP CONFECTIONERS' SUGAR = 4½ oz = 115 g

1 CUP HONEY OR SYRUP = 12 oz

1 CUP GRATED CHEESE = 4 oz

1 CUP DRIED BEANS = 6 oz

1 LARGE EGG = about 2 oz or about 3 tbs

1 EGG YOLK = about 1 tbs

1 EGG WHITE = about 2 tbs

Please note that all conversions are approximate but close enough to be useful when converting from one system to another.

WEIGHT CONVERSIONS

US/UK	METRIC	US/UK	METRIC
½ oz	15 g	7 oz	200 g
1 oz	30 g	8 oz	250 g
1½ oz	45 g	9 oz	275 g
2 oz	60 g	10 oz	300 g
2½ oz	75 g	11 oz	325 g
3 oz	90 g	12 oz	350 g
3½ oz	100 g	13 oz	375 g
4 oz	125 g	14 oz	400 g
5 oz	150 g	15 oz	450 g
6 oz	175 g	1 lb	500 g

LIQUID CONVERSIONS

US	IMPERIAL	METRIC
2 tbs	1 fl oz	30 ml
3 tbs	1½ fl oz	45 ml
¼ cup	2 fl oz	60 ml
⅓ cup	2½ fl oz	75 ml
⅓ cup + 1 tbs	3 fl oz	90 ml
⅓ cup + 2 tbs	3½ fl oz	100 ml
½ cup	4 fl oz	125 ml
⅔ cup	5 fl oz	150 ml
¾ cup	6 fl oz	175 ml
¾ cup + 2 tbs	7 fl oz	200 ml
1 cup	8 fl oz	250 ml
1 cup + 2 tbs	9 fl oz	275 ml
1¼ cups	10 fl oz	300 ml
1⅓ cups	11 fl oz	325 ml
1½ cups	12 fl oz	350 ml
1⅔ cups	13 fl oz	375 ml
1¾ cups	14 fl oz	400 ml
1¾ cups + 2 tbs	15 fl oz	450 ml
2 cups (1 pint)	16 fl oz	500 ml
2½ cups	20 fl oz (1 pint)	600 ml
3¾ cups	1½ pints	900 ml
4 cups	1¾ pints	1 liter

OVEN TEMPERATURES

°F	GAS MARK	°C	°F	GAS MARK	°C
250	½	120	400	6	200
275	1	140	425	7	220
300	2	150	450	8	230
325	3	160	475	9	240
350	4	180	500	10	260
375	5	190			

Note: Reduce the temperature by 68°F (20°C) for fan-assisted ovens.

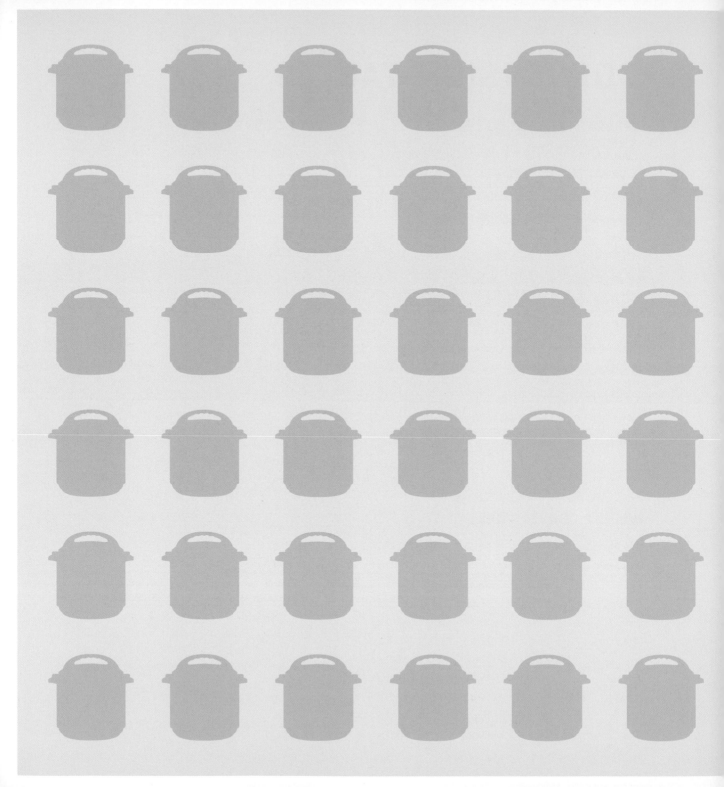

GENERAL PRESSURE-COOKING TIMES

As you start on your own Instant Pot adventures, use this table and these notes to help set cooking times. These numbers are guidelines, not hard-and-fast rules. They will set you on the right path, but as you gain more practice, trust your experience and intuition.

Vegetables: Things happen quickly in the Instant Pot and you don't want to overcook your vegetables. Dense, starchy vegetables such as potatoes will take longer to cook than soft vegetables that contain a lot of water, such as zucchini. Start at the low end of the cooking time and reseal the Instant Pot to cook further if necessary.

Grains: For foods such as oats—which don't remain distinct grains when cooked—use the Natural Release method. Using the Quick Release method can send wet grains shooting up through the release valve, gunking up the works.

Beans and Legumes: Because cooking times can vary depending on the freshness or variety of the bean or legume, take notes on which timing works for you. As with vegetables, start at the low end of the cooking time and increase as needed.

Meat: Health authorities recommend cooking meats to certain minimum temperatures (165°F for all poultry; 160°F for ground meat; 145°F plus three minutes of resting for beef, pork, and lamb. Consult USDA guidelines for a full list). Reaching those temperatures with the Instant Pot happens far faster than in an oven. To determine the temperature, plunge an instant-read thermometer into the thickest part of the meat. Because the Instant Pot cooks from the outside in, taking the temperature of the innermost part is essential, particularly if starting with frozen meat.

VEGETABLES	FRESH, COOKING TIME (IN MINUTES)	FROZEN, COOKING TIME (IN MINUTES)
Artichoke, hearts, medium	4–5	5–6
Artichoke, whole, medium	9–11	11–13
Asparagus, whole or pieces	1–2	2–3
Beans, green/yellow or wax, whole	1–2	2–3
Beets, whole	11–13 (small), 20–25 (large)	13–15 (small), 25–30 (large)
Bell pepper, slices or chunks	1–3	2–4
Broccoli, florets	2–3	3–4
Brussels sprouts, whole	3–4	4–5
Cabbage, red, purple, or green, shredded	2–3	3–4
Cabbage, red, purple, or green, wedges	3–4	4–5

VEGETABLES	FRESH, COOKING TIME (IN MINUTES)	FROZEN, COOKING TIME (IN MINUTES)
Carrots, sliced or shredded	1–2	2–3
Carrots, whole or chunked	2–3	3–4
Cauliflower, florets	2–3	3–4
Celery, chunks	2–3	3–4
Corn, on the cob	3–4	4–5
Corn, kernels	1–2	2–3
Eggplant, slices or chunks	2–3	3–4
Escarole, chopped	1–2	2–3
Greens (beet greens, collards, kale, spinach, Swiss chard, turnip greens), chopped	3–6	4–7
Leeks	2–4	3–5
Mixed vegetables	2–3	3–4
Okra	2–3	3–4
Onions, sliced	2–3	3–4
Parsnips, chunks	2–4	4–6
Parsnips, sliced	1–2	2–3
Peas, green	1–2	2–3
Peas, in the pod	1–2	2–3
Potatoes, cubed	7–9	9–11
Potatoes, whole, baby	10–12	n/a
Potatoes, whole, large	12–15	n/a
Pumpkin, large slices or chunks	8–10	10–14
Pumpkin, small slices or chunks	4–5	6–7
Rutabaga, chunks	4–6	6–8
Rutabaga, slices	3–5	4–6
Sweet potato or yam, cubed	7–9	9–11
Sweet potato or yam, whole	10–12 (small), 12–15 (large)	12–14 (small), 15–19 (large)
Turnip, chunks	2–4	4–6
Winter squash, acorn, slices or chunks	6–7	8–9
Winter squash, butternut, slices or chunks	8–10	10–12
Zucchini or summer squash, slices or chunks	2–3	3–4

RICE & GRAINS	WATER QUANTITY (GRAIN: WATER RATIOS)	COOKING TIME (IN MINUTES)
Barley, pearl	1:4	25–30
Barley, pot	1:3 ~ 1:4	25–30
Couscous	1:2	5–8
Kamut, whole	1:3	10–12
Millet	1:1²/₃	10–12
Oats, steel-cut	1:2³/₄	10
Quinoa	(see page 110)	
Rice, basmati	(see page 211)	
Rice, brown	(see page 216)	
Rice, jasmine	(see page 211)	
Rice, white	(see page 211)	
Rice, wild	(see page 218)	
Spelt berries	1:3	15–20
Wheat berries	1:3	25–30

DRIED BEANS & LEGUMES	COOKING TIME (IN MINUTES)
Black beans	20–30
Black-eyed peas	20–25
Cannellini beans	35–40
Chickpeas (garbanzo beans)	35–40
Great Northern beans	25–30
Lentils, French green	8–10
Lentils, red, split	2–3
Lentils, yellow, split	1–2
Lima beans	20–25
Kidney beans, red	25–30
Kidney beans, white	35–40
Navy beans	25–30
Peas	15–20
Pinto beans	25–35
Soybeans	25–30

MEAT	COOKING TIME (IN MINUTES)
Beef, oxtail	40–50
Beef, pot roast, steak, rump, round, chuck, blade or brisket	20–30 (for small pieces), 35–40 (for large pieces)
Beef, ribs	25–30
Beef, shanks	25–30
Beef, stew meat	15–20
Chicken, boneless breasts	8–10
Chicken, boneless thighs	6–8
Chicken, cut up with bones	10–15
Chicken, drumsticks, legs or thighs	10–15
Chicken, whole	20–25
Cornish Hen, whole	10–15
Ham, picnic shoulder	25–30
Ham, slices	9–12
Lamb, cubes	10–15
Lamb, leg	35–45
Lamb, stew meat	(see page 49)
Meatballs	10–15
Pork, butt roast	45–50
Pork, loin roast	55–60
Pork, ribs	20–25
Turkey, breast, boneless	15–20
Turkey, breast, with bones	25–30
Turkey, drumsticks (legs)	15–20
Veal, chops	5–8
Veal, roast	35–45

RECIPE INDEX

INDEX

Note: Page references in *italics* indicate photographs.

A

Adjust button, 9
All-purpose bone broth, 88–90
Almonds:
    and dried cherries, yogurt
      with, 240, *241*
    and olive oil, mixed
      vegetables with, *264*, 265
    slivered, and chocolate, steel-
      cut oats with, 108, *109*
Apple butter, autumn spice,
    202–3
Apricot-vanilla compote, 206
Autumn spice apple butter,
    202–3
Avocado:
    salsa, 39, *41*
    -yogurt dip, zippy, 238

B

Bacon:
    bacon-y refried beans, 106–7
    and broccoli, Parmesan
      bread pudding with,
      190–91
    corn, and potato chowder,
      81–82
    faux cassoulet, 153–54, *155*
    garlicky white bean soup
      with crispy pancetta,
      186–88, *187*

Balsamic vinegar and parsley,
    sweet potatoes with,
    252, 253–54
Barbecue pork roast, 133–34
Barbecue pork shoulder,
    44, 45–48
Barley-mushroom stew,
    182–83
Basil:
    -Parmesan meatballs,
      125–26, *127*
    and sun-dried tomatoes,
      ricotta spread with,
      230, 232
Bean/Chili function, 12
Bean(s):
    bacon-y refried, 106–7
    black, soup, beyond basic,
      75–76
    chickpea salad, 94–96
    cooking times, notes about,
      73
    crazy-good slow-cooker chili,
      156–59
    faux cassoulet, 153–54, *155*
    flavoring and serving ideas,
      74
    flavoring and serving ideas
      for chickpeas, 97
    fragrant lamb and chickpea
      stew, 49–50, *51*
    pinto, with chorizo, 47–48
    quick chili, *64*, 65–68
    super simple, 70–73
    white, and tomato soup,
      177–78

white, soup, garlicky,
    with crispy pancetta,
    186–88, *187*
Beef:
    barbacoa tacos, *30*, 31–32
    ground, and cocoa slow-
      cooker chili, 159
    Korean-style short ribs with
      garlic and ginger, *120*,
      121–22
    marvelous slow-cooker
      meatballs, 125–29, *127*
    meatloaf, meet the Instant
      Pot, 130–31
    pineapple skirt steak, 33
    quick taco-style chili, *64*, 68
    slow-cooker pot roast and
      carrots, 123–24
    stew, flavoring and serving
      ideas for, 38
    stew, pressure-cooker,
      34–38
    stock, all-purpose, 90
Beer-braised pork roast,
    134–35
Beet and blue cheese salad,
    91–92, *93*
Beyond basic black bean soup,
    75–76
Black bean dip, 71
Blueberry jam, *200*, 201
Blue cheese and beet salad,
    91–92, *93*
"Boil," on LCD screen, 13
Bone broth, all-purpose,
    88–90